THE WORST POVERTY

A History of Debt and Debtors

OTHER BOOKS BY HUGH BARTY-KING

The Baltic Exchange, the history of a unique market
Girdle Round The Earth, Cable and Wireless and predecessors 1851–1979
The AA, the story of the Automobile Association 1905–1980
*HMSO, the first two hundred years of Her Majesty's Stationery Office
1786–1986*
Expanding Northampton (for the Northampton Development Corporation)
New Flame, a social history of Town Gas
Making Provision (for UK Provision Trade Federation Centenary 1886–1986)
A Short History of The River Plate & General Investment Trust 1888–1988
Scratch A Surveyor . . . Drivers Jonas 1725–1975
Eyes Right, the story of Dollond & Aitchison Opticians 1750–1985
Light Up The World, the story of Dale Electric 1935–1985
Cape Asbestos 1892–1952
Food for Man and Beast, the Grain and Feed Trade Association 1878–1978
Honey Not Made From Bees, the story of the Nigerian Sugar Company
Harold Evans's Front Page History 1900–1984 [text]
Round Table, the search for fellowship 1927–1977
GSMD, 100 years of The Guildhall School of Music and Drama 1880–1980
The Drum (for The Royal Tournament 1988)
Quilt Winders and Pod Shavers, the English cricket ball and cricket bat makers
Sussex Maps and History (with Valerie Scott)
Sussex in 1839
Classic Wine Making (with Anton Massel)
A Taste of English Wine
A Tradition of English Wine
Rum Yesterday and Today (with Anton Massel)
Cork on Cork, by Sir Kenneth Cork with Hugh Barty-King

THE WORST POVERTY

A History of Debt and Debtors

HUGH BARTY-KING

Foreword by Sir Gordon Borrie QC

ALAN SUTTON

To Jenny

First published in the United Kingdom in 1991
Alan Sutton Publishing Ltd · Phoenix Mill · Far Thrupp · Stroud · Gloucestershire

First published in the United States of America in 1991
Alan Sutton Publishing Inc · Wolfeboro Falls · NH 03896–0848

British Library Cataloguing in Publication Data

Barty-King, Hugh *1914–*
    A history of debt and debtors.
    1. Consumer credit, history
    I. Title
    336.343509

    ISBN 0 86299 868 9

Library of Congress Cataloging in Publication Data applied for

Typeset in 10/13 Imprint.
Typesetting and origination by
Alan Sutton Publishing Limited.
Printed in Great Britain by
Bath Press, Bath, Avon.

Contents

THE WORST POVERTY

Debt is the worst poverty.

> T. Fuller, *Gnomologia, Adagies and Proverbs*, 1732

I think she [Eleanor Rathbone] would have needed a
lot of persuading that it was other than potentially
disastrous for working class families to become
enmeshed in debt. She wanted to remove the
dependence of the poor on the patronage of the rich,
and I hardly think she cared to see the poor dependent
on the patronage of the moneylender. I suspect she
knew that debt is the worst poverty.

> Sir Gordon Borrie QC, Director General of Fair
> Trading, 'The Credit Society: its Benefits and
> Burdens', Rathbone Memorial Lecture, 1986

There is a very clear dichotomy in the British attitude
to credit/debt. At its most basic assumption, credit is
when you can afford the loan and debt is when you
cannot, but I suspect that a lot of the ambivalence goes
back to the mediaeval Christian theory of the Just
Price and the mediaeval Christian view that usury was
a sin. Certainly approximately 70 per cent of the
population disapprove of debt, and 70 per cent of the
British population are in debt. There is disapproval in
principle and approval in practice, or is it hating the
sin and loving the sinner?

> John Cunningham, Chief Executive of Mintel
> which in 1990 commissioned the British Market
> Research Bureau to research Consumer Attitudes to
> Debt, the main results of which were summarized in
> Mintel's *Consumer Credit Report 1990*.

Acknowledgements

F or helping me to explore this field I am indebted to many: to the staff of The British Library; The Guildhall Library; Lambeth Palace Library; Lincoln's Inn Library and Guy Holborn MA, LLB, ALA, Librarian; Southwark Public Library, Local History and Archives; Birmingham Reference Library, Local Studies; Central Library, Edinburgh; Library of the Religious Society of Friends and Assistant Librarian Sylvia Carlyle; Tunbridge Wells Public Library; Greater London Record Office; Corporation of London Record Office; House of Lords Record Office; East Sussex Record Office; Cumbria Record Office and David Bowcock, Assistant County Archivist (Carlisle); Lancashire Record Office and K. Hall BA, County Archivist.

I am also grateful for the help given to me by Terry Walker, National Association of Citizens Advice Bureaux; Susan Anderson, Consumer Affairs Officer, Building Societies Association; Helen Kinnings, Marketing Department, Policy Studies Institute; John McQueen, Association of Bankrupts; John Moysey, Administrator, Money Management Council; Public Information Unit, The Labour Party; Deborah Leonard, Senior Policy Officer, National Consumer Council; Revd Fred Stevens, St Anne's, Soho; Mrs Kate Beddington-Brown, Administrative Assistant, External Affairs, Institute of Credit Management; John Cunningham, Chief Executive, Mintel; Miss D.C. Rutherford, Assistant Librarian, Office of Fair Trading; Simon Berry, Home Trade Marketing Director, Berry Bros & Rudd Ltd; R.J.W. Gieve, vice-Chairman, Gieves & Hawkes; Kathy Lewis, Secretary, Finance Houses Association; Michael Liley, Director, Consumer Credit Association of the UK; Simon Johnson, National Debtline; G.A. Weiss, Insolvency Practitioners Association; Polly Bide, Thames Television; Mrs Sylvia Morris, Shakespeare Birthplace Trust; Mrs B.J. Peters, Coutts & Co.

And I owe much to Sir Kenneth Cork for providing the platform from which this book sprung.

H. B–K

Ticehurst, East Sussex.

N.B. I have kept to 'he' and 'him' throughout rather than every time putting 'he or she', 'him or her' which of course the reader must infer.

Picture Credits

P. 6 by courtesy of Suffolk Record Office; p. 27 by courtesy of The Shakespeare Birthplace Trust; p. 32 by courtesy of The National Theatre Museum; pp. 34, 52, 58, 59, 69, 91, 114, 115, 145, 156, 157, 158 & 159 by courtesy of The Guildhall Library, City of London; pp. 38, 51, 64 by courtesy of The National Portrait Gallery, London; pp. 43 & 45 by courtesy of Sir Ralph Verney Bart and The Claydon House Trust; pp. 65 & 66 by courtesy of the Trustees of the British Museum; p. 72 by courtesy of the Cumbria County Record Office; p. 90 by courtesy of Swiss Cottage Local History Library, Borough of Camden; p. 93 Dominic Photography; p. 107 & 113 by courtesy of Coutts & Co.; pp. 123, 124, 125 & 126 by courtesy of Southwark Public Library; p. 128 by courtesy of The Religious Society of Friends; p. 151 *Illustrated London News* Picture Library; p. 154 by courtesy of Berry Bros & Rudd; pp. 185 & 195 by courtesy of the *Sunday Times* and Noel Watson; p. 191 by courtesy of the Office of Fair Trading; pp. 193 & 200 by courtesy of Thames Television.

Foreword

by Sir Gordon Borrie QC, Director General of Fair Trading

The new Prime Minister, John Major, once said: 'Give the Germans five Deutschmarks and they will save it but give the British five pounds and they will borrow £25 and spend it.' Perhaps, under his administration, the habits of the British will change. After all, the privatization issues of recent years and the incentives of many kinds to invest must have provided some inducement, some incentive, to save. But it is a big 'perhaps'. Mr Barty-King quotes Mr Major in the final chapter of his fascinating book. The title of this chapter 'The New Orthodoxy' is apt because borrowing rather than saving is the norm of recent years and indeed, whatever the excesses of irresponsibility on the part of some lenders and some borrowers, borrowing has made sound economic sense. Recurring bouts of inflation suffice to demonstrate that.

Modern attitudes are a far cry from the words of King David in the fifteenth Psalm. What sort of person would abide in the Lord's tabernacle and dwell on His holy hill? he asked. He that walked uprightly and worked righteousness, he said, 'he that putteth not his money upon usury nor taketh reward against the innocent.'

Mr Barty-King surveys the changes in attitude over the years with consummate skill and a lot of research. We are reminded that a Christian who practised usury was a sinner and risked suffering the hell fire that awaited all sinners. For centuries it seems to have been a powerful and effective deterrent, at any rate more of a deterrent than the 'extortionate credit bargain' provisions of the Consumer Credit Act! As for the overcommitted borrower, for centuries imprisonment was considered a 'legitimate tool of coercion'. The hardships and cruelties of the Debtors Prison, graphically described in these pages, let alone the injustices and inefficiencies of the threat of prison as a debt recovery system, led to its eventual disuse.

I am deeply concerned with the problems of the present and this very week am responsible for the headline: 'Loan sharks face new clampdown'. Legal action against illegal or oppressive behaviour on the part of lenders and brokers; advice to borrowers and potential borrowers; appeals for more responsible behaviour. These are the stuff of daily activity in advice centres and enforcement authorities. It is salutary for us all to be reminded by the author that debt is not a new problem.

THE WORST POVERTY

It is helpful too to be reminded that it took many centuries for the harshness of the law's treatment of debtors to be ameliorated and for attitudes to change. Sometimes change came by chance. The regulation of pawnbroking, for example, came about in 1800 on the initiative of Lord Eldon who, when a young barrister, often had recourse to pawning his valuables while he waited for briefs. Mr Barty-King has scoured the literature for tales of debt and credit and, as he fairly claims, the same human motivations, the same tragedies, the same over-confidence that all is bound to come right in the end, can be identified.

He brings us up to the present date via Dickens and Oscar Wilde and the words of the Governor of the Bank of England – 'Thrift has gone out out fashion.' He does not offer advice or solutions but his book is a valuable corrective for any sloppy thought that history can teach us nothing.

GORDON BORRIE
December 1990

CHAPTER ONE

Trading Fair

– up to the end of the sixteenth century

'Credit is the exchange of two deferred promises: I will do something for you, you will pay me later. The lord who advanced seed corn to a peasant on condition he were repaid at harvest opened a credit. So did the tavern-keeper who did not claim the price of his drinks from his customer immediately, but put it down to the drinker's account by means of a chalk mark on the wall or notching a piece of wood.' (Fernand Braudel, *Capitalism and Material Life 1400–1800*)

There is nothing more special about a promise to pay next month than a promise to return home next month – nothing more complicated or significant. The person to whom it is made is entitled to assume without any doubt that, made voluntarily, it carries with it the *certain* intention to do whatever is promised. The promise-maker would feel insulted to have that intention doubted. It would be accusing him of being capable of bad faith, of trading on the confidence placed in his word, of being a con man. Unless he *is* a con man, he would be ashamed if his accuser could make any of his accusations stick.

A promise is a simple declaration which needs no reinforcement to make it more forceful. A promise is a promise. The commitment it implies does not become more binding by being clothed with documentation and courtroom procedure, by legislation and religious sanction. The man-in-the-street does not need to be kept to his promise; his making it means he intends to keep it. Institutionalizing the exchange of promises which for Braudel was credit, has not obscured the essentially personal nature of that exchange – two *people*, one trusting another who is conscious of the shame of betraying that trust. It is not being 'conscientious' to keep a promise. It is normal behaviour. There is nothing goody-goody about having scruples. Such attitudes are, and have always been, basic tenets of the rule book by which a civilized community remains civilized.

They are older than the derided Victorian values which today are paraded in articles and speeches as representing an outmoded code of behaviour, out of tune with the aggressive lifestyle of the 1990s. For most, however, having a sense of responsibility towards the neighbours (without having actually to love them),

1

having an awareness of the two-way nature of living together in a community, of there being obligations as well as 'rights', are assets as valuable as they ever were – and in the Middle Ages and earlier they were not just valuable but the mainspring of their 'primitive' society. The key words then were 'fair' and 'just' – terms which the authors of modern surveys and memoranda on debtors and creditors find themselves having to resort to in every other paragraph.

In the comparatively simple society of thirteenth-century Britain a Fair Return for Work Done had meaning. Local craft gilds formed to maintain living standards, and composed of all involved in industry – masters, apprentices and journeymen – gave 'fair' a meaning which related to the reactions of the community as a whole, particularly that part of it who consumed their goods or used their services.

In the Middle Ages there was a just price for everything. It was one which enabled all those who contributed to making and selling the article to earn 'an honest living' suitable to his station in life. For them the law of supply and demand was no reason for raising the price above the sum they considered 'just'. The gilds created a monopoly of trading for their members, but for the benefit of the whole town. They succeeded in reducing (though not preventing) forestalling and regrating (purchasing large quantities to resell at a higher price), which they saw as threatening to undermine their concept of what was fair. They achieved their objective of mutual protection and help, with funds to insure against illness and poverty, without 'muscle'. If a gildsman was imprisoned in another town, his gild would demand his release and go and fetch him home. If a gildsman incurred a debt in a foreign town in the next county and left without paying it, the foreign gild would detain the next member of his gild to visit their town until his gild had forced him to pay up.

A man's affairs were everybody's business. His ill-luck or evil doing were common knowledge, and the community provided the remedy. His failure in trade may, or may not, have been his 'fault', but those with whom he worked and lived felt responsible for him. *It mattered*. In a society, numerically small, bound together as closely as that, a lapse was that much more a personal disgrace. Everyone was liable – the word means 'bound together', the Latin *ligabilis*. The code of conduct had been breached; the side had been let down; the balance upset. It was the spirit of the times.

What fair and just remedies, in conformity with this thinking, were open to the person who allowed another to take away his property on the promise to pay next week and waited throughout the appointed day for the visit that never came? Before the Norman Conquest the attitude was that any wrong believed to have been done by one person to another was best settled between the two of them without the intervention of the state – the King in his Council (*Curia Regis*). King Alfred thought his subjects needed machinery for settling their disagreements at their level not his. When he divided his kingdom into counties, hundreds, manors and tithings, he established a court of judicature in each subdivision. At these courts his subjects could seek redress for their grievances and injuries, including the non-payment of money by those who had failed to keep their promises to pay later.

Tenants of the earls and barons who had had their estates forfeited ('escheated') to the Crown, and from then on held them under the king and had access to his *Curia Regis*, took their complaints to the newly created lower county courts under the supervision of the sheriff or the king's bailiff. It was a maxim of old Common Law 'that matters amounting to or exceeding the value of forty shillings ought not to be pleaded without the King's writ'; and the jurisdiction of these county courts applied to pleas of debt or damages under the value of forty shillings.

The law of Moses prescribed that a debtor was obliged to become the servant of his creditor, who would take his wages as paying off the debt, but that he should not have to serve as his bond slave. Under the feudal system introduced by England's Norman rulers, the king exercised a power of taking, in execution of a judgement that money was owed, not only the debtor's land and goods but his body. Eighteenth-century commentators such as James Bland Burges of Lincoln's Inn (1783) considered this an exclusive privilege, the fruit of an undefined prerogative unauthorized by any existing law. But then in 1216 the earls and barons forced King John to sign Magna Carta, section 29 of which established 'that no man, on whatsoever account can be arrested or imprisoned and can be deprived of his free-tenement, his liberties or his free-customs, or can be out-lawed or be exiled, or be in any manner oppressed or destroyed, unless by the legal judgement of his peers or by the law of the land.' Elsewhere the charter stated specifically:

> Neither the king nor his bailiffs should seize any land or rent for any debt so long as the present goods and chattels of the debtors should suffice to pay the debt, and the debtor himself be ready thence to satisfy it; that the pledges of the debtor should not be distrained so long as the principal debtor should be sufficient for the payment of the debt; and that if the principal debtor should fail in payment of the debt, having nothing wherewith to pay and should refuse to pay when able, the pledges should answer for the debt.

Civil actions between subjects were determined by what was called the Court of Common Pleas, one of the three courts established by King Edward I who came to the throne in 1272. If the person being complained against was already in the custody of the Court of King's Bench, the second of Edward I's creations, then the action was tried by that court. If the man owed money to the king he was tried in the third, the Court of the Exchequer.

3

THE WORST POVERTY

Anyone seeking to recover money owed him through the Court of Common Pleas started the process by securing a writ from the sheriff of his county ordering his debtor to appear in court on a named day – 'an original'. If the man failed to appear, the person who had given him credit obtained a second writ directing the sheriff to 'attach' him. Certain of his goods were taken away or, if he protested that next time he would put in an appearance, his furniture was left where it was, but he had to produce evidence that there were people willing to stand surety for him and surrender the money they had pledged should he fail to appear for the second time. If he left his sureties in the lurch by once again ignoring the order to attend court, they found themselves duly 'amerced'. If some of his possessions had also been taken, these were forfeited. This 'writ of attachment' applied only to the seizure of his goods, not his person.

If he continued to defy his creditor, he would find that the sheriff had received a writ empowering him to take *all* his personal property, which would then be forfeited to the king. Such a writ of *distingas* or 'distress infinite' did nothing to repay the man who had given his buyer credit. It was as if his goods had been stolen from him, which in a sense they had. At this point, the judicial process ground to a halt. Neither the debtor's person nor his land could be seized. Only if the debtor, after an interval of thinking it over, decided to face his would-be benefactor in court, could the action proceed. If judgement was pronounced against him, he found that his creditor could obtain yet another writ, directing the sheriff making good to him both the debt and the costs of the action, out of the sale of his goods and chattels – a writ of *fieri facias*. If the debtor had land, the creditor could levy the debt on his land as well as his goods. The sheriff could go on receiving rent and other income from the land until the debt was paid, but he could not *take* the land.

By the Statute of Acton-Burnel enacted in 1283 in the reign of Edward I, merchants in London, York, Bristol, Lincoln, Winchester and Shrewsbury were given the power to summon anyone who owed them money to appear before the mayor and hopefully acknowledge the debt and name a day on which they would pay it. If, in the event, the mayor was not able to discharge the debt for whatever reason, he could order that as many 'movables' of the man could be sold as would raise a sum equal to the amount owed, calculated 'by a fair appraisement', and the proceeds given to the trusting tradesman. If the buyer on credit was insolvent, the Act said his body could be taken and kept in prison until he was in a position to pay for what he had bought. The creditor's authority for this was a 'writ elegit'. If the debtor was genuinely unable to support himself, the tradesman whom he had let down had to supply him with bread and water.

Burges thought this encroached on Magna Carta and deprived a debtor of trial by jury. It might satisfy the vengeance of the creditor, he said, but answered no good purpose. 'The merchant did not get his money; the miserable debtor irrecoverably forfeited his liberty; his family were left without support; the state lost his labour.'

By the law 25 Edward III cap 17 of 1362 a creditor could obtain a 'writ of capias' compelling the debtor to come to court, but only when other ways of persuasion had proved ineffectual, he had resisted every other strategy to have him face the music before a judge, and by his conduct 'had called for a greater degree of severity by his wilful obstinacy in refusing to appear.'

The man who had already fallen into debt, and saw little immediate prospect of being able to extricate himself from it without ruining himself, could run away from it and from those who were pursuing him for the money he had stolen from them, not by illegally fleeing to the continent but by legally seeking 'sanctuary'.

The ability to take refuge in certain protected enclaves, recognized by the law as a place where a debtor could not be arrested and taken off to prison, had its roots in Anglo-Saxon law.

An absconding debtor who left the kingdom made himself an exile (the cost of which, not only in money, he had to weigh against the cost of facing his creditors), and found that in addition the state had made him an outlaw. That meant that whatever possessions, if any, he left behind him were forfeited to the Crown. The man he had cheated out of the cost of the goods he had handed over to him in good faith felt hard done by, insofar as he received no part of the proceeds of the sale unless he took the expensive and time-consuming course of petitioning the king for his share of the assets. If the debtor eschewed the drastic expedient of abandoning his home and family and fleeing across the Channel he could shut himself up in his house and refuse to come out of his 'castle', since Common Law forbade entry into a man's residence to execute civil process. The middle way – staying in the kingdom though not at home – was availing himself of the protection afforded by the ancient custom of ecclesiastical sanctuary.

Many places were recognized as such. A sanctuary became known as 'Alsatia' after Alsace the part of France bordering on the Rhine which for centuries provided refuge for the disaffected. In London the precincts of the Collegiate Church of St Martins le Grand, founded in 1056, gave sanctuary to refugees from the law. Though the college was demolished in the Dissolution of the Monasteries, the privileges of sanctuary were enjoyed until 1623 when the Act 21 James I cap 28 declared them void. The precincts continued to give shelter to debtors, however, until 1967.

Better known is the sanctuary of Whitefriars beside the Middle Temple, comprising Ram Alley, Mitre Court and what the jokers called 'Lombard Street'.

Medieval money-lender sitting on his money chest – a carved wooden bench-end in Blythburgh Church, Suffolk, symbolizing Avarice.

The privileges derived from it having been an establishment of the Carmelites – the White Friars – founded by Sir Patrick Grey in 1241 after Edward I had given them a plot of ground in Fleet Street to build their church on. At the Reformation it retained its immunities as a sanctuary, and James I confirmed and added to them by a charter in 1608. Thomas Otway featured the Whitefriars sanctuary in *The Soldier's Fortune* (1681); and in *The Squire of Alsatia* (1688), based on Terence's *The Adelphi*, Thomas Shadwell structured his whole play round the place and its inmates. He described his character Cheatly as 'a rascal who, by reason of debts, dare not stir out of Whitefryers'; Captain Hackum as 'a block-headed bully of Alsatia, a cowardly, impudent blustering fellow formerly a serjeant in Flanders, run from his colours, retreated into Whitefryers for a very small debt, where by the Alsatians he is dubbed a Captain.' One of the plates in Laroon's *Cries of London* is 'The Squire of Alsatia'.

Walter Scott gave a fulsome description of life in the Whitefriars sanctuary in his novel *The Fortunes of Nigel* (1831), set in the days of King James I. The lawyers of The Temple – Scott had one of his characters Master Reginald Lowestoffe tell his companion – maintained an amicable intercourse with their neighbours of Alsatia. When Lowestoffe heard the sound of a distant horn followed by a faint huzza, he knew there must be 'something doing in Whitefriars'. 'That is the signal', he explained, 'when their privileges are invaded by tipstaff and bailiff; and at the blast of the horn they all swarm out to the rescue, as bees when their hive is disturbed.'

The debtors and others who sought the sanctuary of Whitefriars governed themselves in a lawless, arbitrary sort of way. Lowestoffe told Nigel he remembered how once Alsatia was governed for nearly nine months by an old fishwoman. 'Then it fell under the dominion of a broken attorney who was dethroned by a reformado captain who, proving tyrannical, was deposed by a hedge-parson who was succeeded, upon resignation of his power, by Duke Jacob Hildebrod, of that name the first, whom Heaven long preserve.'

> The ancient Sanctuary of Whitefriars [wrote Walter Scott] lay considerably lower than the elevated terraces and gardens of the Temple, and was therefore generally involved in the damps and fogs arising from the Thames. The brick buildings, by which it was occupied, crowded closely on each other for, in a place so rarely privileged, every foot of ground was valuable; but erected in many cases by persons whose funds were inadequate to their speculations, the houses were generally insufficient, and exhibited the lamentable signs of having become ruinous while they were yet new. The wailing of children, the scolding of their mothers, the miserable exhibition of ragged linens hung from the windows to dry, spoke the wants and distresses of the wretched inhabitants; while the sounds of complaint were mocked and overwhelmed in the riotous shouts, oaths, profane songs and boisterous laughter that issued from the alehouses and taverns which, as the signs indicated, were equal in number to all the other houses.

The Worst Poverty

The Scottish capital had its sanctuary in the precinct of Holyrood Abbey (now only a ruin) known as Abbey Strand. Three letters S in the road still mark the confines of the once-safe area, which included several taverns and extended over what today is Edinburgh's Holyrood Park. Up to 1560 *anyone* could take refuge there without fear of capture, but after the Reformation it was safe sanctuary only for debtors.

A person without the necessary ready money who wished to affect an air of solvency, if not wealth, could do so by acquiring temporary affluence by borrowing, not from the tradesman who sold goods, but one who sold money. The retailer's profit came from the mark-up with which he charged the price he had paid the wholesaler or producer. The trader in money made his living from the charge he made his customers for the temporary use of his money, a trade known as usury (*usura* in medieval Latin).

Anyone who volunteered to relieve another's financial embarrassment, by handing over some of his money with which to pay the bill which had caused the embarrassment, and then had to wait longer than he had bargained for to get his money returned, could claim compensation for his temporary loss to the extent of 'that which is in between' (*id quod interest*). The phrase referred, in the words of the *Oxford English Dictionary*, to 'the difference between the creditor's position in consequence of the debtor's laches [neglect to repay at once] and the position which might reasonably have been anticipated as the direct consequence of the debtor's fulfilment of his obligation.' It was a principle which harked back to Roman Law. The compensation which became known as interest (*interesse*) was permissible when it could be shown that such a loss had really arisen (*damnum emergens*). Later, loss of profit through inability to reinvest the money (*lucrum cessans*) was also recognized as giving a claim to *interesse*. The sum which could be requested as interest was a fixed one and specified in the contract; though in thirteenth-century England they substituted a percentage of the money which was reckoned periodically to correspond with the creditor's loss.

In medieval England the two procedures were sanctioned only by tradition. However the Christian Church in England, which took its ideas from the Pope in Rome, held that whereas compensating someone who had lent money to another to bridge a temporary shortage of cash was permissible, charging for the use of money lent was not.

It was not just impermissible. The Christian Church's body of rules and regulations on how a Christian should conduct himself, the Canon Law, ruled that usury was 'a sin'. Any Christian who practised it risked dying without 'salvation' and suffering the hell fire that awaited all sinners. While living, no usurer could be admitted to the central rite of the Christian Church – the Eucharist. There was no objection to a Christian lending money so long as he did not charge the borrower for its use.

For non-Christians there was no such ban. In the first five books of the Old Testament, the Pentateuch, from which Jews took their rule of life, they found texts which warned them off giving brother Jews money upon usury and, as the third book of Moses, called Leviticus, put it, 'lending their victuals upon increase'. In the second book, Exodus, they read again that if they should lend money to any of their people 'that is poor by thee', they should not be to him as a usurer 'neither shalt thou lay upon him usury'. But there was no such ban upon charging non-Jews, Gentiles, for the use of money lent. The Word of God, as expressed in the twenty-third chapter of the Book of Deuteronomy, told them, 'Unto a stranger [non-Jew] thou mayest lend upon usury, but unto thy brother [Jew] thou shalt not lend upon usury.' King David seems to have disapproved of it in any circumstances. What sort of person would abide in the Lord's tabernacle and dwell on His holy hill? he asked in his fifteenth Psalm. He that walked uprightly and worked righteousness, he said, 'he that putteth not his money upon usury nor taketh reward against the innocent.'

How Jews earned their living was no concern of the Christian Church, and they became the moneylenders of Christendom. Those that flocked to England in the train of William the Conqueror – there had been few over here in Anglo-Saxon times – brought with them working capital and settled in towns like Norwich and York where they earned their keep by lending out sums on the security of land and rents. They formed syndicates among themselves with what, in his *History of the Jews*, Paul Johnson calls 'layers of borrowing'. In each town with a Jewish community was an Exchequer of the Jews with a chest of money managed by two Jews and two Christians who kept a record of every debt bond. They also had their own courts, the Justices of the Jews.

Their services were in great demand in thirteenth-century England; Aaron of York lent King Henry III 30,000 marks – and died impoverished in 1268. They financed the Christian religious houses, the monasteries and priories established by the Norman barons to ensure their place in heaven. Aaron of Lincoln, 'the most successful Jewish financier in medieval England', lent the Cistercian order a colossal sum in return for mortgages. They reckoned to earn about $12\frac{1}{2}$ per cent on the money they put out on loan each year.

When in 1095 there was a call from France to join the First Crusade to recover Jerusalem from the infidel and everyone thought the world was coming to an end, those who answered it in England firmly believed that whatever debts they had in the home country would be cancelled. Hypnotized by the God-sent opportunity to win 'grace' and obtain 'remission of sins', they sold up their estates to pay for the expensive equipment needed for so hazardous an adventure, and when the proceeds fell short of what was needed, borrowed from the Jews.

Most of the borrowing, however, was done lower down the social scale by country gentlemen who were always hard up and reluctantly resorted to Jewish money-lenders, whom they despised, to keep them solvent. It was there that resentment against the high charges extorted grew into vicious anti-semitism. But there was no lack of persecution at the top. Without the protection of the law, Jews were thrown into prison on little or no pretext and made to pay huge sums to gain their liberty, apart from being exorbitantly taxed. Henry III borrowed 5,000 marks from the Earl of Cornwall and as repayment consigned over to him all the Jews in England. In 1275 his son, Edward I, confiscated and sold the houses and land of the Jews, banished 15,000 of them and robbed them of all they possessed. 'Very few of that nation have since lived in England,' wrote David Hume in the second volume of the *History of England* which he published in 1848,

> and as it is impossible for a nation to subsist without lenders of money, and none will lend without a compensation, the practise of usury, as it was then called, was thenceforth exercised by the English themselves upon their fellow citizens or by Lombards and other foreigners. It is very much to be questioned whether the dealings of these new usurers were equally open and unexceptionable with those of the old. By a law of Richard it was enacted that three copies should be made of every bond given to a Jew; one to be put into the hands of a public magistrate, another into those of a man of credit, and a third to remain with the Jew himself.
>
> But as the canon law, seconded by the municipal, permitted no Christian to take interest, all transactions of this kind must, after the banishment of the Jews, have become more secret and clandestine; and the lender, of consequence, be paid both for the use of his money and for the infamy and danger which he incurred by lending it.

It was dangerous indeed. The medieval view was that money was solely a medium of exchange for articles of consumption, and anyone who put it to any other 'use' was adequately repaid by the return of the same sum as was lent.

The early Christian fathers first of all – at the Council of Arles in 314 and the Council of Nicaea in 325 – forbade all *clerics* to lend money on interest. Then at the first Council of Carthage in 348 and that of Aix in 789, they objected to this method of making profit even by laymen. In the Decree of Gratian, and at the Third Lateran Council in 1179 and the Second Council of Lyons, usury was formally condemned. Martin Luther and Ulrich Zwingli the Swiss preacher both condemned the lending of money for interest, but Jean Calvin allowed it in the case of wealthy debtors.

Someone had to gratify the great demand for cash after Edward I rid England of so many Jews, and their role as money-lenders on a big scale was taken over by the Knights Templar of Jerusalem, the first Christian bankers. Such Jews as were left had to settle for lending considerably smaller amounts, but since, in that never-to-be-forgotten year of 1275, Edward I had also passed a statute making usury of any kind illegal, they certainly contrived to do it as secretly as possible. Those who were discovered were arrested, and in 1278 some 300 of them were hanged.

But apart from surreptitious lending for which they charged twopence to threepence in the pound per week – 45 to 65 per cent – they turned to coin changing and to taking in small pawns or pledges as security for the loan of small sums of money at a low rate of interest. The medieval Jewish pawnbroker in England provided a useful service for the poorer subjects of the sovereign, who himself had no hesitation in pledging his regalia whenever funds were low. Edward III pawned his crown on three occasions, once for eight years. In 1339 he raised a sum on the security of his crown and the queen's; and in 1340 on all the crown jewels. Henry V pawned his crown to the Bishop of Winchester for a hundred thousand marks. Henry VI pledged the jewel in the crown known as the Rich Collar, broken down into three pieces, to pay for his marriage to Margaret of Anjou, and never redeemed it. Richard II put all his jewels in hock with London citizens for *his* wedding.

Every shop had a sign and that over a pawnshop was three golden balls. It was the emblem both of the Italian Lombard family who took over from the English Jews as the country's money-lenders, and of the Medici family whose money-lending made them rulers of Florence. But they, in their turn, took it from the fourth-century Saint Nicholas of Patara in Asia Minor, the legendary Santa Claus who mysteriously filled Christmas stockings. Nicholas was renowned for using the fortune he had inherited to relieve the poverty of others. When he heard a Patara nobleman was about to abandon his three daughters to prostitution to earn dowries, on three nights he secretly threw a bag of gold through an open window in the impoverished family's house. From this legend derives the custom of putting presents in stockings for children to discover on Christmas morning. St Nicholas is often represented as carrying three purses of gold or three golden balls.

By patronizing a pawnshop a poor man hoped to stave off overindebtedness week by week, or perhaps just in an emergency, but he did not always succeed. The balancing act of ensuring he never spent more than he earned was a difficult one, and, when he lost his balance and tipped over into insolvency, he often manoeuvred himself into a hiding place where his creditors could no longer pursue him, not the sanctuary of Whitefriars or Holyrood, but the seclusion of a gaol. In 1419 Dick Whittington, the rich Lord Mayor of London who lent from his fortune to both King Henry IV and V, thought too many were choosing to go to prison rather than pay their debts. Fewer gaols in London would mean less incentive to seek this solution to financial embarrassment, he thought. So on 2 November 1419

Saint Nicholas (Santa Claus), often
represented as carrying the three bulging
purses of gold he gave three sisters to
save them from prostitution – which
became the three golden balls of the
pawnbroker's sign.

he enacted an Ordinance for the abolition of the Debtors Prison at Ludgate 'since
many false persons of bad disposition and purpose chose to go to prison rather than
pay their debts.' Ludgate Prison had not been established for that purpose but 'to
provide a place where poor prisoners might more freely than others, who were
strangers, dwell in quiet and pray for their benefactors, and live on the alms of the
people; and in increase of their merits, by benign suffrance, in such imprisonment
pass all their lives if God should provide no other remedy for them.'

So Ludgate was ordered to be abolished and disqualified as a prison, and the
prisoners sent to Newgate Prison. But it was soon seen to be a mistake, and the
prisoners were all sent back to a re-opened Ludgate because of 'the fetid and
corrupt atmosphere that is in the hateful gaol of Neugate. Prisoners there now dead
but might have been living if they had remained in Ludgate, remaining in peace.'

It was not only poor debtors who found themselves in prison. A law of 1267 known
as the Statute of Marlbridge (52 Henry III cap 23) authorized a lord of the manor
to arrest and detain, pending trial, the man whom he had appointed bailiff to
collect rents from his tenants, if he suspected that the man was not handing over all
that was due to him. The bailiff/rent collector was obviously let out of gaol to

attend his trial, but if he was found guilty of the charge he could not then be sent back to prison as punishment. But James Bland Burges regarded holding him before trial as an outrageous breach of what he called the sacred shield of security against arrest and detention embodied in Magna Carta. The smallest appointment as bailiff to receive the smallest rent was sufficient to bring the victim within the interpretation of the statute. 'A dexterous management, easy to the powerful, supplied the rest.'

> The miserable wretch, unfriended and unable to resist, consumed in gaol his melancholy hours; while his lord, deriving a new accession of his power from his fall, exercised a despotic sway over his trembling dependants.

Depriving a man of his liberty who was accused of failing to pay another what he owed him, once admitted as a legitimate tool of coercion for the ruling class to use when it suited them, soon became the subject of wider and wider application under the system of courts set up, as seen, by King Edward I. That Statute of Acton-Burnel of 1283 gave the bailiff's power of detention to *a merchant* who considered a customer was holding back on payment for goods he had let him have on credit, so that he could make him admit to the debt and agree on a day to hand over the money. If the man had nothing which could be sold to defray the arrears which he had failed to pay on the appointed day, he would be sent to prison, not to punish him, but to put him away in a safe place until he agreed to make a composition with his creditor, or his friends came to his rescue. By the Statute of Merchants of 1285 a merchant could have a man who owed him money put in gaol even if he *did* have enough goods to sell to raise the amount of the debt. The Statute of Westminster II gave a lord of the manor similar powers in the same year to detain his debtor until he reached a composition.

Whether the aggrieved party was a lord or a tradesman, and whoever was the defaulter, indebtedness in those days was seen as an essentially personal matter between the two of them, with imprisonment as a last resort. If a man ran up bills to a number of others, and had the wherewithal to pay some but not all, he could safely wait for a claim to be made by one of them, probably the man to whom he owed the most, and then by another, one at a time. It was first-come, first-served. When the money ran out there was nothing left for the man who came last. There was no question of creditors ganging up to present their claims as a group. With the advent of a more sophisticated society however the one-against-one procedure gave way to collective presentation of claims by all creditors who demanded equal treatment and enforced their rights against the property of the debtor, not his person.

English custom followed that of the medieval city states of the Italian peninsula, who had adapted the Roman Law by which the whole property of the debtor was divided equally among creditors. But forcible restraint, seizure of his body, was still kept as a last resort. Prison brought home to the debtor the consequence of his conduct. As Sir William Holdsworth pointed out in his *History of English Law*, 'it acted as a deterrent to the person with no moral sense who in a world where it is commercially desirable to have credit, has no scruples to take advantage of others' scruples.' It was hoped that restraint would stop abuses of confidence in the long term, though imprisonment was imposed on both the dishonest and the unfortunate debtor. To incarcerate the latter, who had to live on charity, at his own expense or die of starvation, said Sir William, inflicted a hardship which was of no benefit to the creditor. Neither sheriff nor creditor, in later times, were obliged to give the gaoled debtor food or drink. 'If he have no goods he shall live of the charity of others' was the attitude in the mid-sixteenth century, 'and if others will give him nothing, let him die in the name of God, if he will; and impute the cause of it to his own fault, for his presumption and ill-behaviour brought him to that imprisonment.' The dishonest debtor in the next cell, however, could live off the money he had refused to hand over to his creditors, who would be forced to compromise.

The change to creditors presenting their claim as a body came very slowly. As late as 1542, when Henry VIII was exercising his so-called benevolent despotism, a London mercer, Henry Brinklow, had the courage to complain to the all-powerful Privy Council about the first-come, first-served law whereby 'one or two shall be paid and the rest have nothing'. The rich got paid first, he claimed, 'to the great damage and oppression of the pore'. It was, he suspected, because the rich had first knowledge of such things. He wanted a new law by which all creditors fared equally and so 'neyhborly and godly'.

In an age when religion dominated public and private life in a way it is difficult to understand today, the concept of what was godly conduct and what was ungodly was of supreme importance. As religion was a state matter, so was business. Both were strictly controlled, with no personal deviations allowed. Economic and ethical interests were the same; usury was still a sin.

The Tudors forbade the exchange of gold and silver by anyone they had not authorized. They favoured a state-promoted capitalism which depended on granting privileges and concessions to company promoters who paid for them, and by giving royal monopolies – soap-making, textiles and the like – not to those best qualified to run businesses, but to favourites and courtiers with no idea of what was required. There was no place for individual enterprise under the Economic Paternalism of Tudor England, and with the strict control exercised by the state there was little opportunity for speculation. Where it did occur it was severely punished by the Star Chamber. People became rich or poor by leave of the Privy Council who were bent on converting all economic activity into an instrument of profit for the Government and its parasites. The regime regarded the laws on debt, which had lain on the statute book since the Middle Ages, as adequate for people whom the state made sure had little occasion to run into debt either from over-spending or over-borrowing.

The medieval law on debt had overlapped an economic climate for which it became more and more unsuited. But society learnt to make a distinction between the debtor unable to pay by misfortune and one who had brought calamity on his head by recklessness or deliberate fraud.

As a result of Henry Brinklow's complaints Henry VIII's Privy Council enacted a statute in 1542 which is often represented as the first to establish a law of bankruptcy, but in fact was designed to prevent frauds on creditors and generally facilitate execution against a debtor – enforcement by the sheriff of a court's judgement. The objective of 34, 35 Henry VIII cap 4 was spelt out in its preamble:

> Whereas divers and sundry persons, craftily obtaining into their hands great substance of other men's goods, do suddenly flee to parts unknown, or keep their houses, not minding to pay or restore to any of their creditors their duties, but at their own wills and pleasures consume debts and the substance obtained by credit of other men, for their own pleasure and delicate living, against all reason, equity and good conscience . . .

This law of 1542 authorized the Chancellor, on the petition of the creditor, to summon the debtor before him, examine him upon oath and, if he refused to forfeit his possessions to pay off his debt, to have him put in prison until he did. They were then distributed among his creditors. If the sale produced less than the total sum owed, the debtor was not discharged from claims which remained outstanding. If he attempted to flee the country he was declared 'outside of the King's protection', as seen, and anyone who helped him escape could be imprisoned.

It was not until the next reign that a proper law of bankruptcy was introduced, 13 Elizabeth cap 7 of 1570. Henry VIII's Act had failed to deter the persistent fraudster, an admission contained in the preamble to the new measure:

> Forasmuch as notwithstanding [the enactment of the 1542 statute] those kinds of persons have and do still increase into great and excessive numbers, and are like more to do, if some better provision be not made for the repression of them . . .

The Act established a procedure which was to last for centuries. It authorized the Chancellor to appoint commissioners with powers over the person and property of 'a bankrupt'. Only a 'trader' could be declared a bankrupt; everyone else who was found to be without resources was 'insolvent', and the Act of 1570 did not apply to them. The distinction between insolvency and bankruptcy was only abolished in 1869.

The Worst Poverty

In his *Early History of English Bankruptcy*, quoted by Jay Cohen in his article on 'The History of Imprisonment for Debt' in the *The Journal of Legal History* (1982), Levintal explains the initial distinction between traders and non-traders in bankruptcy as arising from merchants being regarded as 'having peculiar facilities for delaying and defrauding creditors'. The landed gentry in England, he adds, were not subject to the law which was essentially punitive in nature.

Who was 'a trader'? The Act called them persons '*as used the trade of merchandize*, in gross or by retail, by way of bargaining, exchange, rechange, bartering, chevisance [making contracts] or otherwise; or *sought their living by buying and selling.*' It excluded shareholders of the three great state trading companies: The East India Company, The Royal African Company and The Hudson Bay Company. No infant could be a trader within the meaning of the statute, nor anyone who did a single act of buying or selling; he had to make a repeated practice of it and make a profit from it.

Who was 'a bankrupt'? 'A trader who secretes himself' or does acts 'with intent to defeat or delay his creditors' such as departing from the realm, taking sanctuary, allowing himself to be arrested, outlawed or imprisoned for debt. The word derived from *bancus*, the tradesman's counter, and *ruptus*, broken, denoting one whose place of business was broken and gone; though some think it is a translation of the French *banqueroute*, meaning one who has removed his *banque*, leaving only a trace ('*route*') behind.

Sir William Blackstone, author of the famous *Commentaries on the Laws of England* originally written in the 1750s but updated in 1876 and thereafter, considered the principal of equal division of a debtor's means among creditors followed the example of Roman Law.

> I mean not the terrible law of the twelve tables whereby the creditors might cut the debtor's body into pieces and each of them take his proportionable share – if indeed that law, *de debitore in partes secando*, is to be understood in so very butcherly a light, which many learned have with reason doubted. Nor do I mean those less inhuman laws, if they may be called so, as *their* meaning is indisputably certain, of imprisoning the debtor's person in chains; subjecting him to stripes and hard labour at the mercy of his rigid creditor, and sometimes selling him, his wife and children to perpetual foreign slavery *trans Tiberim*.

He meant the law of *cession* introduced by Christian emperors whereby, if a debtor *ceded* or yielded up all his fortune to his creditors, he was secured from being dragged to a gaol.

In sixteenth-century England, bankrupts had no alternative but to have their cases judged by commissioners in bankruptcy who, the Act of 1570 stated, shoud be appointed by the Chancellor who thereafter, however, had no control over them. Nor was the Chancellor given jurisdiction in bankruptcy by the Act in his own Chancery court which dispensed moral justice alongside the Common Law courts – the strict Court of Common Pleas whose recorded judgements accumulated over the years to form Case Law.

For Jay Cohen the statute of 1570 formed the cornerstone of bankruptcy law for well over a century.

> Despite its coercive provisions, the statute did introduce a fundamental aspect of modern bankruptcy law, the equal distribution of the bankrupt's assets among his creditors . . . The bankruptcy statutes of 1542 and 1570 imposed severe penalties upon the debtor who sought to evade imprisonment by flight or keeping house, but by the last quarter of the sixteenth century another course of avoiding imprisonment could be followed. The debtor could petition the Privy Council to help him settle his dispute with his creditors . . . The Elizabethan Council established Commissions for Poor Prisoners, in order to secure the release of insolvent debtors. The first commission established in 1576, was staffed by the Chief Justices of Queens Bench and Common Pleas, the Master of the Rolls and others.

This Commission, which sat in Queens Bench Prison, was set up to relieve the prisons of the increasing number of insolvent debtors which had become 'a national problem'. The idea was to bring debtor and creditor together and if possible get them to agree to a composition whereby a debtor would be discharged from his total liability if the creditor could secure immediate settlement of part of it – which was not to be countenanced by the normal bankruptcy courts until the early eighteenth century. The Common Law courts regarded the Commission's activities as highly irregular if not illegal, and it would seem were responsible for the withdrawing of the Commission after the 1590s – a tribunal which in Jay Cohen's view 'represented the most lenient policy towards the insolvent debtor for several centuries to come'.

Another Act, passed in 1604, widened the definition of 'a bankrupt' to mean any trader who had allowed his goods and chattels to be 'attached', that is placed under the control of a court, or one who made a fraudulent conveyance of them. Previous legislation was having less effect than the legislators hoped. The preamble to the 1604 statute showed their concern:

> For that frauds and deceits, as new diseases, daily increase amongst such as live by buying and selling, to the hindrance of traffic and mutual commerce and to the general hurt of the realm by such as wickedly and wilfully become bankrupts . . . (1 Jac cap 15)

The Parliament of James I passed another law (21 Jac 1 cap 19 of 1623) punishing a debtor who could not prove commercial misfortune, or hid or sold his possessions to disrupt the proceedings, by being 'set upon the pillory in some

'Set upon the pillory in some public place'.

public place for the space of two hours and have one of his or her ears nailed to the pillory and cut off.'

The sensible way for a debtor to escape the risk of such a painful and permanent punishment was to persuade creditors to settle for part of what was owed to them – composition. But there was no machinery whereby he could do this unless they *all* agreed. For a long time one obstinate creditor who refused his signature could stop the issue of a certificate of discharge. But in Stuart times, Chancery, by direct command, could compel an intransigent creditor to join in the composition which the majority were prepared to accept.

In theory the commissioners in whom the Chancellor vested the jurisdiction of bankruptcy were 'honest and discreet persons', mostly counsellors in law. But they were also lay citizens and merchants, who were doubtless worthy and upright, but lacked the competency to make the system work as it was designed to do. In the eyes of most of them the fact that the man or woman before them was a debtor made him or her an offender, no matter whether the cause was dishonesty or misfortune. Commissioners could be sued if they acted wrongly, which discouraged the most competent from taking on a job which gave them very great powers over their fellow citizens – disposing of their property, having the doors of their houses broken down if they refused to hand over their possessions voluntarily, having them put in prison if they refused to answer questions. Things had changed since the Middle Ages.

Having heard the case of both parties, they were required to divide the debtor's property pro rata among the creditors – the dividend. And it was as well for them to make sure that, in making their claims, the creditors were telling the truth. If they thought anyone, creditor or debtor, had committed perjury, they could order him to be put in the pillory, as seen, and perform barbarous surgery on his ears.

The rulers had no objection to the principle of their subjects taking away goods and promising to pay later, only the anti-social, unjust, unfair nature of failing to hand over the money within the agreed time. As landowners they frowned on tenants who took pleasure in living in the house, and gaining the produce from the farm they had leased, but thought they could dispense with the less pleasant aspect of the arrangement which was being punctual in paying the rent. They had no objection to people borrowing money, only to those who could not see the justice and fairness of keeping to their side of the bargain, and returning the money lent and paying the charge for using it on the appointed day. As for the lenders, good luck to them so long as their charges were fair and just. History had decreed that the money-lending business was in the hands of a particular group of people. But that was no cause for hostility. It was after all the choice of the Christians to exclude themselves from the activity for reasons best known to themselves.

The Christian Church (of Rome) had no regrets about the stance it had assumed on the issue. The authors of the four Gospels had not reported any guidelines which Jesus had given on the desirability or otherwise of borrowing or lending money, though Matthew recorded that in Christ's sermon on the mount, he advocated that anyone who had happened to run up a debt should settle it quickly, not because that was the right thing to do but for fear of being sent to prison.

> Agree with thine adversary quickly whiles thou art in the way with him; lest at any time the adversary deliver thee to the judge, and the judge deliver thee to the officer and thou be cast into prison. Verily I say unto thee Thou shalt by no means come out thence till thou hast paid the uttermost farthing. (Matthew, chapter 5, verses 25 and 26)

Apart from that, Christ's general attitude seemed to be that anyone who lent money should not be too hard on a borrower who found he could not repay it. In fact he recommended that he should *forgive* him. To illustrate the point he told the story of a king's servant who owed his master ten thousand ducats. When he discovered he could not pay, the king ordered that he and his wife and children should all be sold into slavery, and a sale made of all his possessions, the proceeds from which he would take as payment of the debt. The servant was horrified and begged the king to think again, saying, 'Lord, have patience with me and I will pay thee all.'

The unmerciful servant, who has been forgiven his debt by his lord, forces a fellow servant to pay what he owes him – illustration of the parable reported in Matthew's gospel in a 1720 Bible.

Trading Fair

Then the lord of that servant was moved with compassion, and loosed him and forgave him the debt. But as soon as he was released the servant sought out one of his fellow servants who owed him a hundred pence and took him by the throat, shouting 'Pay me that thou owest!' And the man did as he had done, fell down and asked for patience. If he was given time he would pay all he owed. But the servant would not listen and had him cast into prison where he was to stay until he had repaid the debt. When they heard his fate, all the debtor's friends went to the king and told him what had happened, and the king had the man brought before him. 'O thou wicked servant,' he said, 'I forgave thee all that debt, because thou desiredst me. Shouldest not thou also have had compassion on thy fellow servant, even as I had pity on thee?'

> And his lord was wroth and delivered him to the tormentors till he should pay all that was due unto him. So likewise shall my heavenly Father do also unto you, if ye from your hearts forgive not everyone his brother their trespasses. (Matthew, chapter 18, verses 34 and 35)

The Church saw no harm in Christians lending money so long as they made no charge for its use; it was an act of charity to help another in need and to be encouraged.

As R.H. Tawney has said, by the sixteenth century the Roman Catholic Church (in England as elsewhere) 'maintained the rule that payment could not lawfully be demanded merely for the use of money, and sanctioned such credit transactions as could reasonably be held not directly to conflict with that principle.' It was tolerated so long as the lender shared the risk with the borrower, which made annuities blameless, since the gain was not certain, but contingent. The Church considered it reasonable that the borrower who failed to repay his creditor on the appointed day should submit to a penalty; and that the creditor who lost an opportunity of gain by standing out of his money should receive compensation. The theory of usury, said Tawney, was a special case of the general rule that economic transactions should be conducted in accordance with rules of 'good conscience' derived from religious principles and interpreted by the Church. When the sixteenth century began,

> to live by usury as the husbandman doth by his husbandry was treated as ignominious, immoral and positively illegal. When the century ended moneylending was on the way to enjoy the legal security of recognised and reputable profession. Naturalistic political arithmetic was set in place of theology – part of a revolution that turned religion from the master interest of mankind into one department of life with boundaries which it was extravagant to overstep.

21

THE WORST POVERTY

Tawney made these comments in the Introduction he wrote in 1925 to a reprint of *A Discourse upon Usury* written by Sir Thomas Wilson, Dean of Durham, in 1572, one of many tracts on a subject which exercised the Elizabethans considerably. Wilson's book is thought to have influenced Christopher Marlowe and William Shakespeare in their respective plays *The Jew of Malta* (1589) and *The Merchant of Venice* (1598). 'It is clear', says W. Moelwyn Merchant in his Introduction to the 1967 New Penguin Shakespeare edition of *The Merchant of Venice*, 'that the play is much preoccupied with two matters of Elizabethan concern: Jewry and usury.'

Credit, and the overindebtedness that might arise from it, were as lively issues in the 1590s when William Shakespeare wrote *The Merchant of Venice* as in the 1990s when his topical play is still being staged and has lost none of its topicality. The playwright is not propagating a view but dramatizing a topic of public debate and so giving his audience what they expected. '*The Merchant of Venice* bears not the least resemblance to a pamphlet on usury', says W. Moelwyn Merchant,

> despite the active polemics in the background. Shakespeare rarely takes sides and it is certainly rash to assume that he here takes an unambiguous stand 'for' Antonio and 'against' Shylock.

Shakespeare, like Ben Jonson, author of *Volpone*, says Merchant, had a certain 'social conservatism' in his attitude to an emerging 'capitalist society', but that was all. The dramatist had made his character Antonio, from whom the rake and spendthrift Bassanio wishes to borrow even more money, adopt the stringent rule that usury may not be levied. But Bassanio had caught him at a moment when he had no ready money. 'Thou know'st that all my fortunes are at sea', he tells his friend.

> Neither have I money, nor commodity
> To raise a present sum. Therefore go forth;
> Try what my credit can in Venice do
> That shall be racked even to the uttermost
> To furnish thee to Belmont, to fair Portia.
> Go presently enquire, and so will I,
> Where money is; and I no question make
> To have it of my trust or for my sake.

The Christian merchant Antonio not only disapproved of usury but of the whole activity of Shylock and his customers:

> . . . although I neither lend nor borrow
> By taking nor giving of excess
> Yet, to supply the ripe wants of my friend,
> I'll break a custom.

Henry Irving as Shylock in *The Merchant of Venice*, the play in which William Shakespeare treats of two matters of concern in Elizabethan England, Jewry and usury.

THE WORST POVERTY

Bassanio had got himself into a position with which all the patrons of the theatre on Southbank will have been familiar:

> 'Tis not unknown to you, Antonio,
> How much I have disabled my estate
> By something showing a more swelling port
> Than my faint means would grant continuance.
> Nor do I now make moan to be abridged
> From such a noble rate; but my chief care
> Is to come fairly off from the great debts
> Wherein my time, something too prodigal,
> Hath left me gaged. To you, Antonio,
> I owe the most in money and in love,
> And from your love I have a warranty
> To unburden all my plots and purposes
> How to get clear of all the debts I owe.

The London audience would also have known that the attitude to usury displayed by Antonio and Bassanio in the play was somewhat old-fashioned. As Marchette Chute has shown in *Shakespeare of London* (1951),

> Even more unrealistic [than Antonio's troubles with his ships] is the way the characters discuss usury, which was not only a commonplace in Venice but equally a commonplace in Shakespeare's London. A government decree at the beginning of Elizabeth's reign stated firmly that usury was a sin, but it also went on to state that ten per cent was a legal rate of interest. Half the members of Shakespeare's audience had either lent or borrowed money at high rates of interest, and they knew perfectly well that Shakespeare's *Merchant of Venice* was a folk play that had nothing to do with current economic conditions. As one contemporary remarked, 'He is accounted but for a fool that doth lend his money for nothing', and although in theory the average Englishman still held to the medieval conception of usury as a wicked occupation fit only for Jews, in practice every Londoner made it a part of normal business procedure.

One of those who openly augmented his income as a cloth merchant by lending money at high rates to impoverished noblemen was Sir John Spencer, City alderman, who had been Lord Mayor of London in 1594. In spite of his fortune, 'rich Spencer' as he was known, set himself against yielding to the demands of the profligate Lord Compton who was up to the eyes in debt and sought his heiress daughter's hand in marriage as a way out of his predicament.

Handsome Lord Compton had quickly dissipated the substantial estate he had inherited from his father who had died in 1589. He was then only twenty-one. Over the next ten years he sold off his land section by section to pay his creditors, but by 1599 he still owed at least £10,000. What better way of freeing himself from their constant clamour than by acquiring a dowry for just that sum? So he asked the man who was regarded as one of the wealthiest men in England and he hoped would soon be his father-in-law, for a marriage settlement of £10,000 and a further £18,000 to pay what he had borrowed by mortgaging the parts of his estate he had not yet disposed of.

Sir John refused point-blank to do anything of the sort. As likely as not this dissolute spendthrift would run through his dowry as quickly as the money he had inherited from his father. Sir John's attempt to keep the lovers apart, by hiding his daughter away, led to Lord Compton persuading the Privy Council to have him taken off to the Fleet Prison and kept there for contempt – his daughter and his lordship were after all 'contracted' to each other. Compton may or may not have dressed up as a baker's boy and spirited Elizabeth away in a bread basket, but he was certainly able to ignore the objections of his bride's father and marry the heiress who – for a time at least – would put him out of debt, on 18 April 1599 – and the marriage became the talk of the town.

In that year William Shakespeare was commanded (it is said) by Queen Elizabeth I to write a comedy which told of the amorous adventures of the character Sir John Falstaff who had so pleased her in the two parts of *Henry IV*. In

William Shakespeare, the loving good friend of Richard Quiney, the Stratford mercer who wrote to him asking for a loan of £30 to pay debts he owed in London.

it he used the scandalous affair that all his audience knew about as a plot in *The Merry Wives of Windsor*. The wooing of the impecunious Fenton and the rich Anne Page is by tradition thought to have been inspired by the long drawn-out saga of Lord Compton and Elizabeth Spencer.

In the play, first performed at The Globe Theatre in 1599, Shakespeare has Sir John Falstaff, keen to preserve his reputation as a man of honour, resolutely refusing the entreaties of his rascally follower Pistol for a loan.

FALSTAFF. I will not lend thee a penny.
PISTOL. Why then, the world's mine oyster,
Which I with sword will open. –
I will retort the sum of equipage [repay in instalments]
FALSTAFF. Not a penny. I have been content, sir, you should lay
my countenance to pawn [borrow money on the strength
of my patronage of you]. I have grated upon [pestered]
my good friends for three reprieves for you and your
coach-fellow Nym, or else you had looked through the grate [prison bars]
like a geminy [pair of twin] of baboons.

The playwright knew what it was to be asked for a loan. In 1598 he received a letter from a mercer called Richard Quiney, son of Adrian Quiney who had been High Bailiff of Stratford. The Quiney and Shakespeare families were close friends. Richard's finances were badly affected not only by the general depression of the time but by two fires, and he came to London in October 1598 to apply to the court for a remission of taxes. Before he set out for the hearing of his case, he wrote from the inn where he was staying, The Bell in Carter Lane, to 'his loving, good friend and countryman William Shakespeare' (as related by Marchette Chute) asking him to lend him thirty pounds on good security.

> What Quiney wanted the money for is not quite clear. He told Shakespeare he wanted to pay off 'the debts I owe in London' and that these were disquieting him because he did not like to be 'indebted'. Since he was raising more money to do it, it would seem that Quiney did not consider a debt to Shakespeare as coming within this category . . . Probably Richard Quiney wanted part of the money to pay off old debts and part of it to make some business investments as a mercer; and since he was successful at Court in getting remission of Stratford taxes, it is to be hoped he was equally successful in his attempt to borrow money from his 'loving good friend'.

Borrowing from old friends was a friendly affair. Failing to keep a promise to pay a tradesman later could turn nasty if the customer openly took advantage of the goodwill and good nature of a seller anxious to please and keep his custom. It became even nastier in Tudor times if the non-payer was a grandee who had no

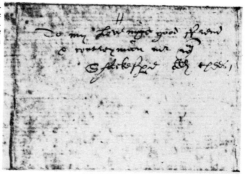

[1598, Oct. 25. Richard Quiney to Shakespeare, pr. *Var.* ii. 485; *H.P.* i. 167; *B.P. Cat.* 45; both with facs. (cf. Plate XVII). Malone describes the discovery in letters of 21 Sept. 1793 to Bp. Percy (*Bodl. Mal. MS.* 26, f. 22) and 15 Nov. 1793 to Ld. Charlemont (*H.M.C. Charlemont MSS.* ii. 220). It was then in a bundle of letters to and from Quiney in the Stratford archives, but is now among the *Wheler MSS.*]

Loveinge Contreyman, I am bolde of yowe as of a ffrende, craveinge yowre helpe with xxx^{ll} vppon Mr Bushells & my securytee or Mr Myttons with me. Mr Rosswell is nott come to London as yeate & I have especiall cawse. Yowe shall ffrende me muche in helpeinge me out of all the debettes I owe in London, I thancke god, & muche quiet my mynde which wolde nott be indebeted. I am nowe towardes the Cowrte in hope of answer for the dispatche of my Buysenes. Yowe shall neither loase creddytt nor monney by me, the Lorde wyllinge, & nowe butt perswade yowre selfe soe as I hope & yowe shall nott need to feare butt with all hartie thanckefullenes I will holde my tyme & content yowre ffrende, & yf we Bargaine farther yowe shalbe the paiemaster yowre self. My tyme biddes me hasten to an ende & soe I committ thys ⟨to⟩ yowre care & hope of yowre helpe. I feare I shall nott be backe thys night ffrom the Cowrte. Haste. The Lorde be with yowe & with vs all Amen. ffrom the Bell in Carter Lane the 25 October 1598. Yowres in all kyndenes Ryc. Quyney. [*Addressed*] H⟨aste⟩ To my Loveinge good ffrend & contreymann M^r W^m. Shacksepere deliver thees. [*Seal*] On a bend three trefoils slipped.

The letter which Richard Quiney wrote to William Shakespeare in October 1598 from The Bell Inn, Carter Lane, London – now in The Shakespeare Birthplace Trust Library.

scruple about pulling rank, a privy counsellor perhaps who made plain that he had the ear of the monarch. He would not hesitate to commit anyone to prison who happened to displease them by suing for just debts. The unhappy creditor, as David Hume relates, 'though he gained his cause in the courts of justice, was commonly obliged to relinquish his property in order to obtain his liberty.'

> Some likewise who had been delivered from prison by the judges were again committed to custody in secret places without any possibility of obtaining relief; and even the officers and serjeants of the courts of law were punished for executing the writs in favour of these persons. Nay, it was usual to send for people by pursuivants, a kind of harpies, who then attended the orders of the council and high commission; and they were brought up to London and constrained by imprisonment, not only to withdraw their lawful suits but also to pay the pursuivants great sums of money.

In 1592 the judges complained to Queen Elizabeth I of the frequency of this practice, but in protecting the lower strata of the queen's subjects from the tyranny of the great and powerful, they had to allow that a creditor committed to prison by special command of the queen was not bailable. Twenty years earlier she had approved the assessment of a county rate for the relief of gaoled debtors. She showed her concern for her humbler subjects at the same time by re-enacting in 1571 the statute, repealed by Edward VI in 1552, which her father had passed in an effort to regulate pawnbroking, which had become as acceptable as money-lending. This fixed the legal rate of interest at ten per cent (57 Henry VIII cap 9).

If the man-in-the-street despaired of surviving without an injection of funds to tide him over, slipping round the corner to the dolly shop with a candlestick under his arm was perhaps the simplest way of obtaining it. No one *chose* to borrow. But needs must when the devil drives. When the sixteenth century came to a close, most of those who wished to be seen walking uprightly in the eyes of the Lord would have agreed with the advice which Edgar, the Duke of Gloucester's son, gave to King Lear:

> Keep thy foot out of brothels, thy hand out of plackets [petticoats], thy pen from lenders' books and defy the foul fiend.

CHAPTER TWO

Mistery and Misery

– in the seventeenth century

The King of Scots, who in 1603 found himself King of England too, in spite of believing that no prince should embark on any considerable undertaking in the first year of his reign, at once summoned Parliament and started issuing proclamations. No one, he proclaimed to his faithful Commons, should be capable of taking their seat in their assembly who had been outlawed for non-payment of debts – or for any other reason.

In 1580 a man called Vaughan had been 'questioned for outlawry'. He told his questioners he had contracted all his debts 'by suretiship', of which he had proof, and that most of them had been honestly compounded. They accepted what he said and he was allowed to keep his seat in Parliament. After thinking about this event for thirteen years, Members of the House staged a formal debate on it, and a majority voted for the motion that Vaughan had been rightfully reinstated, and that anyone outlawed as he had been could be elected and take his seat. In the speech she made to her last Parliament, Queen Elizabeth I expressed her disagreement. Admitting debtor (and other) outlaws, she said, was a great abuse. James I concurred, and in his proclamation of 1604, using his royal prerogative as by divine right, he ordained that in future his subjects would not choose outlaws for their representatives.

What force had a royal proclamation? Was it not an invasion of the privileges of Parliament? Many Members thought just that, and to show their disapproval reversed the Chancellor's decision to vacate the seat of Sir Francis Goodwin, who had been outlawed, and to issue a writ for a new election. They voted for Sir Francis to be restored to his seat.

The argument over who was ruling England, King or Parliament, was gathering momentum. Did not perhaps the new Stuart ruler think that his Tudor predecessor had overreached her powers in appointing commissioners to inspect prisons with full discretionary powers to adjust differences between debtor prisoners and their creditors, to compound debts, and actually to free any debtors they considered honest and insolvent? It was right and proper that overindebtedness

29

should not be a reason for reversing the decision of constituents to make a man their parliamentary representative. But on no account should an insolvent debtor be allowed to circumvent the normal processes of law at the whim of a 'commissioner' acting only on the authority of a despot however benevolent.

Was not Queen Elizabeth's commission contrary to the constitution, to the law? When Members invited King James to express a view on the matter, he suspended the Commission until 1618. In that year there were so many complaints about the abuses practised in debtors' prisons that he felt obliged to appoint a new set of commissioners invested with the same discretionary powers which Queen Elizabeth had given them.

Circumstances made men poor and conspired to keep them in gaol. In Stuart England the gap between rich and poor, with a middling class only just beginning to emerge, was sadly wide. Poverty and want were abhorred of all men, wrote Robert Burton, priest, scholar and librarian of Christ Church, Oxford, in *The Anatomy of Melancholy* published in 1621. To avoid it, he said, people would leave no haven, no coast, no creek of the world untouched, though it be to the hazard of their lives. 'We will turn parasites and slaves, prostitute ourselves, swear and lie, damn our bodies and souls, forsake God, adjure religion, steal, rob, murder rather than endure this insufferable yoke of poverty which doth so tyrannise, crucify and generally depress us.' Commending the happy mean to all his readers as the rule of life that kept melancholy at bay, he bade them pray with Solomon, 'Give me Lord neither riches nor poverty; feed me with food convenient for me.' (Proverbs, chapter 30, verse 8)

He accepted that there could be circumstances which justified people borrowing to relieve want. But not everyone who wanted to – orphans, maids, widows 'or such as by reason of their age, sex, education, ignorance of trading' – knew how to do so. As usual he tried to take a balanced view.

> Brokers, takers of pawns, biting usurers, I will not admit; yet because we converse here with men, not with gods, and for the hardness of men's hearts, I will tolerate some kind of usury. If we were honest, I confess we should have no use of it, but being as it is we must necessarily admit it. Howsoever most divines contradict it (we say "no" with our lips but do not mean it), it must be winked at by politicians. And yet some great doctors approve of it, Calvin, Bucer, Zanchius, P. Martyr, because by so many grand lawyers, decrees of emperors, princes' statutes, customs of commonwealths, churches' approbations, it is permitted etc, I shall therefore allow it. (from his preface 'Democritus To The Reader')

Few would have sympathy with self-imposed poverty. Young women who saw Philip Massinger's satirical comedy *A New Way To Pay Old Debts* performed in London in 1621 might have applauded the trick played by the dashing Frank

MISTERY AND MISERY

Philip Massinger whose satirical comedy
A New Way To Pay Old Debts was first
performed in London in 1621.

Wellborn on his grasping uncle Sir Giles Overreach, and admired him as the hero who thwarted the villain's plot to deprive him of his inheritance. But there was little attractive, though much familiar, in the riches to rags story of the prodigal son who made his first entrance 'in tattered apparel' to be reminded by his father's one-time butler Tapwell of the merry time he had on the family estate as a young man with hawks and hounds, 'with choice of running horses, mistresses of all sorts and sizes'. His uncle had financed his loose living 'with foolish mortgages, statutes and bonds', and then left him.

> Your land gone and your credit not worth a [tradesman's] token,
> You grew the common borrower, no man 'scaped
> Your paper-pellets.

The fictional Frank Wellborn was as much a stock character of early seventeenth-century drama as early seventeenth-century life. Like the real Lord Compton the penniless but handsome young rake found himself being wooed by a woman of wealth, in his case the widow Lady Allworth, with whom a marriage would restore him to his place in society from which he had allowed himself to sink. Uncle Giles encouraged the match since it would remove her ladyship's other suitor Lord Lovell to whom he wished to marry his daughter who, as Lady Lovell, would greatly increase his credit worthiness. Giles is shocked at Frank's appearance and insists on his being allowed to make him more presentable.

Still in the repertoire after three hundred years.

> Because your stay is short, I'll have you seen
> No more in this base shape; nor shall she say
> She married you like a beggar or in debt.
> You have a trunk of rich clothes, not far hence,
> In pawn; I will redeem them; and that no clamour
> May taint your credit for your petty debts,
> You shall have a thousand pounds to cut them off
> And go a free man to the wealthy lady.

Sir Giles sees Lady Allworth's Knave Acre Estate, of which his nephew will become master, as a means of raising more money. Remember, he reminds Frank,

> Upon mere hope of your great match, I lent you
> A thousand pounds; put me in good security,
> And suddenly [at once], by mortgage or by statute,
> Of some of your new possessions, or I'll have you
> Dragg'd in your lavender robes to gaol; you know me,
> And therefore do not trifle.

To lay something in lavender was a cant phrase for pawning.

MISTERY AND MISERY

Frank taunts him – did he do this 'in pure love and no ends else?' – and Sir Giles reacts violently.

> End me no ends! engage the whole estate
> And force your spouse to sign it, you shall have
> Three or four thousand more, to roar and swagger
> And revel in bawdy taverns.

Overreach says he has the Deed of Sale on which he can raise the money, but Frank wants the return of his father's land which he claims was only handed over to his uncle on trust, was never his property and should now be handed back.

FRANK.   You charge me with a debt of a thousand pounds.
                  If there be law (howe'er you have no conscience)
                  Either restore my land, or I'll recover
                  A debt that's truly due to me from you
                  In value ten times more than what you challenge.
OVERREACH. I in thy debt! O impudence! did I not purchase
                  The land left by thy father, that rich land
                  That had continued in Wellborn's name
                  Twenty descents, which like a riotous fool
                  Thou didst make sale of?

Frank reiterates he never 'passed over' the land, though Sir Giles had it for a year or two on trust, which if he discharged

> Surrendering the possession, you shall ease
> Yourself and me of chargeable suits in law
> Which, if you prove not honest, as I doubt it,
> Must of necessity follow.

But Frank, it turns out, is far from frank. He *is* the villain of the piece. Sir Giles has a legally binding conveyance to him of his brother's land, and Frank engages Marall to 'raze out the conveyance' by stealing the document from Overreach's case, applying 'certain minerals incorporated in ink and wax' to obliterate the wording, and putting it back. Evil triumphs, but Massinger labelled it as such and made no bones about his attitude being one of disapproval.

No self-respecting writer could invite readers or playgoers to admire the lifestyle of a Frank Wellborn who arrogantly disdained to benefit himself from inherited wealth – unlike the humble Tim Tapwell who with his stock of forty pounds bought a small cottage which he made into a tavern where he 'gave entertainment'.

33

The Mistery and Misery of Lending and Borrowing. By Tho. Powel, Gent.

London : Printed by Thomas Harper for Benjamin Fisher, and are to be sold at his Shop in Aldersgate streete, at the Signe of the Talbot. 1636.

Setting aside the contemplation of such lending and borrowing as wherby the soule of traffique is breathed into the body of a commonwealth, I descend lower to that practice of mutuation, wherby we accommodate one another for our present necessity in money and other requisites.

First, for the Borrower.

I will first shew who bee the most notable sort of borrowers and book-men.
Next, what method every one holds in his severall way of borrowing and lending.
Then their severall cause of failing and insolvency.
Next, their sundry waies and weapons, with which they fence with their creditors.
Next, their noted places of refuge and retirement.
Then their jubiles and daies of priviledge.
Lastly, the certaine markes of a conscious cautious debtor, with the marshall discipline of the mace according to the modern practise of these daies.

Next, for the Creditor.

I will first shew the charitable extent of the creditors curtesie.
Then his mystery of multiplication.
Next, how the oyster caught the crow.   The hand in the booke bred the wind-collick in the ware-house.
And then, how that winde, being not able to force a passage through the cavernes of his credit, shakt the very foundation of his shop-boord, threatning a most sudden, strange, and stormy eruption.
Next, the signes fore-running the wonderfull cracke.
Then the reparation of the decaied man.
And lastly, the singular comfort which the commonwealth received by him when he was sent forth current from the creditors mint, with a new impression and a second edition.

And of these in order.

The chief and most notable borrowers are,
The courtier, that neither cares for the call of the counting-house nor the checke of the chamber.

VOL. VII.   2 D

The opening of Thomas Powel's tract on lending and borrowing of 1636.

Ridicule by satire was a less-than-heavy way of condemning conduct, which many will have seen as manly, without appearing a prude; and writers like Tho. Powel, gent., who produced *The Mistery and Misery of Lending and Borrowing* in 1636, used it with great effect.

He agreed that there was an aspect of lending and borrowing by which the soul of traffic (trade) was breathed into the body of a commonwealth, but he would set that aside, and descend to the lower practice of mutuation (borrowing) whereby people accommodated one another for their present necessity in money and other requisites.

The plan of his tract was to show who were the most notable sort of borrowers and 'book-men'; what methods everyone held in their several ways of borrowing and lending; their several causes of failing and insolvency; their sundry ways and weapons with which they fenced with their creditors; their noted places of refuge and retirement; their jubilees and days of privilege; and 'lastly, the certaine markes of a conscious cautious debtor'.

In the second part he dealt with the creditor or lender. 'I will first shew the charitable extent of the creditors curtesie; then his mystery of multiplication; next, how the oyster caught the crow, the hand in the booke bred the wind-collick in the warehouse; and then how that winde, being not able to force a passage through the cavernes of his credit, shakt the very foundation of his shop-board, threatning a most sudden, strange, and stormy eruption; next the signes fore-running the wonderfull cracke; then the reparation of the decaied man; and lastly, the singular comfort which the commonwealth received by him when he was sent forth current from the creditors mint, with a new impression and a second edition.'

He listed the four chief and most notable borrowers as first the courtier that neither cares for the call of the counting-house nor the 'checke' of the chamber; then the Inns of Court man that never was a student; thirdly the country gentleman 'no hospitall house-keeper'; and fourthly the city gallant 'that never arrived at his freedome by service.'

The courtier's method was to soften up a prospective lender by inviting him in the first place to eat a fish dish of ling 'with masculine mustard plenty', at court, after which he would show him round the privy and the new banqueting house, and may have a glimpse of 'the robes'. 'Then the great magolls tent in the wardrobe; and so much serves for the first meeting, and to procure him an appetite for the second.'

Next time the lender brought his wife behind him 'like to a broken wicker glasse bottle hanging at his taile'. They all went into the masking-room. As the courtier noticed the lady's spouse become more and more sleepy, the more vigilant he became over his female charge, and by skilfully telling the names of the maskers under their several disguises, purchased an everlasting and indissoluble 'city-consanguinity' with her. The relationship he had now established with the man he sought to borrow from was such that he could visit him in his home and ask him in a familiar and informal way for a loan.

He would build on the trust he had created in this way, so that he could quicken, continue and enlarge his borrowing by pretending that he had received news that a 'faign'd kindred' was very sick, and send the wife a bottle of Frontiniac French wine. That evening he invites himself to drink at their house. Over the meal 'in a cursory way of commending the excellent art of man in manner of manufacture', he recalls how greatly he had admired the stuff of the suit which a great personage at court was wearing. He had had no doubt, he told his hosts, that his cousin's shop stocked just that material and, determined to have a suit made of it for himself, he had visited the shop and been told 'they would lay it by till his moneys come in'.

> Yet, with a very little intreaty, so cleanly exprompted, hee was persuaded to take it along with him, but onely for feare lest the whole peece might be sold by the foolish fore-man unawares before his returne.

The impressed creditor would have felt it impolite not to accommodate the dinner guest who, in passing, had happened to mention this singular episode, and was only too pleased to be the means of enabling a courtier not to miss the chance of buying the material on which he had set his heart.

The Inns of Court man made his first contact with the tailor from whom he wanted credit in the company of a regular customer who always paid promptly, and had agreed to be his accomplice in a straightforward con trick. This known customer took the tailor apart as they were walking down his shop and whispered to him, pointing at the Inns of Court man, that that gentleman was son and heir 'to that worthy knight so potent in the Peake, or that most markable malster of Much Marlborne, or the great grasier of Grimsborrow or the like'. The tailor then called an assistant to bring the would-be customer a stool, and the tailor who wanted custom and the gentleman who wanted to take a suit away without paying for it, excelled each other in playing out the masquerade that the story of the latter's family background, as expounded by the accomplice, was true. The tailor is convinced that he has found a new customer who will shortly come into a fortune, though at the moment he was pinched for cash. 'Alas, you pinch for it!' cries the now completely conned tradesman, 'That shall not need. God be thanked, your creditor is worthy to be rankt in a shop-booke, cheeke by joule, with any debitory disposed gentleman of this towne whatsoever . . . You speake like an honest gentleman. I would all of our customers were of your minde; there be too few such as you are. If you need of any thing heere, either for your wearing or else for conversion, wherein I hope you conceive me, sir it is at your command.'

The country gentleman brought his attorney to London with him, and they went together to the Ship Inn behind the Royal Exchange. The attorney fetched over a scrivener (money-lender) whom he had told of his client's needs and shaken familiarly by the hand 'to insinuate his meaning as unto his share'. At this meeting the lender was more easy in promising than the would-be borrower in proposing, according to the usual practice at a first meeting in a tavern. The attorney told his country client that he would be well to bespeak supper instantly, for 'if he could but fasten that courtesie upon the scrivener for the present', he would be his for ever after, and neither the sum to be lent nor the security could be a matter of any difficulty.

The three of them ate a three-course supper, the country gentleman was presented with the bill. While he is feeling for the money in his pocket, he is asked by the scrivener how much he wants to borrow. There is a horse race at Northampton on Monday week which he will want to bet at; he needs new furniture; he would like to buy the hawk he had seen in Southwark that afternoon, and some new clothes. 'Let's see,' he tells the scrivener, 'a matter of three hundred will doe't, so far forth as my present and most urgent occasions do presse me at this instant':

> As for payment
> And for rayment,
> For hedges and mounds
> And stocking of grounds,
> For corne, for seed,
> Or cattle to breed,
> Or the wolfe at the doore
> And a thousand things more.

The party breaks up. The country gentleman thanks his attorney for procuring the meeting, commends the comely carriage of the scrivener and vows everlasting acknowledgement of his attorney's activity. The three hundred pounds were to be a first instalment of a parcel of a thousand pounds.

The city gallant, 'the Citizen, a Redemptionary Freeman', a youth not altogether free by patrimony, was 'wonderful cautious of borrowing upon record or in the eye of the world'. So he found a young heir who, for a third share of the sum, 'was content to beare the only name and blame of borrower'.

Tom Powel thought each of the four became insolvent for different reasons.

The courtier's cause is his conscience: for he neither can nor cares to pay.
The innes of court man's cause is in his coercence, for he would if he could pay.
The countrie gentleman's cause is his confidence, for he trusts to his countrymen in the city, and had rather they than he should pay.
But the citizen's cause is in his compliance.

They each had different weapons with which to fence off their creditors. The courtier kept them at bay by 'winters journeys and the summers progresse'. But when he was nearer home he kept them at staves length by craving privacy because of an indisposition of his body, having to hold conference with great and honourable personages or employment in the state's wonderful weighty affairs. In fact, says Powel, the conference is about how to pay his laundress; his employment is in and about the taking of a pipe of tobacco. If he found that his creditor was about to close in on him, he swore that he was about to send for him.

The first weapon of the Inns of Court man was a well penned letter excusing his delay; his next his good sword, a watchful eye and a ready hand. The young country gentleman had no occasion to practise a defence. When the day came for him to make payment to the Solomon in Silver Street in London, he, in his better wisdom, was betting of all his white money at the cock-pit in Coventry. The City Borrower handled his weapon with the best grace of them all. His creditor scarce dared to come within his reach but only ask him how he does (how d'ye do?) as he goes by.

The scandal of the lending and borrowing trade had become a commonplace joke for the observers of the social scene as it had always been for rich, frivolous libertines like Sir John Suckling, who was twenty-seven when Tom Powel published his *Mistery and Misery* and knew that others of his kind would share his cavalier attitude to

LOVE AND DEBT

> This one request I make to him that sits the clouds above;
> That I were freely out of debt, as I am out of love.
> Then for to dance, to drink, and sing, I should be very willing;
> I should not owe one lass a kiss, nor ne'er a knave a shilling.

> 'Tis only being in love and debt, that breaks us of our rest;
> And he that is quite out of both, of all the world is blessed.
> He sees the golden age, wherein all things were free and common;
> He eats, he drinks, he takes his rest, he fears no man nor woman.

That overindebtedness was a light-hearted matter, a fit subject for light verse, was held by few whose excesses or misfortunes had deprived them of their liberty and landed them in gaol. Their number in England and Wales, according to a petition presented to Parliament in 1641, was 'about ten thousand'.

In this the distressed prisoners for debt in King's Bench Prison called the legislators' attention to the fact that by assenting to the Petition of Right in 1628 the king had confirmed Magna Carta which was now being breached. Not only that; imprisonment of men's bodies for debt was against the law of God, of Man, of Conscience and Christian Charity and the creditors' own profit.

No law of God in the Old Testament commanded putting debtors in gaol, they said. On the contrary, it expressly forbade it. 'To forgive our brothers debts and

MISTERY AND MISERY

The rich, frivolous, libidinous Sir John Suckling, the poet for whom being in love and in debt were the only things which disturbed his rest.

trespasses as God should forgive our sins, to love our neighbour as ourself . . . must needs exclude all violence, rigour, cruel dealings, oppression, hard heartedness and ruling of one brother over another.'

By Magna Carta the body of a free-borne man might not be imprisoned except by the law of the land – which did not provide for treating debtors in that way. Subsequent statutes were introduced permitting it on the grounds that men made secret estates in trust to defraud their creditors. But once the fraud was proved, the 'secret' estate became liable to the debt. If the law punished the debtor for fraud, what need was there to punish him for debt?

> Let the debtors sufficiency be proved, and forthwith the law gives it to the creditor, whether the debtor will or no; so it is still needless to imprison the body, especially when twenty years imprisonment discounteth never a penny of the debt: and yet the debtor has suffered more misery and punishment upon a mere supposition of fraud or obstinacy than a guilty traitor or rebel suffereth for the highest offence.

Was imprisonment of debtors for coercion (to make them pay up) or for punishment? If the latter, it was against the rule of justice. For to be found a debtor was no criminal guilt. If the former, to enforce a man by way of punishment to do what was not within his power was clearly against justice. It was unjust too to thrust all kind of debtors in a prison together in a heap without respect to their different qualities, to whether they were more or less guilty of fraud or obstinacy, to whether they had an honest or usurious debt. It was unjust to ignore whether a debtor had more or less means whereby he must live or starve in prison.

THE WORST POVERTY

It was contrary to the law of Conscience and Christian Charity to incarcerate anyone who, not knowing how to inform his own case aright, had fallen guiltlessly and innocently by the law, or had done so by the negligence of his attorney, by the perjury of witnesses, the forgery of bonds and deeds, by the corruption of the judge. Anyone could be disabled and become insolvent by casualties and acts of honest and good intention such as standing surety for a friend, lending money which was not repaid, defending a just suit of law in which delay consumed him, suffering shipwreck or robbery, selling land or merchandise unprofitably, making accounting errors. Many had got involved 'by usury which slyly and suddenly eateth up a man's estate ere he be aware.'

> In brief, so frail, insecure and inconstant are all the doings of man in this world that there is no man, in what state or condition soever, but may become insolvent and in debt by one way or other.

Even though a debtor had discharged ninety-nine pounds principal by selling his goods, his body was still subject to be taken till he had paid the whole forfeiture of two hundred pounds. And to do so was in the absolute will and power of the creditor. Once in prison the law did not care whether the person had the means to pay what he owed, or not. It was not concerned whether or not he was able to keep himself in life. Anyone with no means was more likely to starve by famine than to win payment of his debt.

Some had means to pay and were willing to do so but had not the power – their estate, for instance, might be entangled with jointures or embroiled with trustees. There were hardly five hundred debtors who had been imprisoned because of fraud or obstinacy. It was the common slander of creditors to cloak their cruelty and tyranny. Many were shut up on the bare suggestion of a creditor who gave no reason, and had never even spoken to his victim – 'much resembling the course of the foreign Inquisition'. The gaoling of a debtor whose estate would not extend to discharge his whole debt was perpetual, so equal to death or banishment. The ancient Common Law of England was very strict about maintaining contracts, but in those days they were simple and honest documents, and recovery was against the estate only. Usury was not practised by Christians, and there were no penal bonds. However Chancery could mitigate the rigour of the Common Law, and wrong judgements could be reversed by 'Attaint Errors'. It was unreasonable though for a man, disabled by imprisonment, to have to seek a remedy by costly new suits at Law or Chancery. The Statute of Bankruptcy had many provisions for recovery by creditors, but not one act of tenderness towards the debtor.

A man called Frith mortgaged his estate, from which he earned £1,600 a year, to several rich men to whom he became indebted for £8,000. He was stripped of all his possessions and, having pawned his bedclothes and his children's garments, was left with only four farthings. No one would sell him food on credit, so he killed himself with a pistol. Some twelve years previously the landlord of The White Lyon near King's Bench in London, whose name was Allen, was sent to prison, with the two men who stood surety for him in execution of £30 forfeiture and costs, for a £12 principal debt. 'Being mechanical men and not able to pay or maintain themselves in prison, are all three, through want, grief and misery, dead and perished.'

This was the human cost of the laws they had made, said the petitioners of 1641 to the King's Most Excellent Majesty, the Lords Spiritual and Temporal and Commons in the High Court of Parliament assembled. Moreover imprisonment was the cause of much murder and bloodshed; and many were yearly choked up and slain by idle life, ill air, famine and plague in English prisons, and by desperate executions on their bodies for the heavy weight and misery they bore. To gain reward, bailiffs and serjeants would venture life and limb to kill or be killed for the arresting and haling the debtor to prison. Yet, they pointed out, in Germany, France, Italy, Spain and the Low Countries of the 1640s no man was detained in prison for debt for more than a year and a day.

If King Charles's assent to the petition of 1628 was an absolute and legal confirmation of the Great Charter, then it nullified all the statutes which followed, contradicting it and betraying the liberty of the subject.

Within a year the king and the Parliament had more pressing matters to attend to – on the battlefield, as opposing sides in the Great Rebellion, as Cavaliers who became the Tories and then the Conservatives, and Roundheads who became the Whigs and then the Liberals. It was not for another seven years that the Rump could heed the cry of the distress that came from those imprisoned debtors. They had voted to kill their king, abolish the monarchy and the 'useless and dangerous' House of Lords; they had declared the kingdom a republic – or Commonwealth. But now they were only the country's lawmakers in name, or rather only with the agreement of God and the Lord-General. Oliver Cromwell had usurped the absolute power of the late King Charles, and his divine right to it. 'Truly you are called by God to rule with him and for him', he told Members. No one could have been more sympathetic to an appeal for Justice and Christian Charity. 'In every government there must be somewhat fundamental, somewhat like a Magna Charta, that would be standing and be unalterable', he told the Second Protectorate Parliament. There was one general grievance in the nation, and that was the law. The great grievance lay in the execution and administration of the law.

> The truth of it is there are wicked abominable laws that it will be in your power to alter.
> To hang a man for sixpence, thirteen pence, I know not what; to hang for a trifle and

pardon murder is in the ministration of the law, through the ill-framing of it. I have known in my experience abominable murders acquitted. And to come to see men lose their lives for petty matters; this is a thing that God will reckon for . . . This hath been a great grief to many honest hearts and conscientious people; and I hope it is all in your hearts to rectify it.

He had already had them rectify the treatment of insolvent debtors when he made that speech in 1656. As Macaulay wrote of those times in his *History of England*, 'Justice was administered between man and man with an exactness and purity not before known.'

In 1649 Parliament passed the country's first statute which provided for the release of imprisoned insolvent debtors. 'The act', states Jay Cohen, 'became a model of Parliamentary attempts at debtors' relief for the following century.' By it a debtor had to be released from prison if he swore on oath that his assets were not worth more than five pounds, and that he had not transferred part of his estate to a trust from which he would benefit.

No longer was it the creditor who alone dictated his debtor's fate. It was a revolutionary change of attitude on the part of the lawmakers who had hitherto resisted 'interference' with what they regarded as a matter for settlement personally between the parties concerned.

The new procedure was for the judge to tell the creditor that in thirty days' time the man or woman who owed him money, and he had thrust into prison, would be brought from it to his courtroom and swear to the value of his assets and to the absence of a trust. If he, the creditor, confronted with his debtor's declaration on oath, could not refute it, his victim could leave the court a free man. If, having been given a month's notice, the merchant failed to come to court, his debtor was free to go also. A second Act later that year stated that if a creditor did dispute what his debtor had declared, the case must be tried by a jury.

The freed man was no longer a prisoner, but he was still a debtor. He could be sued by the man from whom he had borrowed for the payment of any outstanding debt, if the lender thought the sale of any new goods he bought after his release would raise the necessary amount.

If Tom Verney had tried to get out of prison by swearing his assets were worth less than five pounds no one would have believed him. In *The Verneys of Claydon* (1968) Sir Harry Verney brands him liar and braggart, idle and extravagant, plausible and quick-witted without care or scruple. Born into a distinguished Puritan family, Tom failed to make good in whatever situation he found himself. He failed to make a go of running plantations in Virginia or Barbados (twice) for which his parents lavishly kitted him out at great expense. He was less than a

success as either a naval or army officer. His main failure was to keep out of
mischief, out of debt, out of prison. On the occasions when, in the 1630s, he
returned to Claydon House, the fine family home in Buckinghamshire, 'on leave'
from some overseas misadventure, he found the servants had been instructed not
on any account to lend him money, or indeed a horse which likely as not he would
sell to put himself in funds.

With the outbreak of the Civil War his father thought better of sending him back
to the West Indies for the third time, and Sir Edmund Verney and son Tom both
rallied to the side of the Royalists. As the King's Standard Bearer, Sir Edmund was
killed at the start of the Battle of Edgehill (23 October 1642). Adventuring with the
standard among the enemy in order that the soldiers might be engaged to follow
him, Cromwell's men offered him his life if he would surrender the flag. When he
told them his life was his own but the standard King Charles's, he killed two of
them before himself being slain.

The troop to which Tom was attached was surrounded and forced to surrender
at Chichester. Tom was captured and taken prisoner – for once in military, not
civil, confinement. In January 1643 he wrote to his elder brother Ralph, now the
new baronet, for ten pounds – the brother who had taken an oath of allegiance to
Tom's captors, the Parliamentarians. In his begging letter Tom related a conversation which a friend had overheard in the Horne Taverne in Fleet Street. One man
had said to another he wondered why Ralph Verney, being in so great favour in the

Idle and extravagant Tom Verney,
seldom out of debt, who sided with
Cromwell in the Civil War and was
always being bailed out by his Cavalier
brother Sir Ralph – the portrait which
hangs in Claydon House, the family
home in Buckinghamshire.

THE WORST POVERTY

Parliament House, did not seek his brother's release from his close confinement. He reproached Ralph for making him 'a laughing stock and talk to every unworthy rascall'.

It was not a very clever attitude to adopt towards the only person to whom he could apply for the money which could release him from the debtors' prisons in which he spent so much of his time, and for the necessities which would make life bearable while he was in them.

> To imitate historians in putting prefaces to their books [ran a typical appeal from prison], I conceive I need not, for I am confident you are so very sensible of my want of clothing. Sir, my last request to you is for a slight stuff & coat against Whitsuntide, which may stand you in 50s, the which I will repay you by 3s weekly till you be reimbursed. In former times my own word would have passed for such a sum, but now they require security of me, because I live in so cloudy a condition. God put it in your heart once to relieve my nakedness & you shall find it a most obliging brother of Sir, your humble servant Thomas Verney.

In spite of the abuse, Ralph thought it was his duty to come to the rescue of his wayward brother insofar as he could. He heard from his uncle Dr William Denton, to whom Tom had written, about the action taken by his landlady, and from the good woman herself who took to calling on him. 'Fearing that I should play the knave with her', he told Denton,

> she (not withstanding my then weakness) betrayed me into the prison of the fleet, and I was brought thither by 8 of the clock the last night; which I fear will be a means to put me into a second relapse; for I was forced to walk in the yard all night, having neither fire, money but one poor groat, nor room to shelter me in from the coldness and rawness of the night.

The Fleet Prison, said Tom, was called the grave of the living where they are 'shut up from the world, the worms that gnaw upon them, their own thoughts, the jaylor and their creditors.' He could not face the horrors of the common wards nor pay the great rates exacted by the gaolers for better quarters. In the circumstances Ralph felt obliged to get him a private room, for which the lowest price would be eight shillings a week, plus other fees. He was thankful, but the change of environment did little to relieve his suffering.

> My confinement is so very chargeable, my chamber so extreme cold, my habit so thin, that I did by letter make my desires known . . . Good brother, here is now some cold snowie weather approaching, which incites me to put on warmer clothes. I must confess I am moved for a coat of shagg'd bayes, but you are suspicious my cloak would be then pawned. Hunger will break through strong walls, and I shall be so plain with you as to let

44

Cast into the Fleet Prison by his landlady in January 1652 for being behind with the rent, Tom Verney pens an anguished appeal for help to his uncle Dr William Denton.

you know that rather than I should starve, cloak coat and all that I had should go to relieve nature. But thanks be to God your charities and brotherly affection hath so amply appeared to me that I have not known what hath belonged to want since tuesday last.

Worst livers than himself had seen their errors, and returned home like the prodigal. 'Why may not I? God hath endued me with a reasonable understanding.' He did not question a real conversion since he had so courteous, so kind and so tender-hearted a brother to help him up before he was quite down.

I beg the continuance of a weekly supply during my restraint. Eighteen pence a day, which amounts in the week to 10s 6d, is as low as any one that is borne a gentleman can possibly live at. Let my wants be supplied by noon that I may have a dinner as well as others.

Tom was released before it was time for dinner, but then immediately arrested and taken back. 'I have been now ever since Sunday at night in prison', he wrote, 'and have not come within a pair of sheets or a bed, or have had a fire or any meat to eat but what I bought with my groat; and if this be not hard measure for one that hath been lately desperately sick, let the world judge . . . and if I perish I perish.'

Sir Ralph was moved to pity once more, and Tom wrote in fulsome praise of his long-suffering brother's pious charity which ought to be registered in the chronicle of fame as a memorial to future ages. But his needs were not yet fully satisfied.

One thing more I beseech you take notice of; which is that I must this night and so for the future, lodge without sheets if I pay them not two shillings. For I have lain my foul ones a fortnight; and would, if I could possibly prevail with the turnkey who receives money for his sheets, keep them longer. But that civility I am denied, as I am all others where now I am. Therefore I must pay 2s for a clean pair, which I beg of you to send me. And yet I cannot but blush for my mentioning a thing so inconsiderable and of so small a moment.

On his eventual release from prison Tom Verney considered taking himself off to Barbados yet again – where he would free of his debts as well – but he finally opted for a cheap lodging in Lambeth Marsh which he only ventured out of on a Sunday, the day no debtor could be arrested. He admitted he had come to a very low ebb, 'yet there may come a flood of prosperity which may enable me to express myself grateful.' Tom told his brother he would try and meet him in London next Sunday morning. 'I have made a choice of that day because it is a day of security for me to walk in; otherwise I am very sensible that it is an unseasonable day to visit in.' He asked for ten shillings with which he could buy himself a periwig, a 'must' even for those living in genteel poverty like Tom Verney who had now alienated all his friends. He asked him too, to advance him twenty pounds, to be repaid by four pounds quarterly, which would gain him employment in the Lord Protector's regiment of horse then in the West Country. He said he was as well able to build St Paul's as to raise twenty pounds by credit 'or else how'. He knew the need to play the Roundhead while Cromwell and his cronies were the masters, and only reassume his allegiance to the Cavalier cause when England once more became a monarchy and the House of Stuart was restored in the person of Charles II. Ever aware which side his bread was buttered on, the extraordinary Tom Verney, dedicated debtor, lived till he was ninety-two, blaming his behaviour on want 'the greatest provoker to mischief' but insisting 'I am not naturally inclined to evil'.

Not everyone cared as little for good housekeeping as Tom Verney. On 31 October 1663 Samuel Pepys told his diary of his great sorrow at finding himself £43 worse off than he was the previous month which was then £760 and was now but £717.

> But it hath chiefly arisen from my laying out in clothes for myself and wife; viz. for her about £12, and for myself £55 or thereabouts; having made myself a velvet cloak, two new cloth shirts, black, plain both; a new shag gown trimmed with gold buttons and twist, with a new hat, and silk tops for my legs, and many other things, being resolved henceforward to go like myself.

It was a matter of how people used the talents which were given them, profitably or unprofitably, as in the parable which Jesus told his followers, whether like Tom Verney they spent much of their life in flight from creditors and in misery in cold prisons without sheets or shirts, or like Samuel Pepys they enjoyed the bourgeois comforts that could be earned from keeping their balance. It was mostly, though not of course entirely, a matter of choice. 'Human development is a process of enlarging people's choices', the authors of The United Nations Development Programme were to claim 330 years later. In the days of the Merry Monarch, in the matter of whether or not it was their duty to make ends meet, most people, unlike eccentrics such as Tom Verney, had little choice and acted on religious principles.

The financial failure that led the outsiders of seventeenth-century England to want, to the lack of the necessities of life, to mischief, was considered inexcusable. The Puritans saw in the poverty of those who fell by the way, as R.H. Tawney showed in *Religion and the Rise of Capitalism*, 'not a misfortune to be pitied and relieved, but a moral failing to be condemned; and in riches, not an object of suspicion . . . but the blessing which rewards the triumph of energy and will.' They revolted against the economic paternalism which lingered on for thirty or forty years after the benevolent despotism of the Tudors had been constitutionally replaced. They demanded that business affairs should be left to business men 'unhampered by the intrusions of an antiquated morality or by misconceived arguments of public policy.'

THE WORST POVERTY

Puritan goldsmiths who found their trade as bullion brokers curbed by the re-establishment of the ancient office of Royal Exchange looked to the day when finally economic interests would be separated from ethical interests. Richard Steel's message in *The Tradesman's Calling* (1685) was that there was not necessarily a conflict between religion and business. 'Prudence and Piety', he asserted, 'were always very good friends.' It was a tradesman's duty to use his talents. By a fortunate dispensation the virtue enjoined on Christians – diligence moderation, sobriety, thrift – were the very qualities most conductive to commercial success. The vices of speculation and gambling were the ruin of tradesmen and led to bankruptcy.

The Privy Council relinquished their jurisdiction over debtors during the last half of the seventeenth century, and the legislators assumed the responsibility for relieving the harshness of the law. After the restoration of the monarchy in 1660, distressed prisoners petitioned the now restored House of Lords every other year until an Act, modelled on that of 1649, allowed a Justice of the Peace to have any imprisoned debtor brought before him. Under this statute of 1671, if a man was able to swear that he had not conveyed away his estate to defraud his creditors, the JP was empowered to give him a document certifying this was the case, in return for which he agreed to face the music at the next Quarter Sessions. If his statement on oath could not then be disproved, the Bench gave permission for him to be discharged from prison, unless the principal creditor insisted on his remaining there, which was still his right. However if he did, the new law stipulated that he must pay a weekly sum for the debtor's maintenance. If the creditor agreed that, in the circumstances, the man who owed him money should be set at liberty, he did so in the knowledge that the judgements recorded against him still held.

Further relief came in 1678 when Charles II's Parliament passed an Act allowing labourers who were unable to pay debts of more than £500, and had spent at least six months in gaol, to be moved to the workhouse from which they could demand to be released after two years. There was always the danger, as there had been for some time, that rogues would take advantage of humane laws by seeking the shelter of the debtors' prison to defraud their creditors, and the practice was widespread. There was no way of stopping collusive actions. Legislation had little effect either in stopping the malpractices of gaolers, experienced by Tom Verney, of siding with rich creditors able to afford the biggest bribes. But at least from 1682 onwards a debtor did not have to share a cell with a felon, though it is unlikely that gaolers of crowded and uninspected prisons ever applied that law (22, 23 Charles II cap 20) with any great assiduity.

The fanatical sect of Puritans who called themselves Friends, but others,

MISTERY AND MISERY

For John the Quaker, to owe money and not be able to repay it was against the strict rule of life prescribed in the Society of Friends' *Book of Christian Discipline*.

Quakers (from the convulsions of their enthusiastic preachers), would have been little worried by the company they kept in gaol, the plain diet, the coarse apparel. But few of them were imprisoned for any cause other than the behaviour in public which to many was insulting but their faith demanded. To owe money and not to be able to repay it, was against a strict rule of life that at times seemed to throw them off balance in many bizarre ways, but in this case earned them universal respect. A Quaker tradesman never asked more for his wares than the precise sum which he was determined to accept. The Society of Friends warned him too against being tempted to undertake more than he was able to for fear of it leading to overindebtedness and its attendant miseries.

Let Friends and bretheren in their respective Meetings watch over one another in the love of God and care of the Gospel; particularly admonishing that none trade beyond their ability, nor stretch beyond their compass; and that they use few words in their dealings, and keep their word in all things lest they bring, through their forwardness, dishonour to the precious truth of God. (*Book of Christian Discipline*, 1675)

THE WORST POVERTY

Thirteen years later a printed epistle published after the yearly meeting of 1688 enjoined them not to 'launch forth into trading and worldly business beyond what they can manage honourably and with reputation; and so that they may keep their word with all men, and that their yea may prove yea indeed, and their nay may be nay indeed.'

Even more relevant was the injunction of 1692:

> It is earnestly desired that the payment of just debts be not delayed by any professing Truth beyond the time agreed upon; nor occasion of complaint given to those they deal with by their backwardness of payment where no time is limited; nor any to overcharge themselves with too much trading and commerce beyond their capabilities to discharge with a good conscience towards all men; and that all Friends be very careful not to contract extravagant debts endangering the wronging of others and their families which some have done to the grieving hearts of the upright; nor to break their promises, contracts or agreements in their buying or selling, or in any other lawful affairs, to the injuring of themselves and others, occasioning strife and contention, and reproach to Truth and Friends. And it is advised that all Friends that are entering into Trade or that are in Trade, and have not stock sufficient of their own to answer the trade they aim at, be very cautious of running themselves into debt without advising with some of their experienced friends.

It was the year Daniel Defoe's losses in marine insurance led to his being made bankrupt for £17,000. In 1706 the failure of his brick works at Tilbury bankrupted him for the second time. He should perhaps have taken the Quakers' advice and sought the counsel of experienced friends, though as the author of *The Complete English Tradesman* and having had a stint as accountant to the Commissioners of the Glass Duty in 1694, he should have been able to manage his finances better. It was not as if he was as lacking in business acumen as his fellow writer William Wycherley, author of *The Plain Dealer* and *The Country Wife* who married the rich widow of Charles Moore, second Earl of Drogheda. When Laetitia died the year following his marriage and left him her entire fortune, her family disputed her will. Wycherley spent so much money on lengthy lawsuits contesting their allegations that, without help from either his father or King Charles II (who had given him £500 to convalesce in Montpellier after his illness in 1676), he found himself up to the eyes in debt – and thrown into the Fleet Prison, where he remained a wretched man for several years. His release came when King Charles's brother James II, delighted by a court performance of *The Plain Dealer* in 1685, heard of the author's plight and settled all his outstanding debts – or at least what he *said* was all of them. He remained extremely hard up for some time after his release, but on his father's death in 1697, inherited the family estates and was able to live in reasonable style in London.

Moses Pitt found himself being hounded by creditors when the Revolution of

Laudatur et Alget
Juven. Sat. I.

Daniel Defoe, whose losses in marine insurance and the failure of his brick works at Tilbury at the beginning of the eighteenth century, bankrupted him twice.

Title page of Moses Pitt's tract *The Cry of the Oppressed* (1692).

1688 prevented him from obtaining a clear title to the plot of land in Duke Street, St James's, on which he had built a big house which he let to Judge Jeffreys. He had Christopher Wren handle negotiations on his behalf, but even the intervention of that respected figure was of no avail. A succession of borrowings and lawsuits followed and then, to his horror, he found himself in Fleet Prison for debt. He was so appalled by his treatment that, when he was finally released he wrote to sixty-five other prisons and collated the replies. His book *The Cry of the Oppressed*, published in 1692, painted a terrible picture of the plight of people such as himself caught up in events they had no means of foreseeing let alone preventing; but it failed to stir 'the authorities' to take action.

CHAPTER THREE

Folly and Beggary
– up to the end of George II's reign

No one could have taught William Wycherley or Moses Pitt how to forestall the misfortune which overtook them. Until it started to happen, they had managed their finances – and their lives – with no exceptional merit but as well as most. There were plenty, however, whose attitude to those who brought disaster on themselves obliged them to lecture weak swimmers who chose to wade into a river they knew would be running too fast for them further down and end in a weir; to warn people who did not like the heat to keep out of the kitchen; to point to the need of people with small heads to have small hats; to be scornful about bravado and insist there was nothing prissy about appropriate restraint at the appropriate moment.

In 1705 the Reverend Mr John Kettlewell, Late a Presbyter of the Church of England, wrote a pamphlet entitled *The Great Evil and Danger of Profuseness and Prodigality*. If men did but consider what a reproach profuseness was to their discretion, what a reflection it was upon their judgement, even to support a character, they would live within the limits of their fortunes, he said, and not suffer their expenses to swallow up their revenue lest at some time they should be stigmatized with folly as well as beggary. The last was then only a complete misfortune when people through vanity drew it upon themselves.

The weight of that calamity had at times been so heavy and intolerable that men had chosen to force themselves out of life in a violent manner rather than endure the smart and anguish of it, of which their own age had given too many tragical instances.

His advice, said Kettlewell, was in line with that of the wise Son of Sirach reported in the eighteenth chapter of Ecclesiasticus, verse 33, 'Be not made a beggar by banqueting upon borrowing when thou hast nothing in thy purse, for thou shalt lie in wait for thy own life and be talked on.'

The civil law, he pointed out, treated men of that character very roughly, and ranked prodigals in the class of children and madmen, and appointed curators to the management of their concerns.

FOLLY AND BEGGARY

Let the differences in fortunes be never so great, he will always be *poor* whose expenses are more than his *income*; and he *rich* who can satisfy his desires without exceeding the measures of his revenue. The necessaries and conveniences of life lie in a small compass, but luxury is boundless.

In support of his contention he quoted what Plutarch had to say on the matter in his discourse against running into debt. In Ephesus, the Goddess Diana gave any debtor who fled to her temple freedom and protection against his creditor. But, said the Greek sage who wrote about AD 100, the sanctuary of parsimony and moderation in expenses was always open to the wise and would afford them a long space of joyful and honourable repose. For no usurer could enter into it to pluck them from it and carry them away a prisoner.

After all the bewailing and repentance, the effects of the sin of profuseness would remain to reproach and grieve the debtor and his unprovided-for relations. His debts would always be at hand to upbraid him with his sin when he was most extremely loath to hear of it.

They will set it before your eyes when you most passionately desire it had never been done . . . For debts will not be paid with a sigh or a tear; they are not such things as can be retracted by a wish and undone by repentance; but they will stand upon your score and be ready to break in upon your mind to rob you of all ease and comfort. They will continually be represented to you by the *importunity* of *creditors* who will incessantly be calling on you, representing their own suffering and your shame in your profuseness. All this will set the sin before you and make it live with you till you can suppose men that love money will forbear to demand it where it is due, or you that have it not shall pay it without creating it.

In a printed epistle of 1708, Quakers were reminded to exercise godly care by giving timely caution to any who broke their promises or delayed the payment of their just debts. In another, a few years later, it was earnestly desired that all Friends should be very careful not to run into larger trading and business than their capacities and abilities could well answer; and that they frequently inspected their circumstances and did not live at an expense beyond them. If, through adverse accidents, any should fail in paying their just debts, and after composition with their creditors prospered in their affairs so as to be capable of paying their deficiences, the meeting advised that they did not omit to do so, 'it being agreeable to the command of the gospel and common justice among men'.

It was desirable too that Quakers should avoid all inordinate pursuit after the things of this world by such ways as depended too much on the uncertain probabilities of hazardous enterprises. They were enjoined rather to labour to content themselves with such a plainer manner of living as was most agreeable to the self-denying truth which they professed and was most conducive to that tranquility of mind that was requisite to a religious conduct through this troublesome world.

Robert Nelson saw contentedness as necessary to the right government of the soul, opposing the vice of covetousness which made a man think he never had enough, the heinousness of which was contrary to the foundation of a good life. In *The Whole Duty of a Christian by way of Question and Answer*, he recommended his readers not to suffer their fancies to run on things they did not have.

Q. What's the second branch of covetous injustice?
A. Theft; whereby we sometimes withold that we should pay, and sometimes take from our neighbour what is already in his possession.
Q. How many sorts of debts are there?
A. Two: what we contract by borrowing; and what we contract by our own voluntary promise.
Q. Wherein appears injustice of not paying these debts?
A. In that we keep from our neighbours that which he has a right to; tho' not paying what we borrow is rather the more injurious; for thereby we take from him actually what he once had.
Q. How does a man commit even the sin of theft in borrowing?
A. When he takes from his neighbour upon promise of paying which he knows he is never like to restore to him.
Q. What ought a man to do in such a case?
A. To lay open his disability and see whether his neighbour is willing to run the hazard.
Q. Does justice equally oblige a man to pay those debts he is bound for?
A. Yes, because by being bound he makes them his own; and 'tis likely the creditor was inclined to lend upon the confidence of his security.
Q. Can we without injustice withold that which we have promised?
A. No. 'Tis now the Man's Right, and David makes it a part of the description of the Just Man that he keeps his promise tho' to his own disadvantage. ['He that sweareth unto his neighbour and disappointeth him not, though it were to his own hindrance.' Psalm 15]
Q. What sort of debts may be reduced to this head?
A. The wages of servants, and the hire of the labourer whose complaints cry to heaven for vengeance. Deut. 24. 14, 15.

There was no Christian objection to borrowing on the security of possessions left with a pawnbroker. Pawnbroking was not regarded as immoral – so long as the exercise was conducted honestly. Public pawnshops, with the monopoly to make loans at the legal rate to those who could not afford the rates of the money-lenders, had been opened at such places as Berwick (1598) and Stony Stratford (1624). In 1707 The Charitable Corporation was founded to conduct pawnbroking on a large scale. However, the directors gambled with the money which shareholders had subscribed, and the Common Council of the City of London felt obliged to petition the government to have the corporation dissolved. It collapsed in 1731 when its cashier, George Robinson MP, and another official disappeared, leaving only £30,000 out of the original capital of £600,000.

Regulation of the pawnbroking business came about in 1800 thanks to Lord Eldon who, as a young barrister, had often had recourse to pawning some of his valuables at the times when he was waiting for briefs. The pawnbroking fraternity were so grateful that for many years after his death they toasted his health at their annual dinners.

Under the Act of 1800 interest was fixed at fourpence in the pound per month, with the money being on loan for twelve months. The committee which the government appointed to report on the state of the pawnbroking business in 1870 found that some 200 million articles had been pawned the previous year. Of these around 40 million had been pledged in London. The average value of the article was about four shillings; one in fourteen thousand was pawned dishonestly.

A pawnbroker issued three tickets: one for the customer, one for his records, and one to attach to the article pawned for identification. Many of them used a pen with three nibs, one on the handle and two on extended arms. In this way pawn was effected by 'three hands' with one stroke of the pen.

It was not always the pawnbroker who was dishonest. There is the story of the old lady who pawned her sewing machine every week wrapped in a table cloth. She collected ten shillings on it. 'She came so regularly', said the author of this story, 'that eventually we did not bother to unwrap the parcel. But when she had not returned to redeem it for some time, we traced a bad smell to her parcel, opened it and found not a sewing machine but a sheep's head crawling with maggots.'

People who made a habit of patronizing Uncle provided the regular custom by which the pawnshop survived. They did not do so out of financial misman-agement; it was a cornerstone of their housekeeping. It was only their 'betters' who mishandled their wealth, the folk who earned the scorn of Joseph Addison for disdaining the economy of the merchant and thought it beneath them to act the steward. 'The gentleman no more than the merchant is able without the help of numbers to account for the success of any action or the prudence of any adventure [investment]'.

It is the misfortune of many other gentlemen to turn out of the seats of their ancestors to make way for such new masters as have been more exact in their accounts than themselves; and certainly he deserves the estate a great deal better who has got it by his industry than he who has lost it by his negligence. (*The Spectator*, no. 174, Wednesday, 19 September 1711)

Most gentlemen, unlike the young Eldon, kept themselves out of debt, not by pawning their valuables at the sign of the three golden balls, but by 'depositing'

A three golden balls sign over the words 'Money Lent' marks the door of John Flude's pawnshop in Grace Church Street, London – his trade card, *c.* 1780.

Pawnbroker James Hebbert's receipt for goods pawned by a Mr Allen in July 1762.

them at the sign of the leather bottle in Fleet Street with a banker like Richard Hoare. When the Earl of Nottingham entrusted him in July 1705 with two boxes containing several ingots of silver and pieces of plate, taken round to the bank by his servant, he received a letter acknowledging receipt of the boxes, and telling him he had assayed and weighed them. He had not included in the value of what had been deposited, the covers for the cups or the nozzles for the candlesticks. These would be kept until his lordship came to London,

> but Mr Armstrong may draw bills on me for the value so soon as he pleases (which to be sure will be upwards of £300), and then shall be paid at sight by him that on all occasions will approve himself my Lord.

Others who found their income falling below their outgoings took their wrought plate to the Mint where it was melted down to make coins. The mint, or rather the Exchequer, paid for the plate out of the £60,000 loan made to it by Richard Hoare and others on which it gave eight per cent interest.

Thrifty subjects of the king entrusted their surplus money to his Exchequer and received interest on it. The nation was permanently in debt to these fund-holders, as they were known. In 1715 the amount was around £37 million – the National Debt. It was a new phenomenon created for the most part by the political necessity of participating in the War of the Spanish Succession. As creditors to the nation, these small-time fund-holders felt they could have no security more gilt-edged. But the Government soon found that the burden of keeping up the interest payments became intolerable. Better to liquidate the debt, they said, before the nation itself became bankrupt. But how?

In 1715 a scrivener called Sir John Blunt conceived the idea of a corporation taking over management of the National Debt, in which the Government's creditors, the fund-holders, had shares. The corporation's profits, said Blunt, would soon discharge the debt. What corporation? The Whig Bank of England put up a scheme, but the Government preferred the terms of the South Sea Company which some Tories had formed in 1711. Blunt was a director. Under the terms of the Act of Parliament which established the corporation, purchase of South Sea Company stock was not confined to fund-holders who, moreover, did not have to restrict their purchases to the amounts they had lent the Exchequer. No limit was set on the value of the shares they brought. Any member of the public could invest in the South Sea Company, and as much as he liked. The day the bill was published the value of the stock rose from 130 to 400 – 7 April 1720. The Company was authorized to take in the irredeemable debts of the nation amounting to £16,546,482 7s 1¼d before 1 March 1721 at such rates as they should agree, as well as a similar amount of redeemable debts.

The South Sea operation had no promise of any commercial advantage whatever, but Blunt circulated a report that Gibraltar and Port Mahon were about to be exchanged for some place in Peru to which part of the world English trade would be enlarged. The rumour, entirely without foundation, acted like a contagion. Within five days the directors of the Company had opened their books for a subscription of £1 million at a rate of £300 for every £100 of capital. In a few days the cost of £100 worth of stock rose to £340. By promise of huge dividends it rose to £1,000.

The whole nation, wrote Tobias Smollett, was infected with the spirit of stock jobbing to an astonishing degree.

> All distinctions of party, religion, sex, character and circumstances were swallowed up in this universal concern or on some such pecuniary project. Exchange Alley was filled with a strange concourse of statesmen, and clergymen, churchmen and dissenters, whigs and tories, physicians, lawyers, tradesmen and even multitudes of females. All other professions and employments were utterly neglected; and the people's attention wholly engrossed by this and other chimerical schemes which were known by the denomination of bubbles.

Hundreds of schemes were promoted and thousands were ruined. The £3 million, which together the schemes proposed to raise, exceeded the value of all the land in England. The fever continued until 8 September 1720 when the value of the stock began to fall and people started selling. By the 29th the value had fallen to 150. Several goldsmiths who had lent large sums to customers to invest in it had to stop payment and flee the country. 'The ebb of this portentous tide was so violent that it bore down everything in its way; and an infinite number of families were overwhelmed with ruin.' John Gay the poet, author of *The Beggar's Opera*, reckoned he would make £20,000 but held on too long. He turned down the advice of his friends to make himself sure of a clean shirt and a shoulder of mutton every day, and lost all he invested. Alexander Pope managed to pull his money out in time. So did Jonathan Swift who, looking back on the South Sea Bubble, in which normally sane people had been overcome by greed to put their savings in one of the 150 companies for importing jackasses from Spain, extracting butter from beech trees, manufacturing square cannon balls and other fantasies including A Company To Carry On An Undertaking Of Great Advantage But Nobody To Know What It Is, wrote:

> There is a gulf where thousands fell.
> Here all the bold adventurers came;
> A narrow sound, though deep as hell –
> Change Alley is the dreadful name.
>
> Subscribers here by thousands float,
> And jostle one another down;
> Each paddling in his leaky boat,
> And here they fish for gold, and drown.

Dreams of the profuseness which Kettlewell warned could only lead to misery had made fools and beggars of the doctors, lawyers and tradesmen who fought each other in Change Alley for shares in the company which claimed to have discovered the secret of perpetual motion. When their bubble dream of moving into the fast lane, without having had to work for it, burst, and they came down to earth on the grotty floor of the Fleet Prison, their shock was pathetically traumatic. What sort of private hell was this? Was the Lord Chief Justice of England aware of it? To make sure that he did, they petitioned him, and other members of the House of Lords, in 1723 that

> for the better suppressing Profaneness and Immorality among us, and that the Misery of Imprisonment may in some measure be alleviated by the Observance of good Manners, Cleanliness and Quietude, we humbly pray your lordships would enable us to regulate ourselves in such Manner as the Prisoners in the King's Bench are empowered to do by a Rule of that Court [in 1713].

They also wondered whether their lordships were aware of the extortions of the Warden of The Fleet, Master Huggins. By a law of 14 November 1693 the Warden was entitled to charge £1 6s 8d for liberty of the House and Irons at first coming in, but Huggins charged them £2 4s 4d. He charged a Chamberlain's Fee of 3s instead of the legal 1s; and a 12s 6d Dismission Fee for every Action instead of the 7s 4d to which he was entitled. The old prison had been burnt down in the Great Fire of

London in 1666 but a new one, no less forbidding, had been built on the same site with its garden and ten-foot-deep, tree-lined Foss all round.

Those that were still there five years later might have met a debtor who had suffered a similar misfortune to Moses Pitt, an architect called John Castell, a cultured man 'born to competent estate', author of *The Villas of the Ancients Illustrated*.

Most newcomers spent their first days in the Sponging House known as Corbett's (after the man who ran it), tipstaff of Thomas Bambridge who had bought the office of Warden from Huggins for £5,000. Castell bribed Bambridge to have himself moved out of the overcrowded Corbett's. With more 'presents' he obtained the Liberty of the Rules – ability to walk outside. Bambridge insisted on sweeteners if these privileges were to continue. When Castell refused to pay him any more, Bambridge ordered him to be sent back to Corbett's. When, to his horror, Castell heard that smallpox had broken out in the house, he pleaded with Bambridge as a favour to send him to another house or have him transferred to another prison, since he had never had smallpox and to send him to Corbett's would be sending him to his death. Bambridge was not to be persuaded; Castell was moved over to Corbett's, caught the disease and very soon died.

His death, and its circumstances, came to the ears of his friend James Oglethorpe, Member of Parliament for the Haslemere Division of Surrey, Squire of Westbrook Place near Godalming (still standing) where he planted a large vineyard and made 'wine like Rhenish' from its grapes. Philanthropist and social reformer, he later sailed to America and founded the colony of Georgia as a refuge for people stricken by poverty, including many from London's debtors' prisons, and for persecuted German Protestants. As Brave General Oglethorpe he commanded a part of the army that crushed Bonnie Prince Charlie's Forty-Five Rebellion and retook Preston Pans for King George.

Oglethorpe told the story of John Castell's death to Members of the House of Commons who, on 25 February 1729, agreed to appoint a Commission of Enquiry of fourteen of their number, with Oglethorpe as chairman, to inspect debtors' prisons in London and report on what they found.

When the commissioners paid their first visit to the Fleet Prison unannounced they found a baronet, ironically named Sir William Rich, crouching in a dungeon loaded with irons, a punishment arbitrarily imposed by Bambridge, whom for some reason he offended. They presented their report on The Fleet on 20 March (and followed it with reports on the Marshalsea and the King's Bench Prisons, both in Southwark, on 14 May 1729 and 11 May 1730).

They first probed the circumstances which had led prisoners to write the petition of 1723, and in particular the eleventh prayer concerning profaneness and immorality. When interrogated, John Huggins hit back with accusations of

FOLLY AND BEGGARY

Social reformer James Oglethorpe MP, whose horror at the death of a friend in the Fleet Prison led to the appointment of a House of Commons Commission of Inquiry into debtors prisons in 1729 and the passing of the Debtors Act.

rowdiness and riotous behaviour which demanded stern disciplinary measures to bring under control.

> The Warden saith [ran the Commissioners' report] that the prisoners in general are so very ungovernable that they have tore up the trees around the Bowling Green and cut down several of the Trees in the back part of the Prison set by the warden some years since for the better Accommodation of Prisoners; and also broke down the Stocks in the said Prison, and the Houses of Easement were fitted up lately by the Warden they have torn it almost to pieces and committed other outrages, and most of them, altho' two years in Arrears of Rent to the Warden, refuse to pay him any part thereof, and will by Force and in defiance of the Warden and his Officers, keep in possession of the Rooms and Furniture, and swearing to stand by each other.

They learnt that Bambridge had recovered the £5,000 he had paid Huggins for the wardenship within a year, and made a regular annual income of £5,000 from 'presents' and 'fees' thereafter. When his agent James Barnes spied Thomas Hogg, a prisoner who had been discharged eight months previously, giving charity to debtors at the prison grate, Barnes seized him and forced him into Corbett's Sponging House, and then turned him into the dungeon or vault, a strong room on the Master's Side, with irons on his legs. Hogg's friends stopped giving him money

63

for clothes and bedding. He ate his last meal, grew weaker and weaker and caught a fever. When no longer able to stand he managed to raise threepence to pay the prison's Common Nurse to attend to him. He obtained the liberty of being carried into the Sick Ward where he lingered for a few months and then died. A more dreadful confinement than the strong room was 'coupling the living with the dead', the keepers locking up debtors who displeased them in the yard with human carcases. 'If this be law,' reported the horrified commissioners, 'all England may be made one extended prison.' Warden Bambridge's barbarous and cruel treatment of debtors in his charge, they found, was in high violation and contempt of the law.

The scene of Bambridge's examination before the Committee of the House of Commons was painted by William Hogarth in a picture that shows a prisoner on his knees demonstrating the way Bambridge had fastened his hands and neck together with a metal clasp in order to extract a bribe. As a result of the Oglethorpe Committee's report the House addressed the king on the matter. They asked him

William Hogarth's painting of Thomas Bambridge, the barbarous Warden of The Fleet, being examined (*far left*) by a committee of the House of Commons.

to prosecute the wardens and gaolers of the Fleet Prison for cruelty and extortion, who were at once committed to Newgate for trial. Incredibly John Huggins was acquitted of all the charges and lived to the age of ninety. Even more incredibly Thomas Bambridge was acquitted of the murder of John Castell and all other charges. He lived a free man for another twenty years in which to contemplate his evil life and then took it by slitting his throat. John Huggins and his son William became close personal friends of Hogarth who painted the portraits of both of them. Sir Archibald Grant, the first owner of the Bambridge Before The Committee painting, sold it to William Huggins to pay his debts when he went bankrupt in 1732.

The following year Hogarth embarked on *The Rake's Progress*, eight stages of degradation of which number four was 'Arrested for Debt'. Rakewell was on his

Plate four 'Arrested for Debt' – of Hogarth's series *The Rake's Progress*, eight stages of degradation (1733), showing Rakewell being handed a slip inscribed 'Arrest' while on his way to a levée at St James's Palace, and his mistress, purse in hand, coming to the rescue.

way to Queen Caroline's birthday levee at St James's Palace to seek her patronage, when a sturdy Welshman – it was St David's Day – handed him a slip of paper marked 'Arrest'. His mistress Sarah Young appeared just in time to pay his debts and save him from prison. But stage (plate) seven of *The Rake's Progress* found him finally in The Fleet, having lost all his wife's money at the gaming tables. John Rich, manager of Covent Garden Theatre, handed him a letter saying he had read his play but it would not do. His wife scolded him, Sarah Young fainted, his gaoler demanded 'garnish', his cellmate lost his reason and fell to writing a 'New Scheme for paying ye Debts of ye Nation' – which was exactly what the artist's real life father Richard Hogarth did when *he* was confined to The Fleet. He thought Robert Harley, the Chancellor of the Exchequer, to whom he sent his proposals, would be so impressed as to order his immediate release.

Plate seven in Hogarth's *The Rake's Progress* shows Rakewell in the Fleet Prison, having lost all his wife's money at the gaming tables – 'his talents idle and unus'd/And every gift of heaven abus'd.'

FOLLY AND BEGGARY

More positive outcome of James Oglethorpe's investigations was the Act which he introduced 'for the Relief of Debtors in respect of the Imprisonment of their Person':

> Whereas many persons suffer by the oppression of inferior officers in the Execution of Process for Debt, and the Exactions of Gaolers to whom such Debtors are committed . . .

Enforcement of Charles II's Act for the relief and release of poor distressed prisoners for debt had been lax in the forty-seven years since it was enacted, and this new Debtors Act of 1730 (2 George II cap 21 & 22) promised not only to prevent the malpractices of vile gaolers but to make provision for the ease and relief of debtors 'who shall be willing to satisfy their creditors to the utmost of their power'.

The Act laid down that no sheriff, bailiff or other officer should convey anyone they arrested to any tavern, alehouse or other public victualling or drinking house, or to the officer's private house, without his free and voluntary consent. They could not charge the person they arrested for any wine, beer, victuals or tobacco 'save what he shall call for of his own free accord'. They must not take a greater sum for arresting him than the law allowed, nor take him to gaol less than twenty-four hours after his arrest. They could not receive a sum for a night's lodging or for a day's diet, or other expenses, other than what a JP would consider reasonable.

Gaoler must allow prisoners to send for victuals, beer, ale and food from whatever place they pleased, and have such bedding and linen as they thought fit, and without making them pay for it. They should not take fees except those allowed by law until these had been settled by the Lord Chief Justice. When the new schedule of fees had been fixed, it was to be hung up in an open and public room in every gaol. If any prisoner petitioned in protest of a gaoler's extortions, his case should be heard by a judge. The authorities must discover what gifts had been made to debtor prisoners by charities, and ensure that prisoners were not defrauded but received the full benefit of them.

The most important part of the Act was clause VIII which stated that, if a prisoner with a debt of less than £100 shall be minded to deliver up to his or her creditors all his or her effects towards the satisfaction of his debts, it was lawful for him or her to exhibit a petition to the court of law where his case was considered.

> On receipt of this petition the court must have the prisoner brought before it with the creditors. If creditors choose to appear or not, the court will examine the petition and hear the case for the discharge of the prisoner. Then the court will administer an oath for the prisoner to swear that at no time since his imprisonment or before, directly or

indirectly, sold, leased, assigned or otherwise disposed of or made over in trust for himself any part of his lands, estate, goods, stock, money, debts or other real estate in order to benefit himself or defraud his creditors.

If the court was satisfied he was telling the truth, they could order the man's effects to be assigned to the creditors represented in court in trust for the rest of them. If the debtor signed this assignment, he was released from custody. The creditors divided the man's goods among themselves in proportion to the amounts they were owed, and collectively they paid the gaoler a fee for his release.

If the court is not satisfied the oath is true, then it can remand the prisoner to give them more time and appear another day. If the creditors at this second hearing are still dissatisfied with the truth of the oath, they can insist that the prisoner is detained in prison but must pay him 2s 4d a week. If they fail to do this, the prisoner can apply to the court to be discharged.

Once discharged a prisoner could never be re-arrested for the same debt; but notwithstanding his release from prison any judgement against him still stood. Execution could be taken out against any of his possessions except his wearing apparel, bedding for himself and family and the tools of his trade 'in same manner as if he had never been taken in execution of debt'.

In finding a way to have Britain's debtors' prisons emptied of all those who had been put there for small sums, but had property which could be sold to defray their debts, James Oglethorpe was certainly defying current attitudes. But his courageous and sustained activity had no lasting effect. The law stipulated that a minimum number of creditors's signatures were needed for the certificate of discharge to be operative, and, as usual, there were always too many debtors unable to induce a sufficient number to sign. So they had to stay put, and the object of Oglethorpe's humanitarian statute was nullified.

Life in the Fleet Prison continued much as before.

> A starving life all day we lead
> No comfort here is found,
> At night we make one common bed
> Upon the boarded ground;
> Where fleas in troops and bugs in shoals
> Into our bosoms creep,
> And Death Watch Spiders round ye walls
> Disturb us in our sleep.
>
> Were Socrates alive, and bound
> With us to lead his life,
> 'Twould move his patience far beyond

FOLLY AND BEGGARY

His crabbed scolding wife;
Hard lodging and much harder fare
Would try the wisest sage,
Nay! even make a parson swear
And curse the sinful age.

Thus we insolvent debtors live,
Yet we may boldly say
Worse villains often credit give
Than those that never pay;
For wealthy knaves can with applause
Cheat on and ne'er be try'd,
But in contempt of human laws
In coaches safely ride.

'The Prisoner's Song' of 1738

As much of the unpleasantness emanated from their fellow prisoners as from their guards – the custom of Garnish, Footing or Chummage for instance. Each time a newcomer was admitted, the incumbents demanded Garnish in the shape of

'Garnish' – a newcomer to the Fleet Prison is stripped of his coat which is sold to buy wine for a celebratory orgy – frontispiece of *An Oration on the Oppression of Jailors* (1731).

his coat or other pieces of clothing if, as was usually the case, he could not pay them money. 'Pay or strip' could have fatal consequences, specially in winter when, with little left to sleep in and no bedding to lie on, the Garnishee might well catch pneumonia and die. The gang, of which the alien from the outside world had become a member, sold his clothing, and with the proceeds bought liquor with which they celebrated the new boy's arrival in a night of drunken hilarity.

> Unhappy, friendless man! how hard thy fate!
> Whose only crime is being unfortunate.
> Are jailers suffer'd in such acts as these?
> To strip the wretch who cannot pay his fees?

(*An Oration on the Oppression of Jailors*, spoken in the Fleet Prison on 20 February 1731)

A clergyman imprisoned for debt could always earn a dishonest penny by hiring himself out to an alehouse or brandy shopkeeper within the rules of The Fleet to conduct clandestine marriages without a licence or a bann in a room which became a 'chapel', which was exempt from the jurisdiction of the Bishop of London. He shared the fee with the landlord who acted as Clerk, and the tout who brought in the customers from the streets outside. The marriages were regarded as legal, however, until the Government passed an Act putting an end to the scandal of The Fleet parsons in 1754.

One who rode safely in his coach, was of a fairly wealthy family but no knave, was Sir Thomas Lowther of Holker Hall near Cartmel in Cumberland. In 1723 he had married Lady Elizabeth Cavendish, a daughter of the second Duke of Devonshire who brought him a dowry of probably around £12,000. He sat as an independent country Whig in the House of Commons as Member for Lancaster. With no actual event which could be called a misfortune, he none the less managed to spend the whole of his adult life in debt. He never found a way of making ends meet.

Much of his financial mismanagement was doubtless due to a certain extent to too many drams and too much wine. Today he would be said to have an 'alcohol problem'. He also tended to pay over-generous bribes to electors at the hustings. But he took it all in his stride. He seemed unconcerned that even on reaching manhood in 1720 he was already £300 in debt. Two years later the sum he owed had risen to £570. His main creditor was his own employee, his Estate Steward John Fletcher, which may have been invidious if not humiliating, but at least it meant that it was unlikely that such a person would obtain a writ for the payment of his borrowings and have him taken to Lancaster Gaol.

FOLLY AND BEGGARY

By 1734 his debt to Fletcher, in spite of his lucrative marriage, was up to and over a thousand pounds. He made a stab at reducing it by selling some Holker timber but apparently could only find a buyer able to pay the £410 he was charging in four years. Fletcher had been promised all but £100 of this, and when he heard he would have to wait for it until 1738, he started charging his employer/debtor four per cent interest, and not only on the £310 but on all he owed.

Yet, from a letter he wrote to his cousin and benefactor Sir James Lowther of Whitehaven in June 1735, it would seem that he shrunk from ever finding himself in debt. He did much travelling in his coach, and had been driven down to Bath and then gone to London, where he had hoped to meet his father-in-law the Duke of Devonshire who had been kept at Chatsworth however 'upon account of the Duchess laying in'. He wished to set out for Lancashire as soon as possible, he told his cousin, but could not leave town,

> being we have not yet settled anything & above £400 due to me, & I don't care to go out of this town one farthing in debt, tho' what I owe is so trifling that not one person desires to be pay'd till I return again, for most of the things I buy for house keeping I pay ready moneys for, & who to ask for a small sum of moneys in London I know not. However I shall be easy when the Duke comes up tho' am sorry I can't be down sooner, & it is not everybody one wou'd be oblig'd to, being a thing I never did if it was for less than half a year, it should be pay'd with interest.

Sir Thomas was less in danger of losing what ready money he still possessed from buying stocks in companies which turned out bubbles, than from a footpad in the dark of London's ill-lit streets. 'In coming home lately from taking leave of Mr Trotter', he told Sir James in the same letter,

> I was very near being robbed. A person behind me gave me a blow which brought me down but I immediately recover'd myself & had another from a person which I met at the instant I was getting up that gave me a stroke that partly missed me. I immediately held up my cane when a Lanthorn and two persons came near & the two persons made off. But every night one hears of persons being knocked down in the street.

In Bath, Sir Thomas would have been tempted by the gaming at which losses had been the start of so many journeys to the debtor's prison, but he was probably saved from that by preferring to spend more time drinking Toddy and Hock than playing Hazard, Basset and Faro – in spite of card debts no longer being recoverable by law. He would almost certainly have met Beau Nash however, who, when the cost of his high rate of living started to ruin him, stopped riding in his gilt coach and sold it, along with its six horses, rather than risk the degradation and humiliation of being dragged off to a debtor's prison.

London June ye 19th 1735

Dear Sr.

I writ to you the post after I returned from Bath, & I hope this finds you perfectly well at Whitehaven. I am not yet determin'd when to set out for Lancashire, (tho' I want extreamly to be in the Country) but my leaving this Town, will depend in good deal upon the Duke of Devons return from Chatsworth, being I did not think but that I should have found him in London at my return from Bath, but he went on a sudden, & I hear will be back the first Week, in the Next month upon account of the Dutchess laying in, for till he comes I can't so well leave this place, being we have not yet settled anything, & above 400 due to me, & I don't care to to go out of this Town one farthing in debt, tho' what I owe is so trifling that not one person desires to be payd till I return again, for most of the things I buy for House keeping I pay ready moneys for, & who to ask for a small sum of moneys in London, I know not, however, I shall be easy when the Duke comes up, tho' am sorry I can't be down sooner, & it is not everybody one wou'd be oblig'd to, being a thing I never did, if it was for less than half a year it should be payd with interest —

Sir Thomas Lowther of Holker, who all his life has over-borrowed, protests in a letter to his cousin Sir James Lowther of Whitehaven in 1735 'I don't care to go out of this town [London] one farthing in debt.'

FOLLY AND BEGGARY

Sir Thomas Lowther contemplated no such thing and was content to let his financial affairs go from bad to worse. With his wife showing symptoms of the insanity from which she died, he stepped up his private drinking which for the last two years of his life made him more and more ill. He died in 1745 owing John Fletcher £1,145. With the mortgage to Sir James and several other outstanding loans he left debts of £4,880. Within three years the guardians of his son and heir William Lowther, who was a minor in 1745, had sold more timber, cut back expenditure and collected rent arrears which enabled that to balance the accounts and restore the Holker Hall finances to an even keel.

Though an active member of the Society for the Promotion of Christian Knowledge, Sir Thomas applied little of it to himself, and he would have had little time for the stern admonitions of the Quakers who at the Yearly Meeting of 1732 issued another printed epistle reminding Friends how careful the first members of the Society had been not to involve themselves in business which they did not understand. How circumspect they were not to contract greater debts than they were able to pay in due time!

> But with sorrow we observe that, contrary to their example and the repeated advices formerly given by this meeting against an inordinate pursuit after riches, too many have launched into trades and business above their stocks and capacities; by which unjustifiable proceedings and high living, they have involved themselves and families in trouble and ruin, and brought considerable loss upon others to the great reproach of our holy profession.

Five years later they ruled that no one who should fail to pay their just debts ought to be admitted to act in business meetings or join with Friends in collecting for the poor and the service of the church, until they had made satisfaction to the monthly meeting they belonged to, and done what was in their power to take off the reproach they had, by their imprudent conduct, brought on their Christian principle.

Sir Thomas Lowther chose to live with his indebtedness and, as one who dabbled in necromancy, he might have hoped for some magical relief from them. He also had the option, if he had been so minded, of taking his coach and horses up north and claiming the sanctuary afforded by the Palace of Holyroodhouse in Edinburgh, already referred to. He would have been received, not by the Duke of Hamilton in person as Heritable Keeper, but by the Bailie to whom he delegated the job with the right to collect all the 'fees, casualties, profits, duties and emoluments of the office'.

He would have found others there of the same social standing, probably too many for comfort. 'The number of impecunious persons of every class who availed themselves of the protection from creditors afforded by the sanctuary was by no means few', attests W. Forbes Gray who wrote an authoritative article on the palace in *The Scotsman* in 1935.

> From 1741 to 1752 the persons who registered their names in the books of the Abbey Court-house prior to taking up their abode within the sanctuary numbered 183. For the four years ending in 1770 the figure was 184. From this time onwards the statistics showed a decidedly upward tendency, the peak being reached in the year 1816 when the dwellers in the sanctuary at the foot of the Canongate numbered for twelve months no fewer than 116, a figure which must have increased the small community living within the precincts of the Palace to an alarming extent. Indeed the 'Abbey lairds', as they were jocularly called, must have been huddled together in such a way as to suggest to those who had once known comfortable circumstances whether the placing of themselves in the power of implacable creditors would not be the least of two evils.

It would have been quieter and more dignified, however, than being confined in London's Wood Street Compter where one day in June 1742 a riotous mob broke in to liberate the debtors. Fifteen of them, describing themselves as tradesmen, 'not choosing to avail themselves of so unjust a proceeding, voluntarily came back into custody lest the Sheriffs or Keeper should be damnified by their absence or compulsive escape.'

That was how they described their behaviour after forcible liberation in the petition they presented to the Lord Mayor of London and the Court of Aldermen and Sheriffs, claiming benefit of the Act of Parliament which in such circumstances entitled them to be released by those with the proper authority. For since the extraordinary scenes of 9 June, Parliament had passed a law to indemnify the marshal of the King's Bench Prison and the warden of the Fleet Prison, the keepers of other gaols in Middlesex and Surrey and the City of London against the escape of debtors set at liberty by the mob. The Act, claimed the petitioners, stated that 'every debtor so set at liberty were directed to give in their names and places where in future they were to abide on or before the 1st day of this instant September.' The fifteen signatories, 'tradesmen with large families', had given their names and addresses to the sheriffs of London and the keeper of the Wood Street Compter. So, having voluntarily surrendered before the Act took place and not had the benefit of it,

> Your Petitioners most humbly pray your Honors will be pleased to order them to be released from their confinement pursuant to the said Act which will be of the utmost benefit and utility to them and their families who will reap the benefit of their labor and enable them in some degree to make satisfaction to their respective plaintiffs and become useful members of the community.

Most of the Londoners who signed this petition would have benefited even more

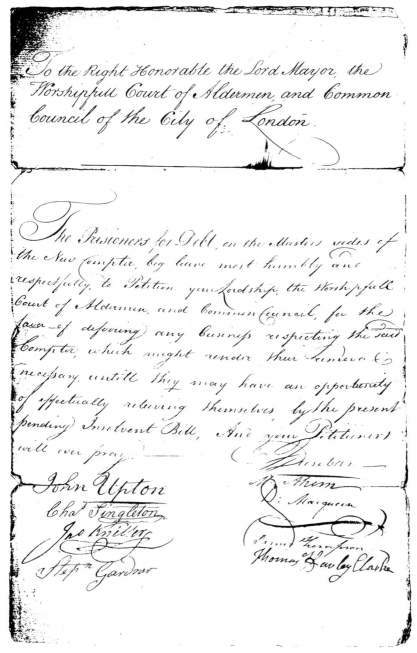

To the Right Honorable the Lord Mayor, the Worshipfull Court of Aldermen, and Common Council of the City of London.

The Prisoners for Debt, on the Masters sides of the New Compter, beg leave most humbly and respectfully, to Petition your Lordship, the Worshipfull Court of Aldermen, and Common Council, for the favor of deferring any business respecting the said Compter, which might render their removal necessary, untill they may have an opportunity of effectually relieving themselves, by the present pending Insolvent Bill, And your Petitioners will ever pray

John Upton
Chas Singleton
Jno Knitter
Stephn Gardner

Prisoners for Debt in the New Compter petition to the Lord Mayor and Aldermen of the City of London in 1742 which defers transferring them to another gaol when the New Compter closes.

from the Small Debts Act which in 1749 established what they called a Court of Requests for Southwark, Newington, Bermondsey, Lambeth and Rotherhithe.

The Act was aimed at deterring creditors who, in the words of Frederick Meymott who became the Southwark Court of Requests' Clerk in the 1830s, 'might be disposed from malicious motives to oppress their poor debtors with the heavy expence of actions in the superior courts.' It declared that if any action were brought in any of his Majesty's Courts of Record at Westminster for any debts recoverable in the Southwark Court of Requests, the plaintiff if successful should not be allowed his costs. If the verdict were given to the defendant/debtor he should be entitled to double costs.

Since nothing contributed more to the promoting of industry and of useful credit than providing an easy and speedy method for recovering small debts, parishioners were authorized to nominate 132 of the most substantial and discreet persons to act as Commissioners of such courts to be held in each of the ten parishes, where lists of their names were to be posted. Three would sit twice a week on Tuesday and Friday. In Southwark they sat in the Court House on St Margarets Hill or some other place so as not to impede or interrupt the business being conducted by assize judges or magistrates. They had the power to award execution, with costs, against the bodies or the goods and chattels of any they gave judgement against 'as to them shall seem just in Law or Equity'. From 29 September 1749 it became lawful for any inhabitant of Southwark and other parishes, and anyone renting a shop, stall or stand or seeking livelihood in the parishes who had any debt owing him not exceeding forty shillings by anyone in the parish, to be warned and summoned by the Chief Bailiff in writing to appear before the Commissioners of the Court, who could make such orders between a debtor and a creditor 'as they shall find to stand with Equity and good conscience'.

> For the more effectual establishing of the Court of Requests and the better enforcing the orders which the Commissioners make, the Commissioners may be invested with proper power and authority and be free and exempt from any Insults or Abuses.

Anyone who contemptuously confronted or insulted a Commissioner while he was sitting would be taken by the Chief Bailiff before a Justice of the Peace to answer for his action, who, if it was proved, could fine him 20s or send him to prison for ten days. The fine would be paid over to the church wardens towards the support of the parish poor. If the abuser was not of the parish he could be committed to Surrey County Gaol to remain there not longer than a month until he paid up. The clauses about insulting Commissioners and the punishments were to be fixed in the most public part of the courthouse 'to the end that no person shall pretend ignorance of the premisses'. The Act did not apply to any debt for rent of land or tenement or any real (estate) contracts, nor to any debts arising from any cause concerning Testament or Matrimony or the Ecclesiastical Court. Nine years later, another Act extended the statute to people in Streatham, Camberwell, Clapham, Deptford and Brixton. The procedure remained unaltered till 1806.

The courts were also known as Courts of Conscience – courts whose interference was requested by the creditor/plaintiff and where the decision was given according to equity and conscience. Meymott held that the first of such courts had been set up in the City of London in the early part of the sixteenth century by an Act of Common Council. Two aldermen and twelve commoners were appointed Commissioners by the Lord Mayor to sit in the Court of Degrees in Guildhall twice a week to hear any matter brought before them for the recovery of trifling debts. The process, on the lines of the 1749 courts, was similar to that adopted in the Hundred Courts, and was confined at first to debts under 40s. But, said Meymott, the Act of Common Council was ruled illegal, and general Acts of Parliament had to be passed establishing the London Courts of Requests on a more solid foundation. The benefits which tradesmen received from the simple, cheap and expeditious procedures in these London courts induced other large towns to obtain Acts of Parliament enabling them to set up courts on similar principles.

There would never have been any cause for tradesmen to request the interference of a court if their customers had read and acted on the advice which Philip Stanhope, 4th Earl of Chesterfield, gave his son in the letter he wrote from London on 10 January 1749.

> Without care and method the largest fortune will not, and with them almost the smallest will, supply all necessary expenses. As far as you possibly can, pay ready money for everything you buy, and avoid bills. Pay that money too yourself, and not through the hands of any servant who always either stipulates poundage or requires a present for his good word, as they call it. Where you must have bills (as for meat and drink clothes etc), pay them regularly every month, and with your own hand.

It echoed that which Richard Steel had given a few years previously in *The Spectator*:

> I cannot much wonder at the endeavour after gain, but am extremely astonished that men can be so insensible of the danger of running into debt. One would think it impossible a man who is given to contract debts should know that his creditor has, from that moment in which he transgresses payment, so much as that demand comes to in his debtor's honour, liberty and fortune. One would think he did not know that his creditor can say the worst thing imaginable of him, to wit *That he is unjust*, without defamation; and can seize his person without being guilty of an assault. Yet such is the loose and abandoned turn of some mens' minds that they can live under those constant apprehensions, and shall go on to increase the cause of them.

THE WORST POVERTY

The Earl of Chesterfield, who told his son in 1749 to pay ready money for everything he bought, but if he had to have bills to pay them regularly every month.

There were circumstances, he said, in which honest natures could become liable to debts by some unadvised behaviour in any great point of their life or mortgaging a man's honesty as a security for that of another. But they were special instances. For one such case there were ten where a man, to keep up a farce of retinue and grandeur within his own house, shrunk at the expectation of surly demands at his door.

> The debtor is the creditor's criminal, and all the officers of power and state whom we behold make so great a figure are no other than so many persons in authority to make good his charge against him. Human society depends upon his having the vengeance the law allots him; and the debtor owes his liberty to his neighbour, as much as the murderer does his life to his prince. (no. 82, 4 June 1711)

He considered that, generally speaking, the gentry of early eighteenth-century Britain were in debt, with many families having put it into a kind of method of being so from generation to generation. Dr Samuel Johnson pleaded with people not to accustom themselves to consider debt only as an inconvenience, for they would find it a calamity.

FOLLY AND BEGGARY

> Poverty takes away so many means of doing good, and produces so much inability to resist evil, both natural and moral, but it is by virtuous means to be avoided . . . Let it be your first care then not to be in any man's debt. Resolve not to be poor; whatever you have, spend less.

In writing about such matters most social commentators of the time took the opportunity to demonstrate their sympathy with the borrower, the buyer who promised to pay later – people they could identify with. The 'plight' of the little man who failed to keep his promise and became an insolvent debtor, was easy to dramatize and pleased the reader. But the lender and seller also resolved not to be poor. To earn a living, let alone riches, he could not afford to take a sentimental attitude to a purely commercial transaction. If he had trusted a customer and found, to his loss, that he had misjudged him, could he trust him not to perjure himself about his assets when he made himself bankrupt? In the present situation of things, thought the anonymous Irish author of a tract of 1757 disguised as *A Letter to Trevor Lloyd Esq concerning a bankruptcy bill*, 'in the present situation I have little or no security from any man I deal with but his honesty, which I should have, in most cases, a better opinion of were it easily in my power to punish him if he deceives me.' Having a bankruptcy bill in Ireland on the lines of that in England, he said, would establish and confirm credit. He had heard it said that a bankruptcy law would encourage perjury because it would put people under temptation of the crime by the great profit they might make by committing it. The fear of damnation in the next world, or of the pillory in this, had kept some men within bounds which they would otherwise have leapt over. As for those whom oaths could not bind, they must be of such profligate principles as not to need the commission of that one crime of perjury to damn them, should they never have the opportunity to commit it.

Many inconveniences would arise from a bankruptcy bill but if they made an objection to its passing, 'I doubt whether we should be obliged to abolish all that is written except the bible, and confine ourselves to the mere law of reason, and rely on the good consciences of the judges who might be appointed to enforce it.' He did not believe that the people of England were tired of their bankruptcy laws. It was scarce to be believed that, ever since the reign of Henry VIII, the legislature had made new acts of parliament against the will of the English people purely to gratify one set of gentlemen, and with so little opposition. Some particular persons were sometimes injured by the villanies committed under sanction of the Bankruptcy Act, but that was the case with relation to almost every law made to secure or ascertain property.

A Bankruptcy Act would facilitate compositions between a bankrupt and his creditor. Moreover,

THE WORST POVERTY

> It will put the honest good-natured man (for whose protection laws should be principally calculated) on the same footing with the crafty hard hearted creditor. It would prevent one man receiving but a third or quarter of his debt, whilst some of his more diligent fellow creditors get half or the whole of their demands.

It was the foolish, open-hearted Young Honeywood's good nature which, in Oliver Goldsmith's comedy *The Good-Natured Man*, led him to stand security for a face he scarce knew. The debtor absconded. His uncle Sir William takes up the security, but to teach his nephew a lesson plans to involve him in 'fictitious distress before he has plunged himself into real calamity, to arrest him for that very debt, to clap an officer upon him and then let him see which of his friends will come to his relief.'

The play which revolves round the whole subject of borrowing and lending, debt and the consequences of overindebtedness, does indeed hold a mirror up to the times. While owing money to his tailor, his mercer and a little broker in Crooked Lane who has lost patience in recovering it, Honeywood has sent ten guineas to a poor gentleman and his children in the Fleet Prison. His monitor, Jarvis, scolds him for having nothing but pressing creditors, false friends and a pack of drunken servants. When, at the opening of Act III, Timothy Twitch the bailiff and little Flanigan his follower come to arrest him, Honeywood insists that he can discharge his trifling debt in three days, and gives them money to stay with him in his house during that time as his friendly guests. He dresses up little Flanigan in one of his blue and gold suits, and the three of them conduct would-be polite conversation with Miss Richland who unexpectedly arrives to borrow a book.

At the first performance of the play, presented by George Colman at the Covent Garden Theatre in 1768, with a prologue by Dr Johnson and without David Garrick who had demanded cuts which Goldsmith refused to make, some of the audience in the pit shouted their disapproval of the scene with the bailiffs. They were shocked by its 'low' and vulgar dialogue, and what they considered its whole indelicacy. The reviewer in the *London Chronicle* criticized the language as 'uncommonly low'. The scene was cut from subsequent performances. A critic said it degraded the good-natured man, whom people were taught to pity and respect, into a low buffoon and falsifier, a character unbecoming a gentleman.

The scene was included in the printed version of the play, however. 'When such an attempt as Honeywood's to pass off the bailiffs for his friends gets condemned as unworthy of a gentleman', wrote John Forster in his *Life and Adventures of Oliver Goldsmith* (1848), 'comedy seems in sorry plight indeed.' But it said a lot for the serious attitude which they considered was more proper for the serious matter of too easy, too available credit, and too lightly falling into debt.

It had been no comic experience for the author of *The Good-Natured Man* to have bailiffs come to arrest him at the instance of his landlady Mrs Elizabeth Fleming to whom he owed £12 10s for three months board in his Islington lodgings, 1s for a pint of Mountain, four gentleman's teas @ 1s 6d, a bottle of port @ 2s 6d for Sassafras, and 16s 10½d for newspapers.

According to James Boswell, he sent a messenger round to Dr Johnson stating his distress and begging to see him. It was early morning and the doctor had not yet risen. He gave the messenger a guinea and told him to return to Dr Goldsmith and give it to him, saying he would come as soon as he was dressed and breakfasted. At Islington he found his friend sitting beside a half empty bottle of Madeira, fulminating against the conduct of Mrs Fleming. Johnson put the bottle away and told him to calm down, whereupon Goldsmith produced the manuscript of a new novel which he said was ready for printing. Samuel Johnson took it to Francis Newbery, who was the writer's publisher/bookseller/accountant, who gave him £60 for it, which he handed over to Goldsmith less what he owed Newbery. Goldsmith then, in the words of his biographer John Forster, 'went and discharged his debt to Mrs Fleming, expostulating in a high tone for using him so ill.'

This had occurred three years before the production of *The Good-Natured Man*; and ten years later, when he was only forty-five, he died of a fever, made more violent, Johnson told Boswell, from uneasiness of mind. His debts had begun to be heavy and all his resources were exhausted. He had raised money and squandered it by every artifice of acquisition and folly of expense. Sir Joshua Reynolds believed he owed not less than two thousand pounds. 'Was ever poet so trusted before?' Likewise Henry Fielding, briefly a London magistrate, wrote his novel *Joseph Andrews* while hiding from his creditors in a room off Charing Cross.

Oliver Goldsmith's self-induced poverty and debt would have elicited even greater pity had Mrs Fleming's bailiffs succeeded in taking him to a debtors' prison and he had died there. The writer of a letter to *The Gentleman's Magazine* in 1760 was one of a long line of social observers to deplore the law that made an insolvent debtor the slave of his creditor, but with the cruel, absurd difference that he was excluded from the common benefits of earth and air which the brute beasts enjoyed above him. In being denied an opportunity to discharge the debt, he was a burden to his injured and resentful creditor and a dead weight to the community.

The property of the creditor however was as much injured, claimed the writer of the letter, as the debtor's liberty.

> But neither of them ought to be over-rated with respect to each other; but a just and equitable compensation established for both. Shall the freedom of our artizans, manufacturers and tradesmen – that freedom which every individual affects to boast as the birth-right of Englishmen – continue to be held so cheap as to be valued at less than the twentieth part of the price of an African slave? God forbid.

THE WORST POVERTY

He thought there must be a more equitable and expeditious method of recovering debts, and preventing the various misfortunes that attended both creditor and debtor by insolvencies, than the arrest for small sums and long imprisonment for sums whether large or small.

The method for many was so to manage their personal finances that there was no, or very little, risk of ever becoming insolvent. Young Jervis, who was to become an admiral and Earl St Vincent, drew a bill for £20 which came back 'protested'. He was mortified at the rebuke and made himself a promise, which he kept, that he would never draw another bill without a certainty of it being paid. 'I immediately changed my mode of living', he recollected later,

> quitted my mess, lived alone and took up the ship's allowance which I found quite sufficient; washed and mended my own clothes; made a pair of trousers out of the ticking of my bed; and having by these means saved as much money as would redeem my honour, I took up my bill, and from that time to this I have taken care to keep within my means.

Arthur Wellesley, Duke of Wellington, chose to do the same. 'I make a point', he told a Mr Gleig, 'of paying my own bills, and I advise every one to do the same . . . It [debt] makes a slave of a man. I have often known what it was to be in want of money, but I never got in debt.'

Which is more than Theodore, King of Corsica could say.

Theodore von Neuhoff was born in Metz around 1696, the son of a Westphalian gentleman of good family. For a time an officer in the French army, he then wandered round Europe in search of adventure. He had his first taste of imprisonment for debt in Livorno (Leghorn) in Italy, and on release fell in with a bunch of men plotting an insurrection to overthrow the Genoese rulers of Corsica. On the strength of his offering to obtain money from the Bey of Tunis to whom he promised exclusive trade with the island and a safe harbour for his pirates, the Corsican conspirators vowed to make him sovereign once the island had achieved its independence.

With guns bought with Tunisian money and loaded with Tunisian ammunition, Neuhoff captured Porto Vecchio from the Genoese but failed to take Bastia. It was enough, however, for the General Assembly, set up by the insurgents, to elect Theodore King of Corsica at a ceremony in which the German adventurer swore to uphold the constitution just proclaimed.

He took the job with due seriousness. He minted new coinage, distributed patents of nobility and created an order of knighthood. He put fear into the hearts of any who contemplated opposition by ordering the execution of members of three leading families who had dared to question his authority. It was a precarious position and he soon tired of it. He made arrangements to delegate his powers temporarily with a regency council and left the island for the mainland, telling the General Assembly he was going to solicit financial aid to bolster the kingdom's flagging economy. He toured Italy, France and Holland where his funds ran out, and for the second time he found himself in gaol for debt. The Jews of Amsterdam procured his release and financed an expedition to Corsica to enable His Majesty to reassume his authority. But in the interval the French had increased their support for the Genoese, and Theodore's attempts to land in 1738 were repulsed, and again in 1742.

No longer a *de facto* reigning monarch, Theodore crossed the English Channel to London where his exploits were sufficiently well known to ensure a sympathetic welcome and ready listeners to stories of the regal life which once he had enjoyed. Plenty of sympathy, but no money. He was obliged to borrow, and when he could not repay the loans, his creditors had him confined to the King's Bench Prison, where he had to stay for several years. There he staged a pathetic display of kingship, holding court under a tattered canopy and receiving visitors with great ceremony. Tobias Smollett described his performance in his novel *Ferdinand Count Fathom*.

Finally, by inviting subscriptions in newspaper advertisements, Horace Walpole and others raised enough money for Neuhoff to pay off his principal creditors, to whom he made over, as an asset, the Kingdom of Corsica, the throne of which he had never abdicated. Penniless and delirious, he was carried from the prison in a sedan chair to no. 5 Little Chapel Street, Soho, the house of a German tailor he had known in better days (and owed money to?), where a few weeks later he died. He was buried in the churchyard of St Ann's, Soho, where there is still be to seen the tablet surmounted by a diadem on which is inscribed the epitaph written by Horace Walpole:

NEAR THIS PLACE IS INTERRED
THEODORE, KING OF CORSICA
WHO DIED IN THIS PARISH, DECEMBER 11, 1756
IMMEDIATELY AFTER LEAVING
THE KING'S BENCH PRISON,
BY THE BENEFIT OF THE ACT OF INSOLVENCY;
IN CONSEQUENCE OF WHICH
HE REGISTERED THE KINGDOM OF CORSICA
FOR THE USE OF HIS CREDITORS.

THE WORST POVERTY

The grave, great teacher, to a level brings
Heroes and beggars, galley-slaves and kings.
But Theodore this moral learned ere dead;
Fate poured its lessons on his living head,
Bestowed a kingdom, and denied him bread.

Theodore may have been one of many who trusted overmuch to the accommodation bills which the Quakers denounced in 1771 as 'the most pernicious practice of raising and circulating a fictitious kind of paper credit with endorsements and acceptances to give it an appearance of value without an intrinsic reality.' So much indebtedness, they said, was due to the ambition of those unwilling to lessen their appearance in the world. Part of Theodore's trouble was doubtless his reluctance to relinquish the trappings of royalty, and the strain of maintaining a semblance of the kingly state to which he had become accustomed. Whatever value he put on his island kingdom in the Mediterranean in mitigation of his debts, his creditors never had the use of it. More than 200 years later, however, some of their descendants may be among those who drink to Theodore's health in The King of Corsica public house in Berwick Street Market near his resting place.

CHAPTER FOUR

An Essence of Fire

– up to George III's Jubilee

S till only insolvent 'traders' could be discharged from their liabilities by bankruptcy. But towards the end of the eighteenth century the courts developed what Jay Cohen calls 'a more expansive definition' of the term, which made many non-traders eligible for discharge in bankruptcy. In the 1770s, however, there were great numbers of ordinary people who overnight had become 'prisoners' of whom few, if any, of the gentry and nobility, let alone Members of Parliament were aware. Fifty years earlier James Oglethorpe had revealed their existence, and now James Neild and Revd Dr William Dodd decided to take over where Oglethorpe had left off.

Their plan was a simple one: pay the imprisoned debtors' debts, plus the fees demanded for their clearance and what they owed the keeper for lodgings and the rest, and they could be released. Dodd outlined their idea, and painted a dramatic picture of the need for it, in a sermon in the Charlotte Street Chapel in Pimlico. The collection taken at the end of the service 'for the benefit of unfortunate persons confined for small debts', amounted to £81 1s. It was the beginning of the funds of The Society for the Relief of Persons Confined For Small Debts, which James Neild, a Londoner jeweller, had founded in February 1772. Dodd preached a second sermon in the Bedford Chapel on the same theme, and the collection, together with the proceeds of the printed sermon, went to the society's funds.

But the main source of money for releasing the poor and insolvent came from the rich and solvent; Neild placed advertisements in the newspapers appealing for donations. The response was immediate. The social conscience of England, it seemed, was shocked at a situation of which it claimed it was not aware. The society's committee were pleasantly surprised at the size of the field of compassion. Many donors declined to identify themselves – 'From an anonymous subscriber, an Heart Blessed with Humanity.' But the Archbishop of Canterbury sent £20; the Bishop of London ten guineas; the Grand Jury of Westminster Quarter Sessions subscribed five guineas. Thirty guineas came from the Earl of Hertford, ten guineas from Lady Frances Coningsby, five from the Earl of Breadalbane. The

THE WORST POVERTY

Earl of Radnor and Lady Windsor each gave ten guineas; John Thornton the notorious City speculator and gambler, twenty pounds. There were donations from Lord Willoughby de Broke and a High Court Judge with a conscience, Mr Justice Nares.

The society also placed advertisements asking for applications to draw on its funds for the purpose of release from debtors' prisons, and backed this up by sending two members of the committee on a tour of London's gaols to receive applications and arrange for the release of 'the most distressed objects, preferring the most useful Artists and Manufacturers, and those who have the largest families.' None were to be relieved who had a right to the benefit of the Insolvent Act currently going through Parliament, except by paying their clearance fees.

Their advertisement inviting applications read:

> It is wished that the Objects [prisoners] recommended may be capable of being discharged for £10, and that in their applications they mention their Age, Business, Family, Name, where confined, the Sums they are indebted and address of creditors.

On 11 March 1772, two weeks after the society had its first meeting on 23 February, they reported discharging five debtors from the Marshalsea Prison in Southwark – the biggest debt was £2 5s 8d – two from the Poultry Compter (biggest debt £6 18s 5d); one from the Kings Bench Prison; five from the Borough Compter; four from the Wood Street Compter; three from Whitechapel Prison; five from Newgate Prison; and one from the New Gaol in Whitecross Street, Southwark.

And so it went on. An unknown benefactor gave them £100, and they received a legacy for £200 'to be distributed to the full list of everyone in Fleet jail'. A Mr Dixon sent five guineas 'for a gentleman who was a benefactor to this charity but is now in great distress with a wife and three children.' In June they released James Matthew Calcott, a surgeon, by paying his debt of £3 10s – 'wife dead in prison, 3 girls, the eldest only 6 year old', read the record. Five of those released on Christmas Eve 1772 had been gaoled for each owing 12s 8d, and were given half a crown (2s 6d) on discharge. By the end of the year they reckoned they had released some 432 men, 180 wives, and 1,341 children. They had paid out some £800.

The society's charitable project soon got round the underworld, and in January 1773 they had a card hung in Westminster Jail stating that their charity was likely to be imposed upon 'by artful and designing villains who cause themselves to be arrested and imprisoned a day before the Society makes a distribution and thus come in for relief designed for the Poor distressed debtors imprisoned for a long time.'

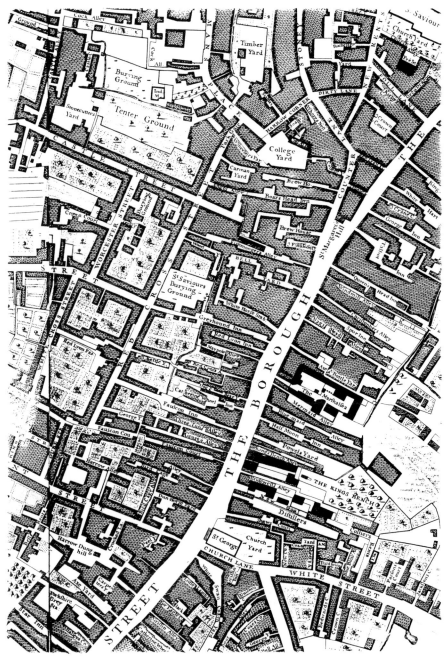

Debtors prisons in Southwark: to the right of The Borough, the Marshalsea, and below it, marked 'New Goal' [sic], the King's Bench Prison; far left, Whitecross Street where another new gaol was opened to relieve the pressure – John Rocque's map of 1749.

North view of the Marshalsea Debtors Prison in Southwark – a print in *The Gentleman's Magazine* of May 1804.

The Committee met weekly at the Thatch'd House Tavern in St James's Street and for that reason became known as The Thatched House Society. Later it extended its operations to gaols outside London. Small debtors remained those that owed less than £10. As a fund raising exercise William Dodd staged *The Debtor Relieved*, a Sacred Ode he had written, with music by a Mr Hook, in the Charlotte Street Chapel, after he had preached another sermon. It was in this vein:

> Thou cruel Creditor, forbear –
> What would'st thou more than All?
> Enough, enough: – The Man in Mercy spare;
> Ah, why his limbs enthrall?
> From his humble home so dear,
> Oh, for mercy do not tear!
> See his wife in sorrow drown'd,
> View his infants weeping round;
> From industry his hands restrain!
> Merciless! – what canst thou gain?
> Shame, disappointment, curses, for thy part;
> While hunger gnaws their soul, and anguish rends their heart!

AN ESSENCE OF FIRE

In 1774 he published *An Account of the Rise, Progress and Present State of the Society for the Discharge and Relief of Persons Imprisoned for Small Debts*. In his Introduction, Dodd reminded his readers that if a person owed only forty shillings, an extortionate litigious creditor could immediately obtain a writ, often by a false malicious oath, and deprive him of his liberty. The very payment of the sum at the instant of arrest would not, on many occasions, prevent him from being taken away. A man's house or apartment was not always a refuge against such malevolent surprises, insults and arrests. Though the law prohibited the forcible opening of a door, yet the bailiffs found means to evade that prohibition by indirect, unjust strategems, treachery or bribery of servants, 'even by force'.

> No person, particularly a clergyman, physician, surgeon, apothecary, officer of the army or navy, magistrate or member of any public department or office of state, court or commerce etc, ought to be liable to the least momentary privation of liberty for debt without three weekly citations or summonses, as in other countries, nor even then in his own house, apartment or shop though the doors be open.

What good could be done by it? Every feeling of humanity reverted from it and it would scarce be believed, in that age and kingdom of philanthropy, that such cruelties were exercised from man to man even for the mean, the paltry sum of eighteen pence.

> All crimes but Debt the hand of mercy spares,
> Nor suffer penance for successive years.
> Why lingers then the *Debtor's* hapless case,
> Who makes ATONEMENT, when he feels DISGRACE?
> Why languish years in close confinement hurl'd,
> Lost to himself and banish'd from the world?
> Whose talents well employ'd wou'd surely give
> The means to pay, and decently to live
> Or, timely fostered by the Good and Great
> Might rise distinguished and adorn the state.
> Yet strange reverse of sense, to shock the mind,
> The means of PAYMENT is to be confin'd!

The Thatched House Society saw their role not only as releasing debtors but making sure they never had to rescue them again. In an Exhortation to Released Prisoners they pleaded with them not to pursue their former vices of Folly, Extravagance and Dissipation. Sin no more, since a second term of imprisonment would deservedly be unpitied. If imprudence, ignorance or unskilfulness caused their debt, want of experience or the common unforeseen occurrences of life, they should frame their future plan of conduct on the principles of prudent care and

89

deliberate circumspection. They should study to improve and grow wary from their past mistakes and inadvertencies, act with caution, advice and consideration.

> Ever willing to take and hear counsel, and to use such discretion in the management of yourself and your concerns that, amidst any of the changes and chances of life, you may at least have the satisfaction to look up to God and to appeal to Men, as having faithfully, honestly, industriously and to the best of your abilities and understanding, done your utmost.

A most unforeseen occurrence cut short the Revd Dr William Dodd's participation in this crusade when, a few years after he wrote his *Account,* he was charged with the capital offence of forgery. After a trial which ended with his conviction, the well-known preacher was publicly hanged – which shocked those who read of it, and even more those that witnessed it, but did not deter James Neild and The Thatched House Society from continuing its fine work.

None of the small debtors whom the Society freed from prison ever considered saving themselves, even though temporarily, from the hounding of their creditors by borrowing. Most of them were used to paying regular visits to the friendly neighbourhood pawnbroker, but on the objects they brought to him they could not

Revd Dr William Dodd, keen promoter of The Thatched House Society for the Relief of Poor Debtors, who was publicly hanged for forgery in June 1777.

expect to raise any great sums. And in any case they wanted them back as soon as possible, and there would be the interest to pay.

Pawnbrokers had a role in society, and it was one which writers in social and literary reviews were constantly querying.

The question is not when the profits of the pawnbrokers are greatest but whether at any time they are just, whether they are not such as must destroy the end for which their

James Grant included 'The Pawnbroker' in *Pictures of Popular People* in 1842, their reputation having improved since the *Gentleman's Magazine* of 1745 which had deplored the pawnbroker's role of living by the miseries of mankind.

THE WORST POVERTY

continuance is permitted, the relief of the necessitous. That they live by the miseries of mankind is notorious; but of how many other employments is that assertion equally true? The only enquiry ought to be whether they contribute to lessen misery or increase it. *(The Gentleman's Magazine,* September 1745)

A mock 'Petition of the Pawnbrokers' said the petitioners who were in the business of lending small sums on pledges were not legally justified in charging more than five pounds for the loan of a hundred pounds for a year. They were not authorized to sell the goods pledged to them however perishable, which meant that many vexatious and expensive lawsuits were commenced against them every day. It would be of much greater service to the honest and industrious poor if the business was regulated, and reputable persons were licensed by a proper authority. It would hinder persons of ill fame acting in the business from whose ill conduct the public odium had arisen. In fact, from 1785 all pawnbrokers had to register.

If the bad image of the pawnbroker kept would-be customers away, many of the small debtors would have been even more reluctant to seek relief from the grander money-lender whose role was not so much, it seems, to relieve the impoverished of misery as to maintain the well-off in their excesses. When in Sheridan's comedy *The School For Scandal* (produced at the Drury Lane Theatre in 1777) Rowley tells Sir Oliver Surface that Mr Moses is below waiting his commands, he explains, 'This is a friendly Jew who, to do him justice, has done everything in his power to bring your nephew to a proper sense of his extravagance.' Money-lenders came to borrowers' houses, not vice versa.

SIR OLIVER.	Sir, I understand you have lately had great dealings with my nephew Charles.
MOSES.	Yes, Sir Oliver, I have done all I could for him; but he was ruined before he came to me for assistance.
SIR OLIVER.	That was unlucky, truly; for you have had no opportunity of showing your talents.
MOSES.	None at all; I hadn't the pleasure of knowing his distresses till he was some thousands worse than nothing.
SIR OLIVER.	Unfortunate indeed! But I suppose you have done all in your power for him, honest Moses?
MOSES.	Yes, he knows that. This very evening I was to have brought him a gentleman from the city, who does not know him and will, I believe, advance him some money.
SIR PETER TEAZLE.	What, one Charles has never had money from before?
MOSES.	Yes, Mr Premium of Crutched Friars, formerly a broker.

Sir Peter Teazle suggests to Sir Oliver Surface that he impersonates this Mr Premium whom Charles had never met, and 'you'll see your nephew in all his glory'. It will be the easier since Premium is not a Jew but a Christian. Sir Oliver is

Moses, played by Oscar Quitak, gives advice to young Surface in the National Theatre's 1990 production of Richard Sheridan's *The School for Scandal*, first staged in London in 1777.

sorry to hear that; but would he not be too smartly dressed to look like a money-lender? Not at all, says Sir Peter, nor would it be out of character if he went in his own carriage – and Mr Moses agrees. But what about the cant of usury and the mode of treating that he ought to know? The main point, said Sir Peter, was to be exorbitant enough in his demands. When Sir Oliver suggests asking eight or ten per cent on the loan, Mr Moses says if he asks him no more than that his impersonation will be discovered.

MOSES.	If he appears not very anxious for the supply, you should require only forty or fifty per cent; but if you find him in great distress and want the moneys very bad, you may ask double.
SIR PETER.	A good honest trade you're learning, Sir Oliver!
SIR OLIVER.	Truly, I think so – and not unprofitable.
MOSES.	Then, you know, you haven't the moneys yourself, but are forced to borrow them for him of a friend.
SIR OLIVER.	Oh! I borrow it of a friend, do I?
MOSES.	And your friend is an unconscionable dog; but you can't help that.
SIR OLIVER.	My friend an unconscionable dog, is he?
MOSES.	Yes, and he himself has not the moneys by him but is forced to sell stock at a great loss.

They agree it would be a good idea to refer to the passing in that year of 1777 of the annuity bill which made void all contracts for annuities made with people under twenty-one. It would be in keeping with Mr Premium to lament that a young man must now be at the years of discretion before he is allowed to ruin himself. Mr Premium, thought Sir Peter, would abuse the public for allowing merit to an Act whose object was to snatch misfortune and prudence from the rapacious gripe of usury, and give the minor a chance of inheriting his estate without being undone by coming into possession.

Richard Brinsley Sheridan was well qualified to write about such matters. He had no income when he married The Maid of Bath, the singer Miss Linley, but he used the £3,000 she had just been given by a disappointed but grateful, rich admirer, to buy a grand house in London's fashionable Portman Square, and furnish it lavishly. With no more resources than Charles Surface, he entertained London society with great panache and little regard for mounting debts. As Guy Boas has described, he would welcome his creditors, immaculately dressed, and 'beg them to share a bottle of the best wine, charm them with the wit of his conversation and send them away exchanging many mutual compliments and almost oblivious of their mission.'

He somehow bought David Garrick's share (with his father-in-law and a friend)

Richard Sheridan MP, who was rarely
solvent and had the bailiffs, who were in
possession of his house, act as waiters
when friends came to dinner.

of the Drury Lane Theatre, and subsequently the whole ownership. In deference
to the apparent madness of King George III he agreed to the Lord Chamberlain's
proposal, as play censor, to omit Shakespeare's *King Lear* from the repertory which
told of a monarch similarly afflicted; but clashed with him over *The School for
Scandal*, the objections to which, however, he managed to resolve, bringing him a
period of near prosperity. He was rarely solvent however. When he stood for
Parliament numbers of poor people crowded round the hustings demanding the
payment of outstanding bills. He remained light-hearted and cracked jokes at their
expense. He gave a dinner to Lord Palmerston and others at which he put the
bailiffs, who were in possession of his house, in livery, and had them officiate as
waiters – reminiscent of the bailiffs' scene in *The Good-Natured Man*. So long as he
was a Member of Parliament he could not be arrested for debt, but bailiffs were in
the house when he was taken mortally ill. One of them proposed arresting him as
he lay on his bed and taking him off to prison with all the bedclothes. Only the
playwright's doctor warning them of their responsibility should he die on the way,
prevented them carrying out so insensitive a duty. Some time later a creditor did
succeed in having him removed to a sponging house, where friends subscribed
£500 to make life more bearable for him. However, when a one-time tenant called
to say his possessions had been seized to pay his debts, Sheridan gave him the £300
which the man said would restore him to his former state.

Sheridan's flippant attitude to the management of his personal finances was typical of the time. 'There is not perhaps any selfish pleasure so frivolous', wrote Adam Smith in *The Wealth of Nations* published in the year Sheridan was writing *The School for Scandal*, 'of which the pursuit has not sometimes ruined even sensible men.' The hospitality of luxury and the liberality of ostentation had ruined many. Among their feudal ancestors however the long time during which estates used to continue in the same family sufficiently demonstrated the general disposition of people to live within their income.

Adam Smith instanced cock-fighting as a pleasure that had brought ruin, but card games probably accounted for even more insolvency. The losses of many players drove them to suicide, not insolvency. When Charles James Fox lost £200,000 at the gaming tables as a young man, his father and others came to the rescue. Others not so fortunate in their relations borrowed from money-lenders who, in this time of gambling mania, set up businesses exclusively devoted to advancing money at extremely high rates for settling gambling debts.

While most eighteenth-century beaux were obviously not disposed to live within their income and affected a bland indifference to the need to manage their personal finances, the tradesmen, the creditors on whose forbearance their insouciance depended, were campaigning against any legislation which seemed to reduce any further the chances of recovering what was owed them.

In February 1780 merchants of Westminster, Southwark and Middlesex petitioned against Lord Beauchamp's bill for amending the so-called Lords' Act (32 Geo II of 1759) to extend the escape route afforded by the bankruptcy laws to non-traders. It amounted, they said, to a total alteration of the law of the land and the establishment of a permanent act of insolvency at a time when trade was embarrassed and credit had sunk to its lowest ebb. Henry Erskine, counsel for the Middlesex committee, said it was a common trick for people claiming benefit of the acts of insolvency, and the bankrupt laws, to bargain for goods to a large amount from strangers to enable their estates to make a better dividend among their old creditors. In that way they secured a majority to sign their certificates. One man who had got himself clear in that way drove in his own carriage by the very commissioners to whom he had but lately surrendered, and splashed both them and his creditors with the dirt of his chariot wheels.

Lord Beauchamp said his bill was not only founded in charity but good policy. Trade would benefit from gaols being cleared of debtors who were of no use to their creditors or the community while in confinement. The only alteration was to relieve debtors who owed larger sums than £100. Instead of putting it in the power of the creditor to prevent his debtor from obtaining his liberty on giving up his all, it vested the right of a negative in the judges in open court, where it was more just to place it than to allow it to remain in the power of the creditor who, from motives of resentment, was less likely to decide impartially in his own cause.

Among the great number of debtors who crowded the gaols of the metropolis there might be fifty who were detained by inexorable creditors animated by motives of revenge, without the least hope of obtaining payment of their debts.

> Let gentlemen, before they declare their opposition to the bill, ask themselves whether the liberty of fifty Englishmen so circumstanced was not an object worthy their attention?

A debtor swearing an affidavit that he had resigned his all would not wipe away the claim his creditor had on him. A debtor who did that and swore that his all amounted to less than £5 would be brought before a court. If the bench believed him, they would set him free. Giving him his liberty would not cancel his debt however. As before, whenever his acquirements enabled him to pay, he would be called upon to do so. No such abuse of the bankruptcy laws was to be dreaded as Mr Erskine had feared. The creditor who had been splashed by his debtor's wheel could have his carriage seized the next day. His bill was intended to deprive the debtor of the power of insulting his creditor on the one hand and to restrain the creditor from tyrannizing over his debtor on the other.

The trading lobby were not to be fobbed off with talk like that. Any new insolvent debtor's bill was rejected one after another. They remained fearful of the opening of any loophole that would more easily expose them to fraud or abuse of the credit they had extended in good faith. It was back to the 'miserable refuge' of the Lords Act of 1759 with its 'great error' in giving all to one creditor, which induced many prisoners to stay and waste their property in prisons rather than by complying with the Act, obtain their discharge and be sent back to prison by other creditors. If a prisoner did not apply in the next term after execution to receive the benefit of the Act, he lost it. If he did apply in time and gave up all to one creditor, he remained a prisoner in the rest of the actions.

The man who in 1788 wrote the pamphlet *New Candid and Practical Thoughts on the Law of Imprisonment for Debt & c*, shared the attitude of the majority in condemning the ability of a creditor to confine his debtor where there was no question of fraud or abuse of credit. And what a long time it took for a tradesman to recover what he was owed! Proceedings invariably dragged on for eighteen months. And then, anyone who owed less than £200 had to wait for the start of the next law term in another four months if he wished to apply for the discharge which would come upon his delivering his whole property to the single creditor who had stayed with the process as long as that. At that point the creditor could still refuse to have the man released from prison and insist of his being kept there, so long as he paid him a groat a day.

Offers of loans at 10 to 14 per cent interest to nobility, gentry, merchants with incomes for life, persons of known properties, heirs apparent to large estates (if not minors) and ladies of character, in *The Times* of 8 June 1792.

AN ESSENCE OF FIRE

But what grieved the author of the pamphlet even more was the cost of it all. Experience showed, he said, that the proportion which debts recovered bore to the cost of the court proceedings was less than one in twenty, and so a burden on trade and business.

> Also, as the writer believes, and he speaks from his experience, there is not one case in twenty where a creditor who sues a prisoner in execution gets a shilling of his debt; and yet if he does not go that length, he might as well never have began. The delay also mocks the suit itself; for if the Debtor went to gaol with any property, in the space of eighteen months, it will either be dissipated, or the man, irritated with the harshness of the proceedings against him, or bad advice gained there, will contrive to defeat the creditor of it. Hence the event almost ever is, where a prisoner goes up to court to take the benefit of this Act, that he has nothing to deliver up. Who then is benefited by all this mummery, affected solemnity and length of proceeding? Why, the *Attorney*! – for doing worse than nothing – for injuring his client to the amount of his bill of costs – and for ruining a man who, on the arrest, would have given up his All to his creditors.

It was not only the tradesmen and merchants but the Lord Chancellor who opposed any bill which tried to remedy defects in the Lords' Act. He and other noble lords admitted the principle of the bill which a Lord Rawdon introduced in 1792 but 'disapproved the mode'. None of them could disagree that it was a species of tyranny that left an unhappy debtor to the mercy of a remorseless creditor whose affluence prevented him from knowing the sorrows of adversity and who, nursed in the lap of plenty, had never heard the call of hunger or knew the cry of distress. They probably could not wholly concur, however, with the pillorying of the legal profession (as the 1788 pamphleteer had done) – 'the rapacity of attorneys whose enormous fees accumulate the debt to such a sum that it is impossible for a debtor once in prison to discharge himself without ruining his family if the value of his possessions equal his debt'. In prison for a debt of £5, how could he pay five plus the thirty of law expense?

> The Lord Chancellor [reported *The Times* of 12 June 1792], on the very same grounds that he has opposed the Insolvent Bills and every other Bill on this subject, gave his decided negative to the present one.

He was at all times happy, said his lordship, to give his assent to any measure that could relieve the unfortunate debtor without giving an opportunity to the adulterer, the swindler etc. to take advantage of the same law – 'for these persons come under the denomination of debtors'.

When the House of Lords reconsidered Lord Rawdon's bill in March the next year they were told that, if they would assent to it, in a short time all debtors' prisons would become the residence of swindlers only. Lord Rawdon felt no one should be arrested for owing less than £20, as it was when George I came to the throne; that a creditor should pay the debtor he had put in prison 4s 8d a week; and the warden of The Fleet and the marshal of the King's Bench Prison (who made around £3,000 a year out of fees) should be compensated if the rules were abolished which allowed them their fees. In short, said *The Times*,

> from the complexion of the Bill, which is a very long one, it wears every appearance of answering those purposes which will save the honest man from prison, destroy the profits of pettyfogging attorneys and . . . do an essential service to public credit, restore the industrious man to society and untenant our prisons.

Lord Rawdon told the Committee of the whole House of Lords, which read his bill clause by clause in May, that he thought a debtor should be able to swear to the real cause of his debt and, if there was no question of fraud or any intention to abscond, he should not be held in custody for more than eight days and be discharged on filing common bail. Lord Kenyon was outraged.

> This is striking at the very foundation of our laws, and will multiply affidavits in such a manner and so increase perjury, as to prove ruinous in the end to the fair trader; it is giving to the courts of law a power to decide on points which come merely within the cognizance of a jury, and therefore defeats the very end which the noble lord has in view.

Lord Loughborough agreed with Lord Rawdon when he said that pettyfogging attorneys were the bane of civil society; they were a pest. A way must be found of ending their practices, but not at the expense of the Constitution. Lord Kenyon was of the same opinion.

> Imprisonment for debt is virtually a part of the British Constitution, and without that, or some other strong mode to compel justice to be done to the creditor, our trade, commerce and, in short, the source of all our wealth, must soon be destroyed. (*The Times* 6 May 1793)

The next day *The Times* carried an announcement headed

LORD RAWDON'S BILL

> At a meeting of the undersigned Traders at the Liverpool Hotel in the Strand on Monday the 19th April to take into consideration a Bill now pending in Parliament which is intitled 'An Act for amending the Law of Imprisonment on Mesne Process; for better regulating the Law and practice of Bail; for the relief of unfortunate, and the punishment of fraudulent, insolvent Debtors'.
> It was Resolved, That the said Bill would, if passed into a Law, in numberless

instances operate as an insuperable bar to the recovery of just and lawful Debts, and would effectually destroy that confidence which is unavoidably necessary in Trade.

Resolved, That by many Clauses in the said Bill the Creditors would be much harassed and put to expence, and numerous advantages given to the fraudulent and designing Debtor.

Resolved, That the Merchants, Traders and others of the Cities of London and Westminster, and the Borough of Southwark, be invited to a General Meeting for the purpose of considering the most effectual means of opposing the passing of the said Bill into a Law.

The twenty-six signatories invited their fellow traders to come to the Crown and Anchor Tavern in the Strand on Thursday 9 May. Lord Rawdon's bill was dropped. Justice to creditors was paramount. And when the person who owed them money was the heir to the throne they still deserved to be treated justly, perhaps even more so. For surely they could be forgiven for believing that a prince's promise to pay later must be firmer than a pauper's? In this, said A. Hanoverian in *A Letter to the House of Peers on the Present Bill depending in Parliament relative to the Prince of Wales's Debts* (1795), they were mistaken. With their bill the House of Commons had just burdened the people of Britain with a near million of debt contracted by the Prince of Wales. Only a maniac, he said, would think that the wretched pittance of the industrious poor should be wrung out of their pockets to pay for the follies and profligate expenses of anyone. No measure had raised such general indignation. Every peasant knew what it was to pay what he spent; every peasant comprehended the character of a prodigal. In 1787 the prince promised the king not to exceed his income and, trusting this promise, Parliament agreed to pay £190,000 of debt. But in 1795 came another demand, so the promise/contract was broken, for he was spending £45,000 a year more than his income. Penitent for this lapse, he dismissed his household and sold his stud. Parliament paid his debts and added another £10,000 to his income. The prince's response was to spend £100,000 more than his augmented income. He obtained money by false pretences, said the pamphleteer, a crime recognizable at common law. If the £190,000 had never been paid, he would have been importuned by his creditors. His furniture, perhaps his carriages, would have been seized; he would have had to hire others. He would not have found it possible to gamble deeply or to accumulate more debt.

The Prince of Wales cannot by law be imprisoned for debt, but those who prevent his feeling inconveniences, which he has exposed himself to, act with malignant indulgence . . . Had the £190,000 of debt not been paid in 1787, the £800,000 of debt could never have accumulated in 1795. Paying the debt can never lessen, but augments this degradation and, by so doing, redoubles the odium in which the Prince is held, excites in the nation disgust at monarchy, and may shake the throne.

THE WORST POVERTY

Parson James Woodforde must have thought the throne was already shaking when, as he described in his diary on 29 October 1795, he saw the prince's father being grossly insulted as he drove in the state coach through St James's Park. King George

> had a very narrow escape of being killed going to the House, a Ball passing thro' the Windows as he went thro' old Palace-Yard, supposed to be discharged from an air Gun, but very fortunately did not strike the King nor Lords.

The rector of Weston-Longville in Norfolk was well placed to appreciate the contrast between the six-figure income of Prinny at Carlton House, the building of which accounted for much of his debt, and the nine pounds annual wage he paid his servant Ben Leggatt. Woodforde was himself meticulous in keeping account of his outgoings and making prompt payment to tradesmen.

> May 14, 1794. Soon after we go to Norwich I walked about the City and paid many Bills that I owed, viz. To Lock, Timber Merchant, pd 1.3.0. To Sudbury, Upholsterer, pd. 5.7.0. To Forster, Taylor, pd. 4.9.6. To Bacon, Bookseller, pd. 0.16.3. To Priest, Wine-Merchant, pd. 2.4.0. To Steward, Attorney, 6.7.1½. To Buckle, Ironmonger, pd. 0.9.6. For two Box Tickets for the Play pd. 0.6.0.

It was not a way of life he would have considered particularly pious; to be content with it, and not strain to improve it, he would not have considered unmanly or unadventurous. Only cynics would have called him stick-in-the-mud or sneered at him being 'worthy'. Paying Your Way made for a comfortable life, with plenty of unsolicited adventure on the way. It was not a conscious avoidance of the Debtors Prison but the more positive, good-humoured attitude which was part of Making Your Bed and Lying On It.

It still behoved the middle class trader to play fair with his customers and not take advantage of good-natured country parsons and ignorant members of the labouring classes. Nor, said Thomas Gisborne in 1795, must he himself disdain to borrow money at the appropriate moment if he is not to put his credit to real and serious hazard. In the chapter 'On the Duties of Persons Engaged in Trade and Business' in his *Enquiry into the Duties of Men in the Higher and Middle Classes of Society in Great Britain*, he said the foundations of a trader's credit were 'property, integrity, punctuality, industry, prudence, openness in dealing, freedom from extravagance, from a spirit of wild speculation and from vice, and the character of the partners and of others with whom he is closely connected.' He should not overrate his resources, the goodness of his debts or the probable sale of his merchandise. 'But above all things let him not seek to bolster up his credit by unjustifiableness. Let him not put off the evil day by accepting deposits, much less by obtaining loans from the unsuspecting. Let him display a mind superior to the suggestion of false shame.'

If people were making demands on him for what he owed them, he should assemble them and lay before them a fair statement of his past transactions, of his present condition and his future prospects. If he thought instant bankruptcy would result from such disclosures, he must be no less earnest to become a bankrupt for the just advantage of his creditors than he would have been resolute not to fail by collusion for the purpose of defrauding them. He must stop paying. For, if he did not, he would have to continue to make partial payments to *some* of his creditors to the injury of others. So long as he was solvent in law, he could not proportion his payments to creditors according to their respective debts. For that he must have the aid of the law. A trader should never act on the presumption of retrieving his circumstances when he had become flagrantly insolvent. If he soldiered on, he was open to the temptation of setting up false credit, to engage in adventurous speculation, to concealing his true situation from his clerks, and to despair of mind. 'A hasty resolution of endeavouring to stand his ground may leave him a prey for life to sorrow and remorse.'

He could terminate his affairs in two ways. A commission in bankruptcy would cost him £100 and be subject to considerable delay; but the consent of a certain proportion of his creditors was sufficient for his discharge for ever from his debts. Under the second method, surrendering his effects under a Deed of Trust, the expense was little. But the signature of *all* his creditors was needed to exonerate him. It was considered the less discreditable way than a commission of bankruptcy, said Thomas Gisborne. A Letter of Licence, by which creditors agreed to postpone claims, brought only temporary respite and did not remove the evil day.

As seen, no such means of escaping their liabilities was available to non-traders. In any case, if Parson Woodforde's manservant Ben Leggatt found himself temporarily 'out of pocket', all he had to do was to pawn the best pair of trousers he had been wearing over the weekend and redeem them in time for church on Sunday.

Since the Act of 1800 pawnbrokers were allowed to charge an annual interest of 20 per cent on all sums under 42s, and 15 per cent on larger sums. A customer who wanted to raise more than ten pounds had first to agree terms and interest with the pawnshop-owner. Many would regularly 'pop their ticker' – pawn the watch they may have bought for five pounds, on which they may have raised forty pounds or more in loans, as Melanie Tebbutt showed in *Making Ends Meet* (1983). Others, who of course never used a bank, would pawn a five pound note for a few shillings, with instructions 'don't break the note' so they could redeem it still in one piece.

Money borrowed from a pawnbroker did not have to be repaid for fifteen months. In 1872 however the period was reduced to twelve months and seven days. Pledges on which less than ten shillings had been lent became the property of the pawnbroker if they were not collected on the appointed day. A pledge on which a loan of more than ten shillings had been made would be put up for auction, but its owner could come and redeem it on any day up to that of the sale.

If Ben Leggatt had earned his living, not as an odd job man at Weston Longville rectory but as a private soldier in one of His Majesty's foot regiments billetted in Bungay, he would have found the shopkeepers overwilling to let him take away purchases on a promise to pay later – had it not been for the 'Crying Down The Credits'. This warned the inhabitants that the average infantryman, in spite of his glamorous uniform, was lowly paid and impecunious. It was in the days before soldiers were housed in barracks and were left to their own devices in the taverns and private houses in which they were billetted. The first day a battalion moved in, the Provost Sergeant would march to the market cross, accompanied by drummers

Clients of a pawnbroker such as this one, illustrated in the 1836 edition of Charles Dickens's *Sketches by Boz*, had fifteen months to repay what they borrowed – reduced to twelve months and seven days in 1872.

and fifers who then started playing to attract attention. To the crowd who assembled, the Provo Sergeant announced that anyone giving credit to members of the regiment which had just arrived did so at their own risk. They were warned of the danger of giving credit – or too much credit at any rate – to mostly illiterate other ranks who were here today and gone tomorrow, and allowing them to run up debts which they had not the slightest chance, or intention, of paying.

When the regiment was about to leave, the same little posse returned to the centre of the town to tell tradesmen they were on the move, and it would be in their interests to stop giving further credit immediately. The likelihood of a hard-up, poorly-paid soldier who had left town for good every returning to pay his debts was negligible. This second ceremony was known as 'All Debts Paid'.

There was no such distrust of the ability to pay later of officers of the army and navy – or their mistresses. Couturiers and provision merchants, caterers and decorators never refused Lady Hamilton, mistress of Admiral Lord Nelson, all the credit she needed. Six months before her husband died in April 1803, she had a letter from Coutts her bankers to say she had outstanding bills for £700 but her current account balance stood at 12s 11d. Sir William Hamilton paid the bills (as the creditors knew he would), and in his will he left her £300 and an annuity of £800, which should have enabled her to live comfortably though not perhaps ostentatiously.

In a codicil Sir William asked Charles Greville, his heir, from whom he had

The luxury-loving Lady Hamilton who, on becoming insolvent after the death of Admiral Lord Nelson, the father of her daughter Horatia, was confined to a Sponging House within King's Bench Prison, Southwark, in 1812.

105

'bought' Emma, to pay the debts she had accumulated since his last settlement. Throughout 1802 she had entertained at Merton Place, where she and Sir William and Horatio had a strange *ménage à trois*, in a lavish style which cost around £65 per week. And when Sir William died she saw no reason to slow down. Nothing in Emma's actions suggested alarm at the deterioration of her resources, says her biographer Hugh Tours (*The Life and Letters of Emma Hamilton*, 1963). 'Nevertheless from the moment of her widowhood the tide of debt which was eventually to overcome her relentlessly started to mount.'

Though she had the money from her late husband's estate and another £1,200 from Nelson for the upkeep of Merton Place, by 1805 she owed £7,000. The death of the admiral on his flagship at the Battle of Trafalgar in October of that year did nothing to stem her spending – of money that was no longer there.

She chose not to reduce the scale of expenditure at Merton, which remained as high as ever throughout 1806 and 1807, and no tradesman saw fit to say No to her. Could she not sustain the momentum, not just on tradesmen's credit but on borrowed money? Her friend Abraham Goldsmid arranged a loan, but it did not last her long. Her admirer, Old Q, the eighty-four-year-old Duke of Queensbury, let her have his house at Richmond at a nominal rent, but declined to buy Merton Place from her. She had hopes of an East India merchant taking it off her for £13,000, and the shock of it falling through brought her to her senses, and to a realization of the depth of the hole she had dug for herself. Her first reaction was to appeal to Greville to get her out of it 'that I may live free from fear [of the debtors' prison] – that every debt may be paid. I think, and hope, that £15,000 will do for everything.' Otherwise lawyers would involve her every day more and more; debts would increase more debts.

> I am lost and most miserable if you do not help me. Only let me pass my winter without the idea of a prison. 'Tis true my imprudence has brought it on me, and villany and ingratitude [of the Government] has helped to involve me, but the sin be on them.

In November 1808 ten of her friends met in London to formulate a rescue plan. They heard that her debts were £8,000 exclusive of the £10,000 needed to pay off annuities; and that her house, land, furniture, books and wine were valued at £17,500. They decided to assign all these assets to five of their number as Trustees for Sale. Six of them lent her £3,700, secured by the Trust with interest, to pay 'all incumbrances absolutely necessary to be immediately discharged'. All her creditors were asked to execute the Debt of Trust, and agree to accept payment out of the Trust Estate. Emma could go on receiving the income from the annuities.

Old Q injected a further £2,500 for old times sake, and when he died shortly afterwards he left her £500 a year. If she calmed down, she might just weather the storm. Early the next year Lord Mansfield told her:

124.

Mess^r Thomas Coutts & Co   2Å July 1810

Having executed my Bond of this date in
favour of The Duke of Queensberry I desire
you will place the amount being Two Thousand
Five Hundred Pounds to my Credit — and pay
the same Sum to Mr Abraham Goldsmid on
my account   He will in conformity to the
plan agreed upon discharge Sundry Bills due
by me amounting to 2641-12.9 with the
2500 £ thus to be put into his hands — & He
will when completed deliver the Bills with
The proper receipts or discharges to you as Agent
for the Duke of Queensberry

Emma Hamilton

Emma Hamilton's letter of 20 July 1810 requesting Coutts Bank to give the £2,500 she received from the
Duke of Queensbury to Abraham Goldsmid who headed the Trust Estate from which her creditors
were to be paid.

The Worst Poverty

You should be cautious not to encrease your expenditure till your affairs are settled, or your creditors will become very troublesome from the apprehension that you will spend your legacy bequeathed to you without their reaping the advantage they expect of being first paid.

But caution was not her style. In December 1812 one of creditors had her arrested for debt, as he was entitled to under the still operating Lords' Act of 1759. She and Horatia, her daughter by Nelson, were taken from their house in Fulham to a Lock-up or Sponging House within the 'Rules' (boundaries) of the King's Bench Prison in Southwark – no. 12 Temple Place on the east side of Blackfriars Road where it joins St George's Circus, one of a terrace of twenty houses. It was the ante-chamber, so to speak, as it was in Tom Verney's day, to the prison itself. There she could call for any food or liquor she wanted, so long as she had the wherewithal to pay the inflated prices demanded by the Sponging House keeper. For the privilege of staying within the rules and not fully 'inside', she paid the marshal of the prison ten guineas. Here at least she would not be hounded by her other creditors. In fact, in her uncomfortable lock-up, she managed to play the hostess to royalty, to HRH the Duke of Sussex, whom she entertained to dinner. She wrote a memorial to his brother George, now Prince Regent, Nelson's friend, reminding him of the codicil which the national hero had made to his will leaving her and Horatia to the nation, and asking for it to be recognized in some tangible form.

After four months Alderman Joshua Smith, president of Southwark Borough Council, secured her release from prison – but not of course from the rest of her debts. When it became known that the Government had said it could not afford to honour Nelson's wishes and help her out, the tradesmen to whom she still owed money closed in. She sold her silver and plate, but the proceeds fell short of what was required. In June 1813 she was back at Temple Place, and she arranged for the auctioning of the contents of her Bond Street house. However, Joshua Smith intervened by buying it all up before the sale, and advanced Emma a sum on its security with which she could pay more outstanding bills. She would have recovered some of her old high spirits if it had not been for a bout of measles and turning more and more to alcohol. She spent the first three months of 1814 in bed.

She persuaded Earl Nelson, the admiral's doctor brother, to give her £250 of the Bronte Pension which had never been paid her, and with this she procured her final release from prison. She had £50 in her purse when she and Horatia took ship to Calais where she brazened it out until January 1815 when she died – not in disgrace but hardly gracefully.

Nell Gwynn played her cards more deftly. Whether or not the Merry Monarch's real last words were, 'Let not poor Nelly starve!' the court saw that that courtesan, once raised from her humble origin, never sank back. Emma Lyon, who made her way up the social scale by similar means, would have found herself in prison earlier had it not been for the lifeline thrown to her by her friends and former lovers. But by the end she chose to overplay her hand and lost the sympathy of those who could have saved her from her last indignities – though perhaps not from the bottle.

None of the Establishment lifted a finger to save William Cobbett from what they considered he well deserved. He was taken to the same King's Bench Prison in June 1810 to await his trial, not for debt but seditious libel in *The Political Register*. He certainly owed money but none of his creditors needed to obtain a writ to have him confined when the Government had arrested him for them. 'Everyone will easily imagine', wrote Cobbett whose 'crime' had been objecting to flogging in the army,

> that every debt that I owed of every description came pouring in for payment. The whole nation was cowed down at that time . . . with several parts of the country actually under the command of Hanoverian generals . . . The sons and daughters of corruption openly chuckled at what they thought my extinguishment. Almost everyone stood aloof except my creditors (never the last to visit you in such a season) who pressed on amain; so that I really forgot I was in prison, so great and so numerous were the torments arising. I was looked upon as a man given over by the doctors; and everyone to whom I owed a shilling brought me sighs of sorrow indeed; but, along with these, brought me his bill.

He was fortunate not to be in prison for debt for, on the tour of British prisons which he made in 1812, James Neild of The Thatched House Society, found debtors were discriminated against. In Dorchester Gaol criminal prisoners were allowed a peck of coal for their common room every day during the six winter months, and half a peck in summer. But there was no allowance of coal for debtors, male or female, except in very severe winter weather, or unless a special order was made by visiting magistrates. In a notice about Neild's *State of Prisons in England, Scotland and Wales* (1812), the *Edinburgh Review* commented: 'A well-fed Mayor, wrapt in warm clothing and braced by exercise will be extremely apt, judging from his own sensations, to pronounce on this subject a decision which a meagre ragged prisoner may feel extremely cruel.'

In the county gaols of Gloucester and Dorchester it was only debtors who were burdened with fees. The Under-Sheriff of Gloucester demanded 6s 8d for the discharge of every debtor. A note under the Table of Fees at Dorchester Gaol read:

> Every debtor who during his confinement has behaved orderly in prison and submitted to the regulations with decent respect and attention, on his discharge is entitled to a certificate of such good behaviour from the Chaplain and a visiting Justice, or Chaplain

and Governor; and this certificate is a complete acquittal from all and every fee payable to the Keeper.

More intelligent inmates of debtors' prisons needed no such inducement to behave themselves. The shock of the change of circumstances was sufficiently numbing to dampen any inclination to run riot, particularly after the painful build up of events which led to the final arrest.

The artist Benjamin Haydon was already £600 in debt when he heard that the Royal Academy would not after all be buying his painting *Macbeth* for 500 guineas. He had been selling his books and clothing to pay for his day-to-day needs, and now he owed his landlord £200. He had just embarked on another huge canvas *Solomon*. Should he abandon it? Sell all, retire to an obscure lodging and do *anything* for a living? But he could never realize enough to pay all he owed. In any case it would be cowardly, he told himself. 'Something instantly circulated through me like an essence of fire, and striding with wider steps I determined to go at once for my model, to begin tomorrow and to make the most of my actual situation. "Well done" said the god within, and instantly I was invincible.' But what would the attitude of others be?

He went to his usual restaurant intending to dine without paying. His heart sank as he said falteringly, 'I will pay you tomorrow.' As he was escaping from the room with a sort of lurking horror, the servant girl called after him. Her master wished to see him. It was, he thought, to tell him he could not trust him. He walked in like a culprit. 'Sir', said the owner, 'I see by the papers you have been ill-used.' He hoped the artist would not be offended, but as he had dined there many years, if it would be a convenience during his present work to dine until it was done, he need be under no apprehension for his dinner. His heart filled. From then on the pretty servant girls eyed him with a lustrous regret and redoubled their attentions. When he told Perkins his landlord of his case, and that it would be a pity to leave *Solomon* unfinished, Perkins blanched when he heard it would take another two years, gave him his fat hand and told him if the painting did not sell after two years, and Haydon still could not pay, '. . . why, sir, we'll consider what is to be done, so don't fret, but work.'

That was in 1812. He sold his *Solomon*, repaid what he borrowed, and four years later felt justified in borrowing again. But, he told himself, it was a fallacious belief, because borrowing had to stop sooner or later. If one was punctual and could pay in the long run, why incur the debt at all? To pay his landlord another £200 he borrowed £100 and paid £22 10s for the favour.

Thus I increased my rent by £22 10s and this is the anatomy of all such detestable transactions. When this bill of £122 10s came due I had received £100 on a commission, so I was obliged to borrow £22 10s to make up the total; for this I paid £5 or £6, so here again was the £6 added to the £22 10s making £28 10s on £200 rent. *(Autobiography, chapter XVII, 1816)*

A reptile of a money-lender from Poland Street offered to accommodate him at 40 per cent, '20 less than any other of the trade.' He advanced £100 for £10 at three months. Five years later happened what he always dreaded.

June 22nd [1821]. A remarkable day in my life. I am arrested. After having passed through every species of want and difficulty, often without a shilling and without ever being trusted; and now when I am flourishing I become a beacon.

His mistake was employing more than one man to decorate his rooms. He paid one of them £300 'who, because I employed another to fit up my last room, out of pique arrested me for the balance.' He told the bailiff who came for him that he must shave, and suggested he stepped into his studio where on an easel he was confronted with the half finished *Lazarus*. 'Oh my god sir!' he exclaimed, 'I won't take you. Give me your word to meet me at twelve at the attorneys and I will take it.' The attorney agreed with Haydon about the injustice of the proceedings, and told him to return that evening to settle the matter finally. But he must remain in the custody of the bailiff, who said however there was no need for it. 'Not he. Let him give me his word and I'll take it, though I am liable to pay the debt.' That night he settled everything, and his expenses were £11.

The following November another officer entered his studio while he was at work on the massive *Crucifixion* and said, 'Sir, I have an execution against you.' But he had paid part of that apothecary's bill that very morning, and the attorney to whom the bailiff took him agreed there had been a mistake. But there was no mistake when on 21 April 1823, while still at work on the *Crucifixion* he had to put the project on hold. The entry in his *Journal* was headed 'King's Bench':

Well, I am in prison. So were Bacon, Raleigh, and Cervantes. Vanity! Vanity! Here's a consolation! I started from sleep repeatedly during the night, from the songs and roarings of the other prisoners. 'Their songs divide the night, and lift our thoughts' – not to heaven.

His creditors met on the 28th and they read a letter from their debtor telling them the law was an enemy he could not conquer. He hoped they could come to an arrangement which would prevent the dishonour of his claiming its protection. 'If I am kept locked up with no power of putting my art into practice what will be the result? – depression, disquiet and ruin. I shall infallibly be destroyed, and how can you be benefited by my death?'

THE WORST POVERTY

He had nothing to offer them, he said, not a shilling. His property was entirely gone; those who were the most severe had possessed it. It was hard to be torn up by the roots, to have his books, easels, prints and materials of study dragged from their places. Want of support was his only failure.

Sir Walter Scott was one of many who wrote to offer sympathy, enclosing a small sum which might stop a leak in a vessel. Haydon should take comfort, said the novelist, from knowing that no species of legal distress could attack the internal resources of genius, though it might for a time palsy its hand.

Haydon failed to come to any agreement with his creditors. But in July a court released him from prison, and two days later he heard that out of 150 creditors none opposed his being discharged. 'One villain entered his name but lost courage. I consider this an ordeal that has tried my character, and I feel grateful for it.' Borrowing on the security of high hopes and honest intentions, as Malcolm Elwin observed in his edition of Haydon's autobiography and journals (1950), and an unsuccessful attempt to live by credit, had brought insolvency and imprisonment, and now he had to make a new start.

When later in 1823 he was once again arrested for debt, he watched fellow debtors in King's Bench Prison perform a mock election which became the subject of a famous painting exhibited in 1828 and bought by George IV for £500 – 'baronets, and bankers, authors and merchants, painters and poets, dandies of rank in silk and velvet and dandies of no rank in rags and tatters, idiotism and insanity, poverty and affliction, all mingled in indiscriminate merriment, with a spiked wall twenty feet high above their heads!' His release on this occasion was secured by friends subscribing to a fund for which Coutts Bank acted as trustees.

In a letter to Mrs Coutts he described the horror and the misery from which the mock election was a welcome diversion.

Ah madam, how prophetic was Mr Coutts when he advanced that 400£. 'My life' he said, 'has been passed in affording Gentlemen of your profession assistance; their hopes have always been disappointed, and my money lost'. I flattered myself that I should be an exception, and my confidence is punished. Since I had had the honour of seeing you at the private view of the Academy, misfortune and ruin have pressed on me with such a merciless vigour, that my credit is inextricably destroyed – my property gone – the labours of years, and all my books, prints, casts and materials of study, lotted and numbered. It was so totally unexpected that I was wholly in the midst of my study, and torn from the delightful occupations of my life, as if in a whirlwind. 900£ had been lent me at the instigation of a pupil by a House in the city. This young man speculated in Spanish bonds and lost 5000£ in one morning. They now applied to me. I paid 100 out of my receipts. I sent them the picture which was their security, and they immediately put it in an Execution on Lazarus, now in Piccadilly.

This was his picture *The Raising of Lazarus* now in the Tate Gallery. When he was arrested in his house he found it impossible to parry any longer such a mass of events, and surrendered to them.

All the savings of my life by this sudden and violent act will be hurried from my grasp, and I shall have again to begin the World, dishonored and degraded!

The King's Bench Prison was a sad refuge as a reward for nineteen years of intense devotion to painting and having his works received with enthusiasm in England and Scotland, and visited by thousands in both countries.

I write this letter that I might explain to you Madam, the utter impossibility of my being able to keep my engagements in August and January, and to hope you will consider the dreadful nature of my condition which renders it so sudden, so totally unexpected. After having lived for years in the silence and solitude of my study, sweetened by the gentle converse of a lovely wife, to be plucked by the roots from such a home, from the endearments of such a Woman, and the smiles of an infant as shining as a star – and plunged into a Prison to herd with Gamblers – is hard – in the midst too of respect and reputation all over the World.

I am gratefully yours
B.R. Haydon

Mrs Coutts

Last page of the letter written by artist Benjamin Haydon to Mrs H. Coutts in 1823 after his creditors had put him in King's Bench Prison – 'a sad refuge' as a reward for nineteen years devotion to painting.

113

King's Bench Prison, Southwark, was for 'Gentlemen Debtors', seen here exercising themselves in the yard at tennis (?), while fellow prisoners watch from the windows – a print of 1825.

He would have had to herd with less congenial characters than gamblers if he had been sent to The Fleet or the Marshalsea. The King's Bench Prison was for gentlemen debtors, for 'men born to property and a high station in life who by their folly and crime reduced themselves to wretchedness and loaded themselves with disgrace' – though James Grant's description in *Pictures of Popular People* could not be said to fit poor Benjamin Haydon. It was melancholy to see in the civil prisons of the metropolis, remarked Grant, men whose birth, education, manners and appearance would have fitted them for occupying the highest positions in society and consequently of proving benefactors to their species, spending no inconsiderable portion of the prime of life amid scenes of deepest degradation. Few ever recovered their status in society, he said, or got rid of the bad habits they contracted while there.

Dandified gentlemen debtors in what, after 1837, became Queen's Bench Prison, depicted by James Grant among his *Popular People* of 1842. For many, non-payment of tailors for their finery was the cause of confinement.

And among the creditors of the gentleman prisoner are always to be found a greater or less number of tailors. His tailor's bill is often indeed the largest individual claim against him; and in many cases it is at his *suit* that he is in prison. Among the sprigs of fashion the poor tailor is thought a peculiarly fit subject for plunder . . . To 'do' a tailor is in his estimation to accomplish some high and honourable feat. The spirit of Sheridan's question when he saw a friend with a new suit which he knew would never be paid for 'Who suffers?' is still preserved. The tailor is an everlasting subject of jocularity among the inmates of the prison.

Grant had never been able to comprehend the reason for this inveterate enmity to the poor tailor. It might be supposed that to injure him by getting deeply into his

debt sufficed to satisfy any unfriendly feelings they might entertain towards him.
'Not so, however. They must needs add insult to injury.'

In sending his contribution to the fund for Benjamin Haydon, Sir Walter Scott
apologized for its smallness, but he had been 'a little extravagant lately'. He had
purchased a lot of land and even more books and 'expensive trifles'. He had already
paid the debts of his brother Tom, an army officer in Canada, but with *Ivanhoe*
selling 10,000 copies at 30s each, he sent the further £800 requested. His financial
position dramatically changed, however, when in 1825 the publishing house of
Constable, in which he had invested, were refused further credit by their bankers.
It came as a great shock. 'I really believe they have not had any capital for twenty
years, but were entirely trading on credit.' Everyone thought they were worth at
least £150,000.

In fact they had unpaid bills amounting to £256,000 on which they were only
able to pay 2s 9d in the pound; their London agents, Hurst & Robinson, only
managed 1s 3d on a debt of £300,000. Scott sent Constable £5,000 and borrowed
another £5,000 on his own and Constable's security. It put him, as investor in these
two as well as Ballantynes the printers who were also insolvent, in deep trouble.
When the Duke of Buccleugh offered to take the whole of his losses on himself he
said, 'I will involve no friend, rich or poor – my own right hand shall do it.' It was
hopeless waiting for miracles, he said. He made an arrangement which, he claimed,
would make him far richer than generals and admirals who led armies and fleets, a
Trust Deed by which his assets were assigned to Trustees who made all the
payments to creditors on the lines of that set up for Emma Hamilton. If he
managed economically he hoped that in five years' time, if the public continued to
buy what he wrote, he would retrieve more than he lost. 'It is a bad business, but
might have been much worse.'

It was bad enough. His creditors who met in the Waterloo Hotel in Edinburgh
on 20 January 1826 were told Scott's liabilities were £104,081 and his estate
available for realization was worth £48,494. His assets were his house in Castle
Street, Edinburgh, his library and furniture, and the value of the life-rent on
Abbotsford the house he had built on The Border. If his creditors allowed him to
be, he would be their vassal for life. He would not put out of the power of his
creditors the mental and literary resources which yet remained to him.

The Trust paid a first dividend of 6s in the pound. He sat down to write himself
out of insolvency with a series of new novels starting with *A Fair Maid of Perth*.
Soon he was earning £20,000 a year. His so-called *Magnum Opus*, the forty-eight
volumes of his novels, generated an income of £5,000 a year. On Christmas Eve
1827 he arrived at Abbotsford which he had left six months before, as he wrote in a

letter, 'in doubt whether I should fly my country and become avowedly bankrupt and surrender my library and household furniture with the life-rent of my estate for sale.'

> But I could not have slept sound as I now can . . . If I achieve my task I shall have the thanks of all concerned and the approbation of my own conscience.

When the Bank of Scotland had threatened to imprison his Constable partner Robert Cadell in Calton Hill Gaol, Cadell took refuge in the debtors' sanctuary at Holyrood – where Thomas de Quincey had also stayed for some time. Walter Scott seriously contemplated doing the same, or perhaps fleeing to the Isle of Man, as his brother Tom had done, but was persuaded that a better way out was the Trust Deed.

When Scott died, after six years of hectic literary activity, he had paid £70,000 of a debt that then stood at £117,000. It took another fifteen years to wipe out the debt completely.

His attitude was that of one the soldiers whose income by the sword he said he would better with his pen. When Arthur Wellesley was in command of the British troops in Spain he refused to pay for their upkeep by pillage and plunder. But it meant their being overwhelmed with debts. 'I can scarcely stir out of my house', he told his political masters in Whitehall, 'on account of public creditors waiting to demand payment of what is due to them.' Relating the story of the future Duke of Wellington in *Self-Help*, Samuel Smiles commented that the general had no intention of acting grandly or nobly, 'merely regarding the punctual payment of his debts as the best and most honourable mode of conducting his business.' The old campaigner's sense of what was honourable in such matters was more acute than the three sons of George III who, in the words of the author of the tract *The Royal Criterion* (1814) 'resorted to every mode of raising money without a scruple as to the means.' The Prince of Wales, he claimed, wanted money to support his horse racing; the Duke of York to pay his bets and preserve his credit at Mucklow's Tennis Court where he spent much of his time and lost a great deal of money estimated at £200,000. The Duke of Clarence was also always overspending.

The three brothers raised a sum upon Post Obit Bonds through one Louis Weltzie, Clerk of the Prince of Wales's Kitchen, and a man who had been a Lottery Office Keeper near Carlton House, called Annesley Shee. They also enlisted the help of John Cator MP 'a mean, avaricious money-lender very much employed by men of fortune in trafficking for annuities, reversions and post obits.' Cator engaged to pay them £10,000 down against a bond for treble that amount, £30,000, which the holder of the bond would be paid when 'a certain event' took place – the death of the king and the succession of any one of the three royal borrowers. Much to William Pitt's disgust Cator sold the bond by public auction to a solicitor called Yates.

King George thought his sons should be able to live on their official incomes which he was not prepared to augment so they could indulge their more frivolous pastimes. Any spare cash he preferred to donate to more worthy causes. In 1809 he celebrated his Jubilee, fifty years on the throne. In that year the secretary of the Society for the Relief of Persons Confined for Small Debts received a letter from Spencer Perceval the Prime Minster (who was later to be assassinated by a bankrupt, John Bellingham) to say that His Majesty had graciously given orders to present The Thatched House Society with £2,000 from his private purse. In addition the king gave £1,000 for the liberation of prisoners confined for small debts in Scotland, and another £1,000 for those in Ireland. The Corporation of London and the Merchants of London also marked George III's Jubilee by donating £2,000 to The Thatched House Society.

JUBILEE

PRISONERS for DEBT in the Prison of the Marshalsea of His Majesty's Household

There are now confined in the above prison in the Borough of seventy-two persons (from the age of 23 to 74, leaving 53 wives and 203 children) for various debts from seven guineas up to £140. The total amount of the whole sum is £2,092. Many are in great distress and objects of charity, every way worthy the notice of a generous and feeling public who are interesting themselves in the cause of suffering humanity against the approaching Jubilee.

This advertisement in the *Morning Post* of 23 October 1809 asked for money towards a fund for offering compositions to creditors which would effect the debtors' release – 10s in the pound for every debt under £20; 7s 6d under £50; 5s above £50.

CHAPTER FIVE

No Longer a Crime
– up to 1869

T he law, which Benjamin Haydon regarded as an enemy, remained hostile to insolvent debtors throughout this time. Since the lawmakers were mostly of the creditor class, their attitude was to retain a statute by which they could obtain a writ for the arrest of their debtor and his detention at their will. The old Lords' Act was a long time a-dying; and non-traders were still unable to claim the benefits of bankruptcy open to traders.

There were changes however. By an Act of 1808 (48 Geo III cap 123), anyone who had been a year in prison for a debt of less than £20 was thought to have suffered enough and must be allowed to go home. A creditor could no longer stop the release of anyone, however short their confinement, who was willing to pay what he owed. On discharge he was still not free of his debt, but the Act greatly improved the insolvent debtors' lot. An even greater improvement came in 1813 with 53 Geo III cap 102 which created a scheme involving a new 'Court for Relief of Insolvent Debtors' which, as Sir William Blackstone saw it in his famous *Commentaries*, 'first provided permanently for the relief of insolvent debtors'. Its purpose was to hear prisoners' petitions for release. It was the court which Benjamin Haydon appeared before and ordered his release. Either the debtor or the creditor could appeal from the decision of the court to a single-judge Court of Appeal which gave a final decision. The judge was chosen from among the judges of King's Bench, Common Pleas or Exchequer.

Anyone who was prepared to submit himself to a debtors' prison for a token period could apply from The Fleet or the Marshalsea for the help of the Insolvent Debtors Court. He then had to stay in prison for two months while a schedule of his debt was prepared, he was examined by the court and he agreed to surrender his property. His debt did not have to be less than £20; it could be for any amount. He was immediately released from his confinement, but he was still liable to the man who had given him credit in the belief he could keep his promise to pay later.

Not everyone had sufficient assets of sufficient value to cover what he still owed, or was willing to surrender them, but the new scheme certainly benefited a large number. 'Even so', said W.R. Cornish and G. de N. Clark in their *Law and Society in England 1750–1950*, 'there was a growing feeling that a system which sent 10,000 or so debtors into prisons each year (a quarter or more on the mesne process*) was too expensive, too indiscriminate, too open to abuse and over-weening pressure.' The mesne process allowed a creditor to have his debtor arrested and detained before the case came to court and judgement was made on it.

Apart from anything else, the procedure became a method of habitual fraud. Unscrupulous operators took the two months' imprisonment in their stride. They cynically referred to it as 'college' where they picked up further tips in the arts of fraud from their cell mates. However it did enable anyone who was in fact a trader, but the law did not recognize as such, to achieve something resembling the benefit of bankruptcy. In fact the procedure was similar to bankruptcy procedure, with the debtor's property transferred to an assignee who had to pay the creditors in proportion to what they were owed. Charles Dickens described the scene in *Pickwick Papers*.

> In a lofty room, badly lighted and worse ventilated, situate in Portugal Street, Lincoln's Inn Fields, there sit, nearly the whole year round, one, three or four gentlemen in wigs, as the case may be, with little writing desks before them constructed after the fashion of those used by judges of the land, barring the French polish. There is a box of barristers on their right hand; there is an enclosure of insolvent debtors on their left; and there is an inclined plane of most especially dirty faces in their front. These gentlemen are the Commissioners of the Insolvent Court, and the place in which they sit is the Insolvent Court itself.

It was the common resort and daily place of refuge of all the destitute shabby-genteel people in London. A casual visitor might suppose it to be a temple dedicated to the genius of seediness. The barristers' wigs were ill-powdered and their curls lacked crispness.

> But the attorneys who sit at a large bare table below the Commissioners are after all the greatest curiosities. The professional establishment of the more opulent of these gentlemen consists of a blue bag and a boy; generally a youth of the Jewish persuasion. They have no fixed offices; their legal business being transacted in the parlours of public-houses or the yards of prisons; whither they repair in crowds and canvass for customers after the manner of omnibus cads. They are of a greasy and mildewed appearance; and if they can be said to have any vices at all, perhaps drinking and cheating are the most conspicuous among them. Their looks are not prepossessing and their manners are peculiar.

---

* Pronounced 'mean', the part of a law suit that intervenes between the primary and final process.

No Longer a Crime

All sorts of dodges were resorted to for 'surrendering' property. The clever ones soon discovered that while banknotes could be seized a bank balance could not. As E. Welbourne showed in 'Bankruptcy Before the Era of Victorian Reform', 'men in prison who had stripped themselves of all they had, could produce £2,500 in notes from under the bed.'

But the misery of those who could not obtain their release, either honestly or dishonestly, by appearing before an Insolvent Debtors Court and agreeing to assign their property, still drew sympathy. The debtor might have been reduced to his inability to satisfy his creditor, asserted Thomas Foxwell Buxton,

> by the visitation of God, by disease, by personal accidents, by the failure of reasonable projects, by the largeness or the helplessness of his family. His substance and the substance of his creditor may have perished together in the flames or in the waters. Human foresight cannot always avert, and human industry cannot always repair, the calamities to which our nature is subjected. Surely then some debtors are entitled to compassion. *(An Inquiry whether Crime and Misery are Produced or Prevented by our Present System of Prison Discipline, 1818)*

The reviewer of his book in the *Edinburgh Review* thought half of the thousands of imprisoned debtors had been reduced to their state by 'venial errors' or innocent misfortune. Clearly all inflictions beyond that of mere detention were illegal; fetters were contrary to the law. For the Quakers their fall illustrated the danger of making haste to be rich and deviating from safe and regular methods of business. No one could expect the blessing of the Most High for such pursuits.

Now that the law embraced the principle of what lawyers called *cessio bonorum* – yielding up of goods – some thought imprisonment should be regarded as punishment and not just a way of preventing the debtor absconding. For anyone with few possessions who chose to contract a variety of debts, said Lord Althorp in a Commons debate in February 1820 on a Bill that would refine the 1813 legislation, it would only be 'a slight visitation' to have to surrender them to his creditors. But was it not partly the fault of tradesmen?'

> I am perfectly ready to admit the too great facility of credit which is always extended, particularly by the tradesmen of this metropolis. This is an evil; but the remedy must be provided in some other way than by placing those tradesmen in a situation in which they would so severely suffer for their confidence.

Lord Redesdale wanted to see a revision of the procedure in small debts courts. Their jurisdiction should be raised from 40s to £10; similar courts should be set up in every county; the jury should be reduced to four. John Bright wanted the benefit extended to crown-debtors who should be released after a full disclosure and a discharge of all claims above £200. In that way, said the Attorney General, the revenue would be defrauded with impunity. For the law applied to smugglers, and they were rarely men of property. Individuals on the other side of the water would pay five or seven hundred pounds to procure their discharge, which could not be expected to continue if they could be released by other means.

It worried Lord Auckland that a court could now refuse to free a prisoner whom his creditor wished to see released. In the debate on Lord Redesdale's insolvent debtors bill in 1820, he said he would like to see the debtor the creditor's prisoner once more, not the court's. And should not those in Sponging Houses, who squandered what properly belonged to their creditors, be removed to the actual prison? The discipline there would put a stop to any more of *that*.

And maybe they would be cowed not only by the discipline but by the man who wielded it. Any who were unfortunate enough to find their lives being ruled by James Spencer, keeper of the Debtors' Prison for London and Middlesex, soon learnt to keep their wits about them.

Spencer's conduct at the new Debtors' Prison in Whitecross Street, where in 1828 he had been keeper for six years, was the subject of a Memorial from James Neild's Thatched House Society to the Lord Mayor and Court of Aldermen of the City of London. They accused him of altering the figures on receipts for money they had given for the release of prisoners, handing over a smaller sum to creditors and pocketing the difference; charging prisoners for candles; taking £5 out of the Poor Box to free a prisoner; lending them money on their plate and watches which belonged to their creditors. But James Spencer's most improper conduct, said the petitioners, was towards Solomon Neete and his wife, a dealer in smuggled silks and other contraband goods,

> to whom [in the words of the Memorial] Spencer advanced money for a chaise, harness and a Newfoundland dog, while on his way to the Insolvent Debtors Court, which chaise etc were the property of his creditors; his having allowed the Neete's three children called Silver, Frederick and Napoleon to remain constantly in the prison five or six weeks but interdicting other prisoners from seeing *their* children (except on Wednesdays and Sundays) when he discovered that Neete's wife had obtained her husband's chaise and harness when he, Spencer, was absent, which so exasperated him that his rage fell upon the whole of the prisoners confined at that time.

The Court of Aldermen investigated these allegations, but before they had finished them they received a grovelling letter from the keeper of Whitecross Street Gaol tendering his resignation. The painful state of his feelings rendered him incapable of personally addressing them. He would not attempt to vindicate the incorrect manner in which he had acted and sincerely lamented. Imprudence which could not be pardoned had blighted his life. He, his wife and seven children were left without any means of support . . . and so on and so on.

The City aldermen accepted his resignation and appointed Samuel Barrett, a glover, in his place.

By 1830 the number of towns which had obtained Acts of Parliament to have their own Courts of Requests or Courts of Conscience, on the lines of those established in London in 1749, had risen to fifty-four. The Southwark Court of Requests was still functioning, and the process there was initiated by a tradesman or individual lodging a complaint against another for non-payment of money owed, after less formal requests had been ignored. He went to the court where he found himself dubbed the plaintiff, paid a fee and a deposit for which he received a receipt. If he was suing for less than 20s in 1830 he left a deposit of 5s; 7s 6d for one between 20s and 40s; 10s between 40s and 60s, and 12s 6d for 60s. He gave the Clerk of the Court his name and that of the person he was suing whom the clerk called the defendant.

SUMMONS.

GEO. IV. REX.

No.

COURT OF REQUESTS for the Town and Borough of Southwark. and Eastern Half of the Hundred of Brixton, in the County of Surrey.

To C. D.

Amount of
Debt claimed.
s.   d.

You are hereby summoned, and in his Majesty's Name strictly enjoined and commanded personally to be and appear before the Commissioners of the said Court, at the COURT HOUSE, in Swan Street, Trinity Street, near Stones' End, Borough, on TUESDAY (or FRI-DAY) next, at a Quarter before Eleven of the Clock in the Forenoon precisely, to answer the demand of A. B. for the Debt owing by you, as stated in the Margin. Herein fail not.

Dated this   day of   , 1830.

MEYMOTT & DREW, Clerks.

Summons form of 1830 used to order a debtor to attend Southwark Court of Requests to answer a creditor's demand for payment of what he claimed he was owed.

BRING THIS SUMMONS WITH YOU.

Note.—If you have any Set-off, you must deliver an account of it to the Plaintiff before the day of Hearing—and also be prepared with the best evidence to substantiate the same before the Court.

123

THE WORST POVERTY

This action by the creditor set in motion the issuing, by the clerk, of a writ or summons which was formally delivered to an officer of the Chief Bailiff who served it on the defendant at his house. It told him to come to the court on a certain day to defend himself before a Commissioner and the man who said he owed him money. If he failed to turn up, the Commissioner had the power to hear the plaintiff's case only and give immediate judgement on it. But he almost always gave the defendant a second chance, and sent him a second summons to appear the following week. If he was absent again, the plaintiff declared on oath the amount of the debt, whereupon the Commissioner could order an 'execution' either against the body or goods of the uncooperative debtor.

If for any reason the plaintiff was unable to come at the time fixed for his hearing, he became 'non-suited', and the man he hoped to sue could collect the deposit he had left with the clerk on starting the action. If the plaintiff/creditor was unable to prove his case and had judgement given against him, he also lost his deposit to his debtor. But if the defendant lost, he was ordered to pay his

ATTACHMENT, WITH NOTICE TO THE PLAINTIFF.

GEO. IV. REX.

COURT OF REQUESTS for the Town and Borough of Southwark, and Eastern Half of the Hundred of Brixton, in the County of Surrey.

At a Court holden on , the day of 1830, at the COURT HOUSE, *Swan Street, Trinity Street,* near *Stones' End, Borough.*

To C. D.

No.

Amount of Debt claimed.

s. *d.*

IT appearing to this Court, that you have been duly summoned to attend here this day, to answer the demand of A. B., for a debt owing by you, as stated in the Margin, and although duly called, came not : *You are therefore attached for Contempt.—And are hereby peremptorily commanded,* personally to be and appear before the Commissioners of the Court aforesaid, at a Court to be holden on TUESDAY (or FRIDAY), the day of 1830, at Eleven o'Clock in the forenoon precisely, at the Court House aforesaid, to hear and abide such order as shall then be made touching such demand.————— Herein fail not ; as in case of default, Execution will immediately issue for such Debt as shall then be awarded against you, together with Costs.

By the Court,
MEYMOTT & DREW, Clerks.

Mr. A. B.

No.

You are hereby required to appear at the COURT HOUSE, in *Swan Street, Trinity Street,* near *Stones' End, Borough,* on TUESDAY (or FRIDAY) next, at Eleven o'Clock precisely, to substantiate your Debt against C. D. otherwise your claim will be dismissed.

Dated this Day of 1830.

E. F. *Officer.*

N.B. Bring this Notice with you.

Notice of Attachment sent to a debtor in 1830 who failed to respond to a Summons to attend Southwark Court of Requests to answer a creditor's demand for payment.

outstanding debt by instalments and if he defaulted on any one of them, he had to pay over the rest in one lump.

The debtor who refused to go and defend himself against his creditor's charges risked having some of his possessions seized and sold to pay what he still owed. He also risked being arrested and put in gaol. Frederick Meymott, Clerk of the Southwark Court of Requests, whose *Analysis* of 1830 has already been referred to, thought the latter was the most usual and advisable course. However unpopular such a measure might at first appear, the long experience of the commissioners had shown them not only the inefficacy in most cases but also the cruelty of issuing executions against the *goods* of defendants – 'as regards the wives and children of debtors by selling their beds from under them, and the expense and oppression attending the levy'.

Proof of that was to be found in the returns to Parliament during 1826 and 1827 which showed that out of sixty-seven executions ordered against goods only forty produced payment. The remaining twenty-seven were obliged to be withdrawn in

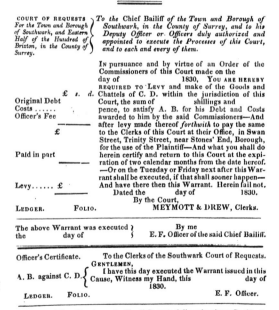

Warrant of Execution against the Goods of 1830 issued to Southwark Chief Bailiff requiring him to levy from a debtor the sum the Court of Requests had declared he owed a creditor, or 'make of', i.e. sell, enough goods and chattels of his to raise the sum.

EXECUTION AGAINST THE BODY; WITH THE OFFICER'S CERTIFICATE.

COURT OF REQUESTS For the Town and Borough of Southwark and Eastern Half of the Hundred of Briston, in the County of Surrey.

To the Chief Bailiff *of the Town and Borough of Southwark, in the County of Surrey and to his Deputy, Officer or Officers duly authorized and appointed to execute the processes of this Court,—* To the Keeper *of the County Gaol of Surrey, commonly called Horsemonger Lane Gaol—and* To the Keeper *of the Prison called the Borough Compter, within the said Borough, and to each and every of them.*

	£.	s.	d.
Original Debt	:	:	
Costs	:	:	
Officer's Fee	:	:	
£			
Paid in Part	:	:	
Levy	£		

IN pursuance and by virtue of an Order of the Commissioners of this Court made on the   Day of   1830, YOU ARE HEREBY REQUIRED to take C. D. if he shall be found within the jurisdiction of the said Court, and him safely lodge and detain, (if his residence shall be within the Town and Borough of Southwark) in the said Gaol or Prison, called the *Borough Compter*—And (if his residence shall be within any other part of the Eastern Half of the Hundred of Brixton) then in the said County Gaol of Surrey—for the space of   days, Or until the sum of   Shillings and Pence, due to A. B. is sooner paid—And what you shall do herein Certify and return to the Court at the expiration of two calendar months from the date hereof—Or on the Tuesday or Friday next after this Warrant shall be executed, if that shall sooner happen —And have there this Warrant. Herein fail not.
            Dated the   Day of   , 1830.

LEDGER   FOLIO

By the Court,
        MEYMOTT & DREW, Clerks.

The above Warrant was executed } By me
the   Day of   }   E. F. Officer of the said Chief Bailiff.

OFFICER'S CERTIFICATE.
            To the Clerks of the Southwark Court of Requests.

A. B. against C. D. }
{ GENTLEMEN,
I have this Day taken the Defendant under the Warrant of Execution issued in this Cause, Witness my hand, this   day of   1830.

LEDGER   FOLIO
                E. F. Officer.

Notice.—The Officer is required, in all Cases, to deliver the above Certificate, (properly filled up and signed by him) to the Defendant, immediately after the execution of it.
The Defendant is particularly requested to take or send it (without delay) to the Office in Swan Street, Trinity Street, near Stones' End, Borough, that the Debt may be regularly discharged in the Books.

Warrant of Execution against the Body of 1830 requiring the Chief Bailiff to take a debtor 'and him safely lodge and detain' in Surrey County Gaol or the Borough Compter until he paid his debt.

consequence of action brought or disputed ownership. But in the same period upwards of 10,000 executions were ordered against the *bodies* of defendants. Of that number considerably less than one-tenth were actually imprisoned for the full period specified, the mere ordering of the execution against the body having produced the almost immediate payment of the debt in nine cases out of ten. But this was not always so. Obtaining judgements against unemployed ironstone miners in the Merthyr Court of Requests, and writs for bailiffs to seize goods, was a cause (among others) of the fearsome Merthyr Rising of June 1831. Armed with guns stolen from gunshops, they revenged themselves on creditors who had 'restrained' their property. When a detachment of Argyll and Sunderland Highlanders tried to restore order, twenty-four of them were killed and seventy wounded.

Whether or not attitudes changed in the next ten years, by the Act 1 & 2 Victoria cap 110 of 1837 abolished arrest by 'mesne process' by which, as seen, a debtor could spend time in prison *before* his case had been tried in court and judgement

126

made on it. In the speech which he made in the House of Lords debate on the bill, Lord Brougham pointed out that one half of the cases where 'serviceable process' had been used were settled before even an appearance was entered.

> How many do your lordships think are settled where the body has been seized in the first instance and has been saved from prison by finding bail? Just one-sixth. Surely this is a striking illustration of the view which friends of the present measure take that the efficacy of arrest on mesne process has been overrated, and that it has not the tendency to produce payment of debts really due which has been urged as the principal reason for its continuance.

Many opinions in its favour on that ground had been advanced by tradesmen. A grocer with dealings of £200,000 a year once favoured arrest on the mesne process as favourable to creditors. Then he set off the expense of having a debtor arrested in this way, which failed to produce payment of the debt against the sums he recovered. There was no balance left. The money he had fruitlessly spent was equal to what he successfully gained.

> A fact like this is worth a thousand opinions and lets in the broad day-light of actual experience to dissipate apprehensions and imaginations from which so many inferences had been drawn.

Lord Lyndhurst had argued that fear of imprisonment operated beneficially to both parties by deterring men from imprudently contracting debts. But the power of arresting made tradesmen more ready to lend. For they knew that they could, in an instant, pounce upon their debtors and obtain payment for themselves even if all other demands went unsatisfied. Payment under pressure, moreover, prevented any narrow scrutiny of its amount or its justice.

> Everyone knows that the practical effect of this is an increase of the disposition to give credit . . . that credit is thus imprudently given, to the real injury of the customer who is induced to buy what he cannot pay for, and to the injury also of those who do pay what they owe but pay the dearer in proportion to the bad debts which the tradesman is led to let others contract with him.

Parliament passed the bill and thereafter a creditor no longer had the power to detain a debtor already in prison at his pleasure, since the man could at once petition the Court for Relief of Insolvent Debtors for his discharge on the terms of his whole property, present and future, being given up for distribution among his creditors – and not only in London but to Commissioners who made circuits to hear such petitions in country districts.

THE WORST POVERTY

For a tradesman or businessman to allow himself to become over indebted to the extent of being taken to court, let alone jailed, remained a slur if not, at least temporarily, a disgrace and a mark of unreliability. In 1837 the Committee of The Baltic Exchange, where the owners of cargo ships met shippers wanting cargo space, ensured that everyone who struck a bargain on the floor at St Mary Axe was in a financial position to honour it, that no one was admitted who was insolvent. In that year they introduced a new rule which stated:

> Members having the misfortune to fail or who compound with their creditors, after the adoption of these rules, to be by that act excluded from the Society, but to be re-eligible on the same footing as new members after they have obtained their discharge or settled with their creditors.

It was a rule they later applied also (in the face of considerable opposition) to the guests whom a member signed for in the Visitors Book and introduced on to the floor of the Baltic Exchange. The Society of Friends were equally severe about members who fell into debt. Quaker businessmen were meant to act with integrity

Quaker tea merchant Joseph Fry, husband of prison reformer Elizabeth Fry, who was disowned by his monthly meeting when he went bankrupt in 1828 – a portrait by C.R. Leslie, 1820.

and caution. When Quaker tea merchant Joseph Fry went bankrupt in 1828 his monthly meeting disowned him. His Quaker wife, the famous prison reformer Elizabeth Fry, felt members of her own family were also giving him the cold shoulder when they heard he was being 'investigated' by the Ratcliff and Barking monthly meeting. The failure of Frys Bank – a new venture for the tea importers – was due, said his investigators, to dangerous advances made 'to persons not worthy of such credit, by which the property of others confided to their care was unjustifiably risked' resulting in 'great and lamentable loss' to a large body of creditors. Quaker creditors showed great tolerance to those who were tardy in paying their bills. At the end of 1836 the Quaker biscuit-makers, Huntley & Palmers, were owed £466, a third of their total credit sales. A year later unpaid bills amounted to £590 on credit sales of £1,300.

For working class folk wanting to borrow sums between £2 10s and £100 to keep them out of debt or buy something special, the Government passed legislation in 1835 (5 & 6 William IV cap 23) creating Loan Societies. A second Act of 1840 amending the original law set out twelve 'schemes' in three columns.

Amount of Weekly Instalment	Day on or after which the lst is payable	Sum which may be taken by way of Interest at the time of advancing loan
2s per £5	11th	6s per £5
6d per £1	16th	12d per £1
18d per £1	21st	10d per £1
4s per £5	38th	4s per £5
10d per £1	21st	8d per £1
1s per £1	35th	8d per £1
2s per £1	70th	8d per £1
2s 6d per £1	77th	8d per £1
4s per £1	62nd	6d per £1
5s per £5	66th	6d per £1
10s per £1	73rd	6d per £1
20s per £1	76th	6d per £1

The Act stated that all instalments after the first were to be paid weekly. The borrower had to pay a shilling for a promissory note stamp and a fee of two shillings for enquiring into the sufficiency of his security. The first loan society opened for business in 1838, and within five years there were 150. The Act stated that other schemes could be formed from the schedule of twelve by advancing or postponing the day of payment of the first instalment, provided that the first payment was not made sooner than the eleventh day, and that not more than one penny per pound was added to the interest for every thirteen days of such postponement. Thus scheme six, for instance, might be altered by making the first instalment payable on the 22nd day after the loan and taking 7d per pound for interest.

In fact few were conducted in strict accordance with the Act. The director of each society was required to submit its rules for approval to Mr Tidd Pratt the barrister who certified Saving Banks regulations, and afterwards to have them approved by the magistrates at quarter sessions. The number of sureties needed was in proportion to the sum borrowed, one housekeeper for £5, two for £10 and so on. Societies deducted the interest at the time so never paid the full amount of the loan, which greatly enhanced their profits. The security search fee was non-returnable even if a loan was not granted, and increased by a shilling for every mile the searcher had to go beyond two miles. There was an additional charge of twopence a week for the secretary's salary and office expenses. Anyone borrowing £5 would in fact collect only £4 10s, on top of which he paid around 18s in fees and expenses. If he failed to pay one instalment, he was fined a halfpenny for every shilling, which became a penny after the second omission when the loan society secretary sent him a circular letter for which a fee of threepence was exacted. If he accepted the letter he had to pay 2d postage, but more and more of these 'loan letters' were returned to the loss of the Post Office. *The Times* was highly critical of what it called 'these usurious companies', but their creation was a genuine attempt by the government of the day to provide the less privileged members of society with a state money-lender which hopefully they would find more trustworthy than the neighbourhood pawnbroker; and presumably each society's secretary was able to provide some kind of money management advice to those who needed it.

The second version of the Insolvent Debtors Act did not prevent anyone who mismanaged his finances, or who was commendably cautious but overwhelmed by catastrophe, from being forced to spend two months in prison. Whatever the outcome, he not unnaturally regarded his time in gaol as a stigma, as a stain on his character. The tradesman who put him there knew this, and hoped that by being removed to such unfamiliar and unpleasant surroundings his debtor would soon see the sense of agreeing to do what would immediately return him to the comparative comfort of his own home, namely to surrender, in settlement of his debt, the real estate which the law did not allow the trader to touch. The 1837 statute (1 & 2 Victoria cap 110) only applied to those already in prison. But then, as Blackstone pointed out, the opinion gained ground that it would be to the advantage of trade, and of creditors in general, if debtors outside the scope of the bankruptcy laws who were on the point of insolvency could also surrender their property for the benefit of their creditors, and in return be protected from legal process. This protection from the impending danger of imprisonment was afforded by the so-called 'Protection Acts' (5 & 6 Victoria cap 116 and 7 & 8 Victoria cap 96). Under these a relief, similar to that given to prisoners for debt, was afforded on the same terms to traders owing less than £300 and to all other insolvents.

> There were thus two distinct systems in operation, one intended for the benefit of those who sought relief from actual imprisonment, the other for *traders* owing less than £300, and for all insolvents not yet incarcerated. The proceedings were in either case analgous to those in a bankruptcy, with this essential point of difference however, that whereas the bankrupt was relieved from all claims upon him whatever, so that he began the world again without incumbrance, the insolvent remained burdened with the whole amount of the debts, which his present property was unequal to discharge, and all future acquisitions which he might make were for the benefit of his creditors until they were fully paid. The result was that a *trader*, however reckless, could as a bankrupt be ultimately freed from all his obligations; while a *non-trader*, however unfortunate, had no effectual means of escape from the pressure of his liabilities. (*Commentaries*, chapter 31)

Many tried and failed to introduce legislation to remedy the situation. The Whigs rejected Lord Lyndhurst's bill of 1842 for a small debts court, and the Lords shelved Lord Cottenham's bill which *The Times* called 'as masterly a measure as was ever submitted to Parliament', in deference to a pet bill which Lord Brougham had drafted. But while the legislators were vying with each other to amend insolvency laws which all were agreed were far from fair or just, in 1842 they were able to agree on the need to do away with the notorious symbol of that unfairness and injustice, the Fleet Prison. News of the passing of the Act for the demolition of the gaol in Farringdon Street (5 & 6 Victoria cap 22) was celebrated by Philip Ball, a Chancery prisoner, with

THE LAST DAYS OF THE FLEET

A Melancholy Chaunt
Air. 'The Fine Old English Gentleman'

> I'll sing to you a bran new song
> Made by my simple pate,
> About the end of the good old Fleet,
> Which on us now shuts its gate.
> It has kept confin'd the choicest lads
> That e'er together met –
> Of merry, jolly, rattling dogs,
> A regular slap up set.
> Of jovial Fleet prisoners,
> All of the present day.

THE WORST POVERTY

To racquets, skittles, whistling shops,
We must soon say farewell;
The Queen's assent to her prison bill
Has rung their funeral knell;
And Bennett, Gray and Andrew too
Must close their welcome doors,
For sing song and tape spinning now,
This damn'd new Act all floors,
For the jovial Fleet prisoner,
All of the present day.

Philip Ball and his fellow prisoners feared that life in the stricter Queen's Bench Prison (so named since 1837), to which they would be transferred, would be less jovial. No beer or ale, victuals or food could be sent in to the Southwark gaol 'except as may be reasonable and expedient to prevent extravagance and luxury.' But the country would save £15,000 a year by The Fleet's demolition, stated *The Times*, 'besides getting rid of an ugly object'. Judges would have difficulty in removing the prisoners by habeas corpus however, and a short bill would be needed. The Commissioners of Woods and Forests invited tenders for the one acre site, and it was sold to the Corporation of the City of London for around £29,000. When the prisoners were moved, two of them had been in The Fleet for thirty years. The site was not finally cleared until 1846.

There were still plenty of ugly and unpleasant prisons attached to Courts of Requests outside London, like that at Kidderminster, a dungeon with an exercise yard of only twelve square feet. It had one small room which acted as both day-room and bed-room. The authorities provided neither fire nor blankets in the winter, and gave prisoners no food other than the regular allowance of a half-quartern loaf for two days and water, with maybe a little tea. The beds were of loose straw, and the debtors were locked up from six in the evening to nine the next morning. There was no resident keeper. They were in the custody of the court beadle who lived some distance away. There was no way they could call for help if any of them fell ill.

In the Marshalsea Prison in Southwark on the other hand, Charles Dickens (whose father spent a time there in 1824) made clear in *Little Dorrit* the prisoners were able to find help of every kind within the prison's walls. When one prisoner who had been there six months found his wife was about to have a baby, he was taken by the turnkey to the room of a shabby man dressed in a torn and darned rough-weather sea jacket who had once been a surgeon on a passenger ship but was now 'a ghastly medical scarecrow', Dr Haggage. The three of them ran downstairs to the debtor's room where they were joined by a fourth helper, Mrs Bangham, charwoman and messenger who volunteered her services as flycatcher and general

132

The Father of the Marshalsea, resident there for twenty years, says goodbye to the plasterer who settled with his creditors and was released in a week – illustration by J. Mahoney for Charles Dickens's *Little Dorrit* (1858).

attendant, and fanned the patient with a cabbage leaf throughout her delivery. The prison was populated with people of every trade and profession only too pleased to give advice and apply their skills, from all sections of society, thrown together by the common circumstance of overindebtedness and reconciling themselves, some willingly some reluctantly, to its consequences. They had little alternative but to stay there 'for as long as it takes'. The plasterer dressed in his working clothes of fustian splashed with white lime, seen in the *Little Dorrit* illustration saying goodbye to the Father of the Marshalsea, managed to settle with his creditors after only a week. But the man whom he promised to come back and visit had been there for twenty years, the oldest inhabitant, 'brought up as gentleman, he was, if ever a man was, ed'cated at no end of expense' as the turnkey would tell newcomers; he could play the piano and speak fluent French and Italian.

THE WORST POVERTY

Crushed at first by his imprisonment, he had soon found a dull relief in it. He was under lock and key; but the lock and key that kept him in kept numbers of his troubles out. If he had been a man of strength of purpose to face those troubles and fight them, he might have broken the net that held him, or broken his heart; but being what he was, he languidly slipped into this smooth descent and never took one step forward.

How did he get there? His case, as described by Charles Dickens, was probably typical in arising not from sinister intent or even negligence, but from pure confusion.

> The affairs of this debtor were perplexed by a partnership of which he knew no more than he had invested money in it; by legal matters of assignment and settlement, conveyance here and conveyance there, suspicion of unlawful preference of creditors in this direction, and of mysterious spiriting away of property in that; and as nobody on the face of the earth could be more incapable of explaining any single item in the heap of confusion than the debtor himself, nothing comprehensible could be made of his case.

To question him in detail and endeavour to reconcile his answers, to closet him with accountants and sharp practitioners learned in the wiles of insolvency and bankruptcy, was only to put the case out at compound interest of incomprehensibility.

The legislators, said *The Times* in May 1844, were equally confused. They had been unable to decide whether creditors preferred the property or the carcase of their insolvent. They had indulged them with a capricious dominion, sometimes over the one, sometimes over the other object of desire. They showed a mercy to house and land which they denied to flesh and blood.

> If the English creditor has not taken his knife with Shylock or the old Roman usurer, he has wielded a scarcely less formidable machinery of bolts and bars. Engines of infliction he had in plenty, degradation and confinement for all, and starvation besides for the truly insolvent debtor. But the misfortune always was, he was yet without that for which all these instruments of evil were given him – a remedy.

It was but lately that realty had been made liable for the debts of its deceased owner. The greater part of the property of Britain used to be surrounded by a kind of magic circle within which the law of honesty could not penetrate. Instead of boldly breaking the charm and paying every man's debts out of his property, the legislature attempted to turn the flank of the evil – to extort justice by persecution, to arm the creditor with powers of vexation instead of powers of sale, to satisfy his vindictiveness instead of his bill delivered. The principle of the old law was that the rich man who had property to pay his creditors was allowed to spend it comfortably in The Fleet or Marshalsea. On him the squeezing was neutralized. On the

THE STARVED OUT SHERIFFS' OFFICERS.

(*Vide* LORD CAMPBELL'S BILL FOR THE TOTAL ABOLITION OF IMPRISONMENT FOR DEBT.)

. One of the effects of Lord Campbell's Bill for the Abolition of Imprisonment for Debt was the closing of most of those infamous dens of extortion, the sponging houses in London.

Punch's reaction to Lord Campbell's abortive bill for the total abolition of imprisonment for debt which would have led to the closing of 'those most infamous dens of extortion, the sponging houses of London' – 25 May 1844.

135

penniless alone fell the horrors of imprisonment. The screw was only allowed to be effective where nothing could possibly be effected by its application.

The new Insolvent Act had made considerable inroads on the whimsical principles of those days. But in some ways the law was worse than it was ten years ago. Then you could catch your knave speedily and keep hold of him.

> Now the paraphernalia of notice, appearance and other legal delays which intervene between your claim and his imprisonment, give him ample time to take himself and all he has beyond your reach, if only he plays his cards with tolerable dexterity, long before you have arrived at that desirable consummation . . . We can fairly say that the present law is at once unjust and unavailable – inefficient against those who wish to escape it, oppresive upon those who stay to suffer by it; and we are heartily glad that we are to have no more of its useless vexations. (*The Times*, 2 May 1844)

But Lord Cottenham's bill, to which this leading article referred, was not to have the easy passage through the legislative machine the writer looked forward to. The minds of the legislators were still in a state of confusion. Read the first time on 12 February 1844, his creditors and debtors bill was read a second time on 30 April. When it came up for its third reading on 21 June it was referred to a select committee who on 18 July reported that they were of the opinion that the bill ought not to be proceeded with.

When he next turned his attention to the matter, *The Times* leader writer had to explain to his readers that the law of debtor and creditor was as yet only in a transitional state and that a very unsatisfactory one.

> We are passing on from a state of barbarism into one of civilization, and have as yet only laid aside the blunt and butcherly weapons of the one without having substituted the more polished and, it is to be hoped, not less efficient armoury of the other . . . We have long since got rid of the pillory and the scaffold, and we are now, it is hoped, fast getting rid also of the hardly less inhuman practice of taking in execution indiscriminately the person of the debtor without reference to the origin of his liabilities, whether in misfortune or in fraud. (*The Times*, 19 July 1844)

They were renouncing the wholesale cruelty which, with a uniform and general severity of punishment treated all, the unfortunate dupe as well as the designing knave, alike as guilty. They had already renounced the more savage brutalities which less refined times reserved for the particular distinction of fraud and knavery. But they were still as far from anything like a real and right discrimination between the guilty and the unfortunate. 'And we seem disposed now to frame our laws as if everybody were alike innocent.'

The passing of the Insolvent Debtors Act in August 1844 (7 & 8 Victoria cap 96), abolishing imprisonment for debts of less than £20, however, was widely

TO THE EDITOR OF THE TIMES.

Sir,—On reference to the Insolvent Debtors' Act, it will be found not only to favour such characters as "Jeremy Diddler," and "Charity begins at Home," who have lately in your valuable columns confessed the boon Lord Brougham has given them, but to hold out protection to any one who has the knavery to impose on unsuspecting tradesmen by obtaining goods to an amount under 20*l*., taking care to give an acceptance, making it a debt, and thus keeping within the pale of the criminal law, who may afterwards sell the goods at less than cost price, or more, and pocket the plunder without the unfortunate creditor having any remedy against him. It will, perhaps, be recollected that Sir James Graham on its passing, in answer to the alarm expressed by an hon. member that had been created relative to the 20*l*. abolition of imprisonment clause, particularly alluded to the protection given by the clauses for the punishment of fraud, and Lord Brougham in his circular appears quite angry with some papers for having misrepresented the act, and points out that if fraud have been committed, the debtor will undergo imprisonment by the sentence of the court. There is the protection held out by Sir James Graham and Lord Brougham to the creditor, and now comes the important question.—I should be glad to know how the creditor is to avail himself of this boon? How is he to bring this knave of a debtor, who has contracted debts, however fraudulent, before the court, to suffer punishment and put a stop to his fraudulent career? The creditor has no power, and thus the knave and many other unprincipled persons holding situations averaging from 100*l*. to 500*l*. a-year, or more, living in furnished lodgings, taking advantage of a creditor's troubling them by calling once too often, will be enabled to contract as many debts as they please under 20*l*., without the fear of any law before their eyes to compel them to pay or to punish them, and if the creditors delay suing for six years, although the debtor has no goods during that time, the statute of limitations will for ever bar them. Even where the debtor contracts debts above 20*l*., the unfortunate creditor is compelled to bring his action, and perhaps a vexatious defence is set up (and, by the by, for which there's no punishment), thus putting him to an expense of 60*l*. or 70*l*. before he can obtain execution to arrest the debtor in order to drive him to come before the court under this act for his discharge; and even then it is quite optional; and if his debts are very fraudulently contracted he might prefer to remain in a debtor's prison rather than risk being sent to the treadmill, and this, if at all, to get at the creditor's boon! What creditor would like to adopt this alternative? Verily this is a onesided piece of legislation, and well might it be quoted by "Jeremy Diddlers." Lord Brougham, in his anxiety to assist the unfortunate debtor, has certainly overlooked the unfortunate creditor. Why should not the creditor under 20*l*. have the same remedy as the creditor above 50*l*. has under the bankrupt law, in bringing a debtor summarily before the court (but at a cheaper rate), with a clause to punish for fraud !

I fear I have trespassed too much on your valuable paper, yet I feel from your sense of public justice, if you should consider these remarks worthy the notice of your readers, you will give them publicity, as they might operate as a caution to honest tradesmen as to what protection is afforded them, that they may mind whom they trust.

A LOVER OF EVEN-HANDED JUSTICE.

One of the many letters to *The Times* on the Insolvent Debtors Act pointing out the importance of protecting unsuspecting tradesmen from knaves obtaining goods worth less than £20 to whom the Act would not apply – 20 August 1844.

The law of debtor and creditor in this country is as yet, to use a geological metaphor, only in a transition state, and that a very unsatisfactory one. We are passing on from a state of barbarism into one of civilization, and have as yet only laid aside the blunt and butcherly weapons of the one, without having substituted the more polished, and it is to be hoped not less efficient, armoury of the other. Time was when any fraudulent concealment or embezzlement of his property and effects by a bankrupt was punishable with death as a felony; and, to use the words of Sir W. BLACKSTONE, the great apologist for whatever was law in the reign of Queen ANNE, "un-"less it appeared that the inability of the "bankrupt to pay his debts arose from some "casual loss, he might, upon conviction by indict-"ment of such gross misconduct and negligence, be "set upon the pillory for two hours, and have one of "his ears nailed to the same and cut off." We have long since got rid of the pillory and the scaffold, and we are now, it is to be hoped, fast getting rid also of the hardly less inhuman practice of taking in execution indiscriminately the person of the debtor, without reference to the origin of his liabilities, whether in misfortune or in fraud. But we have as yet got nothing in the room of these things. We have now no indictments at all for fraud— no penal laws whatever against the polite pickpocket who steals duly under all the forms and regularities of law. We are renouncing the wholesale cruelty which with a uniform and general severity of punishment treats all, the unfortunate dupe as well as the designing knave, as alike guilty ; and we have already renounced the more savage brutalities which less refined times reserved for the particular distinction of fraud and

Start of a leading article in *The Times* of 19 July 1844 stating that, as regards the law of debtor and creditor, Britain was passing from a state of barbarism into one of civilization.

welcomed. It also had the effect of materially abridging the business of loan societies, most whose loans did not exceed £20. They could no longer have anyone who defaulted on a loan put in prison, and had to take proceedings against his goods, a process *The Times* described as 'uncertain, expensive and tedious'. Up to the passing of the new Act, the loan societies recovered money owed to them either by a summons to a Court of Requests or to a Police Court. But now, neither commissioners nor magistrates would issue any more summonses against debtors who owed less than £20.

Few tradesmen were happy with the state of affairs. But if the operation of the Act should prove as detrimental to the interests of trade as many of them imagined, said 'A Merchants Clerk' in his letter to *The Times* of 22 August 1844, they were surely powerful enough to cause their just complaints to be heard. Had they considered the previous state of the law?

> Have they never known of creditors insisting upon their 'bond' under circumstances which proved nothing but the inability of the indebted and the selfish heartlessness of his pursuer? Have they never heard of a young man's prospects blasted and his after life made wretched by the impatient rapacity of those who would not forbear when forbearance might have saved, who were vindictive when they should have remembered mercy, who punished misfortune as a crime, and who refused all sympathy with the poor struggling debtor, as though vengeance for an unpaid bill was a Christian duty, and incumbent on them as Christian men and citizens?

'Another Clerk' wrote the next day to say the first writer must be blind to his own interests. For now he had lost the friend who five weeks before the quarter day used to discount a bill for £10 'at something like a trifling interest of 200 per cent.'

Most early Victorian men of commerce saw their priority in balancing their books, leaving the achievement of justice and other abstractions to their betters. Recovery was the name of the game. They could take those who still owed them large sums to the Insolvent Debtors Court. From 1846 they could sue those who owed them small sums under £20 in county courts, created for that purpose in that year. When he heard that one of these new county courts was to have its first sitting in County Hall, Lewes on 27 April 1847, Thomas Bance, a leading tailor of the town, was quick to register claims against eight customers who had delayed paying for their suits longer than most thought it traditional to do so. James Brown only owed Bance 8s 6d which, if he had paid earlier, he would not have found increased by 3s 6d costs which Judge William Furner ordered him to pay in monthly instalments of 4s on top of his debt. He was one of only three 'defendants' of Bance's claims to appear personally. In the leather-bound Minute Book, solicitor Edgar Blaker, Clerk of the Court, entered the words 'Default – Service Proved' against the names of the absentees. They were all ordered to pay what they owed the creditor/plaintiffs, plus costs varying from 14s 2½d to 3s 10d. The largest debt was £9 1s 6d which incurred 33s 6½d costs. James Lower was ordered to pay £4 at once and then 5s a month. Few defendants were represented by attorneys.

The reporter from the *Sussex Express*, who described the novel scene, was impressed – and surprised. Many of the debts sued for, all undefended, had been outstanding for three, four, five and six years, or even for a longer period. 'The unfortunate creditors, it was obvious from the nature of the cases, could never have recovered the debts, had not the County Court been established.' Though forty-five causes were entered in the list for the March session, 'so efficacious did the mere issuing of the summons prove, that this number was reduced by a third before the opening of the court.'

> We were never present in a Court of Justice in which we felt more thoroughly satisfied that substantial justice was being done to plaintiffs and defendants. That this is owing to a great degree to the happy admixture of firmness and conciliation with which Mr Furner discharged the duties of his office, we have no wish to deny; very much is also owing to the excellent constitution of the Court itself, which appears to be precisely what everyone required. Indeed, it appears surprising how English tradesmen could allow the wretched state of things previously existing to continue so long.

Those who were called upon to defend non-payment of what they owed beyond the promised date were, as they had always been and were to go on being, in the minority. Most, like Miss Matty in Mrs Gaskell's novel *Cranford* about life in Knutsford in the 1850s, were proud of the way they 'managed'. When catastrophe hit her in the shape of the Town & County Bank stopping payment, she was ruined. When she tried to explain that she would now have to live on five shillings a week, she could not restrain a few tears.

> 'I am not crying for myself, dear' said she, wiping them away, 'I believe I am crying for the very silly thought of how my mother would grieve if she could know; she always cared for us so much more than for herself. But many a poor person has less, and I am not very extravagant and, thank God, when the neck of mutton and Martha's wages and the rent are paid, I have not a farthing owing.'

What had happened was no fault of hers, and she set herself to live with it. And it won her admiration. For her, as with George Eliot's Caleb Garth in *Middlemarch*, it was a matter of making the exertion. For years Caleb conducted his failed building business entirely for the benefit of his assignees,

> exerting himself to the utmost that he might after all pay twenty shillings in the pound. He had now achieved this, and from all who did think it a bad precedent, his honourable exertions had won him due esteem.

No Longer a Crime

Unlike one of those characters whom Charles Dickens described as taking 'Night Walks' in *The Uncommercial Traveller,* the well-to-do, clever, suitably married man who

> like some fair-looking houses and fair-looking ships . . . took to Dry Rot. The first strong external revelation is a tendency to lurk and lounge . . . to do nothing tangible but to have an intention of performing a variety of intangible duties tomorrow or the day after . . . When this manifestation of the disease is observed, the observer will usually connect it with a vague impression that the patient was living a bit too hard . . . a certain slovenliness and deterioration which is not poverty, nor dirt nor intoxication, nor ill-health but simply Dry Rot. To this succeeds a smell as of strong waters in the morning; to that, a looseness respecting money.

Should society sit by and allow 'characters' who chose to be loose with their money to get away with it? People who maybe started by being genuinely forgetful of the date on which they had promised to pay later and then, when they became too dangerously indebted, developed a sense of cunning in their schemes to evade their obligations? Their medieval neighbours who considered their conduct unneighbourly, unjust and unfair, would have had no hesitation in attempting to tighten their looseness in the interests of the common good. In the 1840s the aim would have been not so much to save the debtor's soul as to save his creditors the expense and boredom of having to sue him.

Some saw old laws which gave a creditor tyrannical powers of coercion over his insolvent debtor as the barbarous expedients of a rude age which were both unjust and inhumane. One of them was John Stuart Mill who feared, however, that the reform of them which was taking place in the 1840s was being taken as an affair of humanity only, not of justice. The then modish humanity had gone into a violent reaction against the ancient severity, 'and might almost be supposed to see in the fact of having lost or squandered other people's property a peculiar title to indulgence.'

> Everything in the law which attached disagreeable consequences to that fact was gradually relaxed or entirely got rid of; until the demoralising effects of this laxity became so evident as to determine, by more recent legislation, a salutary, though very insufficient, movement in the reverse direction. The indulgence of the laws to those have made themselves unable to pay their just debts, is usually defended on the plea that the sole object of the [insolvency] law could be to get at his property and distribute it fairly among his creditors.

The mitigation of the law was at first carried so far as to sacrifice that object, said J.S. Mill. He agreed with *The Times* that imprisonment at the discretion of the creditor was a really powerful engine for extracting from the debtor any property he had concealed or done away with. Had the law furnished a sufficient equivalent? he asked. The doctrine that all the law was expected to do was to put creditors in possession of debtors' property was a totally inadmissible piece of spurious humanity.

> It is the business of law to prevent wrong doing and not simply to patch up the consequences of it when it has been committed; to take care that insolvency should not be a good pecuniary speculation; that men should not have the *privilege* of hazarding other people's property without their knowledge or consent, taking the profits of the enterprise if successful and throwing the loss on the rightful owners if it fails. (*Principles of Political Economy*, 1848)

No debtor, he said, should find it an answer to make themselves unable to pay their just debts by spending the money of their creditors in personal indulgence. Anyone who became insolvent by keeping no books, never taking stock and going on year after year without knowing how their affairs stood, was like a child at school who found to his surprise that he had but one halfpenny left in his pocket.

A case of Dry Rot?

No one wished, said Mill, to curtail 'commercial credit', but 'that which is given by retail dealers to unproductive consumers is no doubt, to the excess to which it is carried [in 1848], a considerable evil.'

The usefulness of large and long credits by tradesmen to suppliers was well known to the businessman who was secretary to several railway companies and later the editor of the *Leeds Times*. Narrow-mindedness in living and in dealing was short-sighted and led to failure, wrote Samuel Smiles in his best-seller *Self-Help* (1859), but every man ought to live within his means. It was of the very essence of honesty. For if he did not, he must be living dishonestly on the means of somebody else.

> Those who are careless about personal expenditure, and consider merely their own gratification, without regard for the comfort of others generally find out the real uses of money when it is too late. Though by nature generous these thriftless persons are often driven in the end to do very shabby things. They waste their money as they do their time; draw bills upon the future; anticipate their earnings; and are thus under the necessity of dragging after them a load of debts and obligations which seriously affect their action as free and independent men.

The proverb said that an empty bag could not stand upright. Neither could a man who was in debt. It was also difficult for a man who was in debt to be truthful; hence it was said that lying rode on debt's back. The debtor had to frame excuses to his creditor for postponing payment, and contrived falsehoods. The facility of incurring the first obligation became a temptation to a second.

> Very soon the unfortunate borrower becomes so entangled that no late exertion of industry can set him free. The first step in debt is like the first step in falsehood! almost involving the necessity of proceeding in the same course, debt following debt, as lie follows lie.

Smiles quoted Benjamin Haydon as dating his decline from the day he first borrowed money. Haydon realized the truth, he said, of the proverb, 'Who goes a-borrowing goes a-sorrowing'. The painter told a young man joining the navy, 'Never purchase any enjoyment if it cannot be purchased without borrowing of others. Never borrow money; it is degrading.' Haydon's autobiography, said Samuel Smiles, showed but too painfully how embarrassment in money matters, produced poignant distress of mind, utter incapacity for work and constantly recurring humiliations. And the minority who chose to behave in this way were mostly aware that they had no one to blame but themselves – which made it all the more painful. It led to the condition of which William Cowper wrote in *The Winter Evening*:

> But poverty, with most who whimper forth
> Their long complaints is self-inflicted woe,
> The effect of laziness or sottish waste.

Most had no occasion to change their lifestyles in accordance with such advice; they had always acted on it instinctively. Those few who consciously risked the consequences of disregarding it, or allowed themselves unthinkingly to slide into overindebtedness, could still suffer the degradation of what went for life behind the walls of the Marshalsea or the Kidderminster dungeon. In 1859 the legislators were still wrestling with (so far) insuperable objections to abolishing imprisonment for debt. After seeing his 1853 bill side-tracked by a Royal Commission, Lord St Leonards was moving the second reading of another debtor and creditor bill in the House of Lords in 1859, but once again many of their lordships found it all too complicated, and wanted it examined by a select committee.

The Lord Chancellor said the bill was entirely one of principle: abolition of imprisonment for debt except in cases of fraud, no more distinction between traders and non-traders, debtors able to liquidate their liabilities by private arrangement or by a public enquiry in the Insolvent Court. Lord Brougham held that a debtor should also still be imprisoned if he refused to pay what he owed when he could do so by executing a deed, or if he was culpably extravagant or reckless in contracting debts which he had no reasonable expectation of being able to pay. The debtor was prima facie in the wrong and the creditor in the right, and it was up to the former to extricate himself from the charge to which he had laid himself open. Lord Cranworth agreed, but held the House should remove the anomaly that no MP or Peer could be imprisoned for debt. Sir John Pope Hennessy, an Irish adventurer, successfully claimed immunity from arrest for the recovery of the huge debts he accumulated while the Member for King's County in the 1860s. When defeated in the election of 1865, he had to go into hiding. He accepted Disraeli's offer of the post of Governor of Labuan – 'about as far from his creditors as he could get'. He stayed in the South China Sea four years and was Governor of the Bahamas and Hong Kong, all safe sanctuaries, until in 1883, following investigation of his activities as Governor of Mauritius, he was ordered home.

Parliament did not finally merge bankruptcy and insolvency until 1861 (24 & 25 Victoria cap 134) following the report of the House of Lords' Select Committee. It was only in certain cases however that a non-trader could be adjudicated bankrupt. And some acts committed by a trader were considered misdemeanours which, committed by a trader, were no offence at all.

The Act of 1861 abolished the Court for Relief of Insolvent Debtors and transferred its jurisdiction to the Court of Bankruptcy. The final chapter in the story of imprisonment for debt came eight years later with the simultaneous passing in 1869 of the Debtors Act (32 & 33 Victoria cap 62) and the Bankruptcy Act (32 & 33 Victoria cap 71). Under the Debtors Act no one could be imprisoned except (and then for only twelve months) for default in payment of a penalty; default by a trustee ordered to pay a sum in his possession; default by an attorney in payment of costs; or default in the payment for the benefit of creditors of any income which a court ordered or any other sums.

Fraudulent acts would be tried as misdemeanours and punished by up to two years in prison with or without hard labour. A typical fraudulent act was withholding information from a trustee administering a debtor's estate for the benefit of his creditors, or failing to give a trustee all his books and papers.

The Bankruptcy Act ended distinctions between trading and non-trading debtors. It defined traders as all persons using the trade of merchandise by way of bargaining, exchange, bartering, commission, consignment or otherwise, in gross or by retail, or who sought their living by buying and selling, by buying and letting for hire or by the workmanship of goods and commodities. A farmer was not considered a trader, but those who were included apothecaries, bankers, brokers, innkeepers, millers, printers, shipowners, stockbrokers, warehousemen, victuallers, ship insurers and scriveners.

As Jay Cohen has pointed out, after the promulgation of these two statutes all insolvents who had contracted debts by non-fraudulent means could discharge their liability through personal bankruptcy.

Last release of debtors from the Whitecross Street Prison in Southwark after the abolition of imprisonment for debt in 1869 – from *The Graphic*, 15 January 1870.

Creditors were predictably reluctant to abandon the remedy. Even in 1869 a member of the House of Commons continued to argue for the retention of civil imprisonment in the same manner as centuries before. Perceptions of trade, credit and risk of default gradually changed over the course of the nineteenth century and rendered obsolete Blackstone's sentiment that it was 'an unjustifiable practice for any person but a trader to encumber himself with debts of any considerable value.'

'New Years Day 1870' recorded solicitor G. Manley Wetherfield in *A Manual of Bankruptcy and Imprisonment for Debt under the Bankruptcy and Debtors Act 1869* (1870), 'will bring to a close that power of imprisoning their debtors by way of satisfaction which creditors have more or less fully possessed for above five centuries.'

The 'Act for the Abolition of Imprisonment for Debt, for the Punishment of Fraudulent Debtors and other purposes', to give it its full name, was, said Wetherfield, a very short, simple and sweeping measure, 'a great innovation upon what we have become accustomed to as the legal relations of debtor and creditor.' Since those relations were daily growing in importance with the increase in trade, it was becoming more and more essential that all should try and give life to that necessary fiction of government that every man knew the laws of his country. His manual was a contribution to that worthy objective.

In 1861 the Insolvent Debtors Court had been abolished, he said, but imprisonment for debt continued. Now both had been swept away and under the new Act a debtor could only be adjudicated bankrupt on his creditor's petition. He could not make himself bankrupt. The new Act abolished the old method of arranging with creditors by a deed of composition, assignment or otherwise 'which has for so long a time disgraced our law'. Creditors would no longer have the absolute right of imprisoning their debtors upon a judgement over £20 'which they have for so many years possessed and in some cases abused'. The best remedy for a creditor owed more than £50 was to make his debtor bankrupt. If fraud could be proved, the debtor could be punished criminally. The new Act gave creditors more authority over their debtors' estates. In place of an 'assignee' came the 'trustee in bankruptcy' who was one of themselves, and responsible to a Committee of Inspection.

Since the abolition of direct imprisonment for debts not exceeding £20, the Insolvent Debtors Court and, after its abolition, the Bankruptcy Court in London and the county courts in the provinces, had possessed the power of imprisonment for forty days or less upon proof of means to pay or fraud. 'It has been the aim of the Debtors Act of 1869 to simplify this rather complicated machinery.' It seemed to Wetherfield to follow that where a creditor had proved his debtor's means, he might have him committed to prison, and that he could then levy on those means, if tangible and available, to obtain payment of what was owed him.

No Longer a Crime

It is a moot question whether the total abolition of imprisonment for debt is desirable, but we venture to say that the Act of 1869, professing to abolish such imprisonment, will be very far from effecting that object, if indeed it does not increase the number of prisoners for debt. To bring a debtor within the penal clauses of former statutes, it has always been necessary to prove that he committed the acts specified with 'intent to defraud'. This is the old-fashioned and very sound notion of presuming a man to be innocent until he is found guilty, but by the new Act it is reversed and certain acts of a debtor are made misdemeanors *prima facie*, and until the accused has shown his innocence.

Formerly, intent had to be proved by the prosecution, but after 1870, claimed Wetherfield, it would be *implied* and 'thus the onus is thrown upon the debtor of proving that the act done by him, though suspicious, was committed with an innocent intent.'

While aware of its shortcomings, *The Times* welcomed the Act as a promising experiment which should be tried. To do away at a blow with the protection against dishonesty, which the power of arrest and detention had been supposed to afford, it declared in its leading article 2 April 1869, would appear little short of revolutionary to anyone who had not followed the course, and watched the tendency, of modern legislation. Half a century ago it would have been so in fact. Then the doctrine common to all ages and nations had been that insolvency was a crime, and that the debtor might be properly made to pay in person the penalty for his offence. It was a doctrine which had grown obsolete. The presumption that insolvency was criminal was no longer allowed. The principle of bankruptcy law was that the debt was essentially a charge on the debtor's property and not on his person.

The unfortunate liberty conferred by the Act of 1861 on debtors to make themselves bankrupt on their own petition has made it now especially incumbent on Bankruptcy Reformers to deal with this collateral or alternative right of Imprisonment at present enjoyed by creditors. It is allowed on all hands that bankruptcy on the debtor's petition is an incubus on the Courts and a public scandal.

The debtor had no personal claim to a change in the law. There was no reason why the contract by which a debt was undertaken should not imply the liability to be imprisoned in default of payment. He was free not to contract the debt. Dishonest people would now be free of the salutary fear which alloyed their admiration of the confiding temperament of tradesmen. They might well be inspired with the hope that the millennium of impecunious debtors was at hand. The public interest would hardly suffer by the curtailment of temptations to give or accept credit which were likely to follow the abolition of so dubious a guarantee of honesty as furnished by the liability to imprisonment. No legislation could be expected to make ready-money dealings the universal rule. There was sure to be a considerable though decreasing number of households to which the credit system was indispensable, and whose custom tradesmen must lose if refusing to accede to these terms.

The main drawback of the bankruptcy laws as they stood was the high cost to creditors of realizing the estates of their insolvent debtors – between 30 and 40 per cent of the amount they hoped to recover. At the end of it all little was left for the tradesmen who had resorted to the complicated machinery. Of the 9,123 adjudications in 1868 there had been 6,489 in which no dividend had been realized. How did that come about?

> The great majority of insolvents go on spending and speculating until cash and credit are exhausted. A few stop while yet something is left of their estate, and that little disappears in course of process through the Court. Some by post-nuptial settlements secure to their family what belongs to their creditors; and others manage to conceal valuable assets which, after their discharge, they enjoy without let or hindrance.

The result was disastrous and a scandal to the country's law and trade. It was clear to *The Times* that bankruptcy was far less of a protection to creditors than a licence to dishonest traders to speculate with other persons' property. That being the case how did it happen that a system which worked so ill had not been altered long ago? 'Chiefly, no doubt, the extraordinary complexity of the subject.' To master the details of bankruptcy law was a task requiring not only skill but assiduous and prolonged attention. There was not time to have so complicated a measure thoroughly discussed in both Houses in a single session. But the 1869 Bankruptcy bill was a third of the length of its predecessor. It was framed on the principles of modern political economy. A free system of administration was substituted for an official system. Court rules and restraints were done away with. The functions of the judge were curtailed and his quasi-criminal jurisdiction transferred to a criminal court. Inducements were offered to the debtor to confess his insolvency and be frank in his discussion of assets. The system of management by a Trustee was the main feature of the bill. His accounts underwent a double audit every quarter and his acts could be reversed by a court on the application of the bankrupt.

County courts could still, in spite of the 1869 Acts, commit small debtors to prison, on the principle that imprisonment was a penalty which should be reserved for what was in the nature of the crime. The penal jurisdiction of the county courts was to apply only where the debt had been contracted under circumstances which implied an intention to defraud (which upset Wetherfield) or where the debtor had the ability to pay but would not. These, as *The Times* said, 'may be plausibly construed as approaching very near the confines of crimes.'

No Longer a Crime

In the House of Lords debate on 27 July 1869, Lord Romilly deprecated continuing the power of imprisonment for debt in the hands of county courts. Credit was given for goods sold in the ordinary way, he said, only because the vendor believed the purchaser would pay, and fear of imprisonment benefited no one but the tallyman who forced his credit on the unwary poor.

His objections were overruled. Judge Furner was still presiding over the county courts at Lewes after twenty-two years, and he continued to order defaulting and mostly absent debtors to be punished by having to spend short terms in the county gaol, for some time after New Years Day 1870. It was part of the routine he had got used to. At the first session of the court in January 1869 he gave judgement to James Sprinks, who had sued Harry Carroll for 7s 6d to be paid the full amount plus almost as much in costs, 6s 3d.

Order: Committed for Ten Days having had the means to pay but refusing so to do, suspended for one month.

He showed no such leniency to Edward Childs who, unlike Carroll, appeared in person, and was sued by Edmund Geering for 14s 6d. Furner gave judgement for 14s 6d with 3s 6d costs.

Order: Committed for Ten Days having had means to pay but refusing so to do.

Three years later he was still exercising the same power. On 9 January 1872 the Minute Book kept by the clerk now called Registrar, recorded the commitment of Richard Piper sued by Henry Pierpoint for 5s (money lent on 14 November 1871). Judgement was entered for the 5s plus 3s costs. Half was to be paid in fourteen days and the balance in a month. But Dick Piper stood his ground. He had seven days in Lewes Gaol to consider the consequences of his 'having had means to pay but refusing so to do.'

CHAPTER SIX

For Debt Read Credit

– into the twentieth century

T he lower classes were not of course alone in making a habit of over-indebtedness, nor indeed were the middle classes. While Dick Piper was hard pushed to find the five shillings he had borrowed from Harry Pierpoint, the father of the princess who was to become Queen Mary was jibbing at paying tradesmen's bills which he had allowed to grow to around £20,000.

Prince Teck, later the Duke of Teck, and his wife Princess Mary Adelaide, had apartments in Kensington Palace where they entertained lavishly. They had an annual parliamentary grant of £5,000 and another £5,000 from the princess's mother, the Duchess of Cambridge. They should have been able to live on that, but Teck was worried about losing his status at court if he did. In 1870 he persuaded Queen Victoria to let him, in addition, the substantial White Lodge in Richmond Park which doubled his household expenses. Reckless extravagance? The Queen was far from amused when they soon got themselves grievously in debt, and refused to help them. Baroness Burdett-Coutts lent them £50,000 and the princess's mother made regular contributions. But the more the Duchess of Teck received the more she spent, and shopkeepers, who had sent round goods on a royal promise to pay later, started pressing for payment now. She demonstrated her apparent unawareness of her position in the speech she made at the opening of the church hall in Kensington to which the grocer John Barker, from whom she bought provisions, had contributed. 'And now', she said, 'I must propose a special vote of thanks to Mr Barker to whom we all owe so much.' Her husband vaunted what he called his 'poverty', without, of course, ever explaining its cause. When asked by playwright Joseph Comyns Carr to chair a dinner in aid of the Actors Benevolent Fund he said, 'My dear fellow, it is not possible. If I do it I must give at least ten pounds and I simply haven't got 'em.'

Just when their creditors were on the point of issuing writs the Tecks left England for the continent, insolvent and heavily in debt.

It was the traditional way of avoiding the consequences of such cavalier an attitude to the obligation of Paying Your Way. Their son Prince Francis (Frank)

The Duke and Duchess of Teck with their daughter Princess May, who became Queen Mary, and three sons (Prince Francis second from right). To escape their creditors the royal couple fled to the continent.

inherited the habit, and as an officer with his regiment in Dublin he soon amassed debts of up to £1,000. No need to worry. He knew of a 'sure winner' in the Stewards Plate for two-years-olds at The Curragh race meeting. He placed £10,000 which he did not possess on a 10 to 1 favourite, Bellevin, to win £1,000. Only four horses were entered for the five furlong race, and he saw Bellevin beaten by Winkfield Pride. So now he owed £11,000. It was June 1895. To avoid family disgrace, his sister's husband, then HRH the Duke of York and later to become King George V, agreed to help pay his debts, and Frank was packed off to India.

No shame, just a bit of a lark. Owing large sums of money and not caring a damn, as Anthony Trollope recorded in *The Way We Live Now* (1875), was one way of making sure there was no doubt about being one of the top people.

> 'My income is becoming less and less every day', Lady Carbery told her daughter, 'I already owe money to your cousin and I owe money to Mr Broune.'
> 'Money to Mr Broune?'
> 'Yes – to Mr Broune. I had to pay a sum for Felix which Mr Broune told me ought to be paid. And I owe money to tradesmen. I fear that I shall not be able to keep on this house.'

Augustus Melmotte, the rich entrepreneur hero of the book, feared his debts would not allow him to go on living anywhere, and killed himself. Asked why she thought Melmotte had spent such a lot of money, Lady Carbery said, 'because he thought he could conquer the world by it and obtain universal credit.'

It was the childlike attitude which Walter Bagehot alluded to in *Lombard Street, A Description of the Money Market* (1873). Writing of the credit system of those times, he said:

> We do not always manage it with discretion. There is the astounding instance of Overend Gurney & Co to the contrary. Ten years ago that house stood next to the Bank of England in the City of London; it was better known abroad than any similar firm – known perhaps better than any purely English firm, the partners had great estates which had mostly been made in the business. They still derived an immense income from it. Yet in six years they lost all their wealth, sold the business to the company and then lost a large part of the company's capital. And these losses were made in a manner so reckless and foolish that one would think a child who had lent money in the City of London would have lent it better.

The great grandchildren of those who had been gulled by the infantile speculative ventures on offer during the manic South Sea Bubble phenomenon had obviously been conditioned to react in the same wild way.

For the man-about-town of the 1890s betraying concern at owing money to tradesmen was bourgeois, boring and absurd. Oscar Wilde had his Algernon Moncrieff in *The Importance of Being Earnest* (1895) – the original four-act version – fob off the solicitor Gribsby who came to serve a writ on him, with frivolous repartee.

GRIBSBY.	I am very sorry sir, but we have a writ of attachment for twenty days against you at the suit of the Savoy Hotel Co Limited for £762 14s 2d.
ALGERNON.	Against me?
GRIBSBY.	Yes, sir.
ALGERNON.	What perfect nonsense! I never dine at the Savoy at my own expense. I always dine at Willis's. It is far more expensive. I don't owe a penny to the Savoy.
GRIBSBY.	The writ is marked as having been served on you personally at The Albany on May the 27th. Judgement was given in default against you on the fifth of June. Since then we have written to you no less than fifteen times without receiving any reply. In the interests of our clients we had no option but to obtain an order for committal of your person.
ALGERNON.	Committal! What on earth do you mean by committal? I haven't the smallest intention of going away. I am staying here for a week.
GRIBSBY.	I am merely a solicitor myself. I do not employ personal violence of any kind. The Officer of the Court, whose function it is to seize the person of the debtor, is waiting in the fly outside. He has considerable experience in these matters. That is why we always employ him. But no doubt you will prefer to pay the bill.
ALGERNON.	Pay it? How on earth am I going to do that? You don't suppose I have got any money? How perfectly silly you are! No gentleman ever has any money.
GRIBSBY.	My experience is that it is usually relations who pay.
ALGERNON.	Jack, you really must settle this bill.
JACK.	Kindly allow me to see the particular items, Mr Gribsby . . . £762 14s 2d since last October. I am bound to say I never saw such reckless extravagance in all my life.

It was beneath people like Algy to carry 'ready money', let alone pay anyone with it except cabbies. Traders like tavern-keepers in the Strand and wine merchants in St James's Street, learnt to expect and tolerate late payment, and to ensure that any steps to obtain settlement were taken with the greatest diplomacy.

Henry Berry, grandfather of Anthony Berry who retired as chairman of wine merchants Berry Bros & Rudd of 3 St James's Street in 1990, waited three years for what one of his noble customers owed him. At last, his patience exhausted, he reluctantly sent his lordship a letter threatening legal action unless the debt were paid.

This brought a reply from the peer's butler saying that his lordship had been so surprised and upset to receive such a letter that the only thing that could restore him to good spirits would be a case of our best brandy. It was decided to take a chance and despatch the restorative, whereupon payment was made by return for three years' supplies, including the brandy. (*Number Three St James's Street*)

Later, Berry Brothers introduced discount schemes to encourage early payers by making their wine purchases cheaper. The firm's Wine Lists stated 'Terms Cash'

Berry Bros, the old-established West End wine merchants, charged two shillings in the pound extra to customers who asked for credit in 1909, and those who still had not paid after twelve months 5 per cent interest.

but printed parallel columns of the 'Price for Cash' and the 'Price for Credit'. Two shillings was added to every pound for credit, and five per cent interest charged after twelve months (which became six per cent in the 1920s).

Such attitudes were far removed from the world of the fictional Sir Joseph Bowlem in Dickens's *Chimes* short story who boasted 'I allow nothing to be carried over into the New Year; every description of account is settled in this house at the close of the old one', and the real life employee of Manders the Wolverhampton paintmakers who scribbled on the flyleaf of a 1896 catalogue:

> Sum up at night what Thou hast done by day,
> And in the morning what thou hast to do.
> Dress and undress thy soul, mark the decay and growth of it.
> If, with thy watch, that too be down, then wind up both,
> If it be true That we shall be most surely judged.
> Make thine accounts agree.

Crafty debtors might escape their obligations by crossing the Channel and going to live on the continent where their creditors could not reach them, like the Duke and Duchess of Teck. The unsophisticated and desperate ones brazened it out by maintaining a facade of affluence or normalcy by borrowing.

The reader who signed his letter to *The Times* in February 1869, 'J.W.', offered a word of warning. He had had some experience, he said, of the extent to which thoughtless, incautious young men were 'victimized and not unfrequently involved in utter ruin on the very threshold of their career by money-lenders who prey upon their credulity and inexperience.' A young friend of his, aged nineteen, needed a loan of £150 to pay horse-racing bets. As a great favour, the well-known proprietor of a cigar shop he frequented introduced him to a 'gentleman' with a den in Piccadilly who offered to 'help him out of his difficulty' by lending him the money. Hearing that the young man was the only son of a gentleman of wealth, the money-lender begged of him never to hesitate in coming to him again whenever he stood in need of a 'friend'.

The Piccadilly money-lender gave the young man not only the £150 he needed but a £10 diamond ring and an £8 gold watch. In return the borrower gave

> first, his acceptance at 17 months for the trifling sum of £550 (being £400 interest for a loan of £150 for 17 months); secondly, he gave his acceptance on a blank 10s bill stamp; and thirdly, signed a letter admitting the debt and pledging his word and honour as between 'gentlemen' to pay it, notwithstanding his minority; and authorising this cormorant [the fashionable word for a money-lender], in the event of the first acceptance not being paid, to fill up the blank acceptance for £550, at one month, with interest at 5 per cent per month, or 60 per cent per annum.

The young man, with no means of meeting the acceptance when it came due, took fright and told the whole story to J.W. who told his father who, on the advice of his solicitor, consented to pay back the borrowed £150 with interest at five per cent per annum, and to return the trumpery jewellery which luckily his son had considered too worthless to sell.

Most of the minority who were suddenly faced with 'pecuniary embarrassment' would have taken fright and felt a sense of failure, if not disgrace – sometimes needlessly, and for the most part would not have displayed it openly. By resorting to a money-lender it became more difficult to conceal their embarrassment – than if they had merely run up bills with retailers. 'To a man who has been accustomed to obtain credit from those who have supplied him with goods', wrote Thomas Farrow in *The Money-Lender Unmasked* (1895),

> it [a Bill of Sale] means an immediate stoppage of his accommodation and this is often followed by the destruction of his business. He is met by neighbours who are not slow to remind him that he is in the hands of a 60 per cent Money Lender. He is called upon immediately to settle his accounts, rates and taxes; the landlord keeps a sharp eye on him while, in the case of farmers, they are unable even to remove their cattle for pasture to another farm without the usurer's consent.

In the chapter he headed 'Cost of Captivity' Thomas Farrow gave a List of fifty money-lenders and their rate of interest. At the top was James Frederick Townend trading as The Strand Bank and Pall Mall Bank, London: 60 per cent per annum.

Most of them charged 60 per cent a year or 5 per cent a month. However John Edwards – 'Union Deposit Bank' – of King William Street off the Strand charged 120 per cent. To illustrate the way many of them operated he cited the case of a

---

THE CLERICAL & MEDICAL BANK.

This Bank grants to Medical Men overdrafts WITHOUT SECURITY, and has no competitor in the size of its business with PROFESSIONAL MEN throughout England, Scotland, and Ireland.

Prospectus on application.

Bills discounted. Deposits received.

Address Manager, Clerical and Medical Bank, Bath.

References to Medical Men if desired.

MONEY LENT ON NOTE OF HAND FROM

£10 TO £5,000 LENT

PRIVATELY at a FEW HOURS' NOTICE to Persons of Position, Tradesmen, Hotel Proprietors, Farmers, and Householders,

Upon Note of Hand Alone,

WITHOUT SURETIES.

NO FEES,

DISTANCE NO OBJECT.

APPLY PERSONALLY OR BY LETTER, TO

Mr. J. FORD, 1, BANK PLACE, NORWICH.

NO FEES.   STRICTLY PRIVATE.

MONEY

LENT

From £2 to £500.

AT A FEW HOURS' NOTICE, to Professional and Private Gentlemen, Tradesmen, Farmers, Cowkeepers, Market Gardeners, Working Men, Householders (Male or Female), and others.

ADVANCES made upon BORROWER'S OWN NOTE OF HAND, without any SURETIES, BONDSMEN, or PUBLICITY. Advances also made upon Deeds, Life Policies, Reversions, Jewellery, Plate, and Furniture without removal, at a low rate of interest. Repayments to suit borrower's convenience.

Intended borrowers will find it to their advantage to apply to a local office, and to a firm that is known for their straight-forward way of doing business. London offices, as a rule, should be avoided. NO FEES of any description charged. NO DEDUCTIONS. No genuine application ever refused. TRADE BILLS discounted. DISTANCE no objection. Prospectuses free. Office hours, 9 to 9 daily. Established 1886. Apply personally, or by letter,

THE MANAGER,

BEDFORDSHIRE LOAN COMPANY,

9, CASTLE LANE, BEDFORD.

BORROW FROM SCOTCHMEN.—No Exposure or Loan Office Formalities, no Sureties, and on Best Terms ; £3 to £500 Lent Privately without delay, on own signature alone, and on borrower's own security. Householders, Tradesmen, Shopkeepers, Farmers requiring Cash should, before applying elsewhere, Call or Write to MACPHERSON BROS., 6, Dixon Street, off St. Enoch's Square, Glasgow. Hours 9 to 7.

LOANS.

THE ABBEY LOAN and DISCOUNT BANK, 110, Middle Abbey-street, Dublin (oldest established Loan Bank in Ireland), makes private advances to all classes of borrowers on their own signature, without bail. Special loans to enable persons to pay rent, debts, and to enable persons to enter into business. Loans can remain out ten years as long as the interest is paid. Distance no object. Apply personally, or write for prospectus, stating amount,

W. MALONE, Manager.

MONEY.—Clerks and others requiring loans, without fees or risking their situations, should apply to Mr. DENT, 26, Moorgate-street, E.C. Existing debts paid off and matters settled for those in financial difficulties.

Money-lenders' advertisements of 1895 – reproduced by Thomas Farrow in *The Money-Lender Unmasked*.

widow who in 1894 borrowed £50 from a London loan bank on the security of her furniture which was valued at £250. She had repaid £35 in seven monthly instalments of £5, when she asked for a second loan. The money-lender gave her £20 and took a further charge on her furniture – Bill of Sale no 1.

First advance	£50
Interest @ 60% for 8 months	£20
LESS repaid in 7 instalments of £5	£35
Balance due on first Bill of Sale	£35
Second advance	£20
	£55
Interest on £55 for 17 months	£46 15s
STILL OWING	£101 15s

THE MONEY-LENDER.

PROSPECTUS.

ADVANCES MADE WITHOUT DEDUCTIONS, FOR SHORT OR LONG PERIODS IN ANY PART OF ENGLAND OR WALES.

From £20 to £2,000,

ON SIMPLE PROMISSORY NOTE ALONE, WITHOUT BILL OF SALE OR ANY PUBLICITY.

Also upon Furniture, Stock in trade (without removal), Farm Stock, Plant, Growing Crops, and to assist persons into Business, at 5 per Cent. Interest, from One Month to 10 Years.

Private and Professional Gentlemen, Manufacturers, Merchants, Tradesmen and other persons (Male and Female), although in good positions and of the highest respectability, occasionally find themselves liable to· unexpected demands, and notwithstanding the fact that they are in receipt of large incomes, require, at certain periods, temporary accommodation, which they are unwilling to obtain from their Bankers or Private Friends. In all such cases the ——— Deposit Bank offers a strictly confidential, reliable, and trustworthy source from whence to obtain the necessary assistance without favour or formal introduction, the object of the Borrower being in every way promoted and facilitated, and his convenience consulted by a free choice of repayments. (*See other side*).

If any further information is required the Manager will have much pleasure in giving same, either by letter or personal interview, any day between the hours of Ten and Four o'clock, Saturdays between Ten and Two,

MONEY-LENDERS' BAITS.

Scale of Interest and Repayments

For every £100 or part of £100.

TWELVE MONTHS.

Money Advanced.	Interest Added.	Monthly Repayments.	Quarterly Repayments.
£	£ s. d.	£ s. d.	£ s. d.
20	1 0 0	1 15 0	5 5 0
30	1 10 0	2 12 6	7 17 6
40	2 0 0	3 10 0	10 10 0
50	2 10 0	4 7 6	13 2 6
60	3 0 0	5 5 0	15 15 0
70	3 10 0	6 2 6	18 7 6
80	4 0 0	7 0 0	21 0 0
90	4 10 0	7 17 6	23 12 6
100	5 0 0	8 15 0	26 5 0

EIGHTEEN MONTHS.

Money Advanced.	Interest Added.	Monthly Repayments.	Quarterly Repayments.
£	£ s. d.	£ s. d.	£ s. d.
20	1 10 0	1 3 11	3 11 8
30	2 5 0	1 15 10	5 7 6
40	3 0 0	2 7 9	7 3 4
50	3 15 0	2 19 9	8 19 2
60	4 10 0	3 11 8	10 15 0
70	5 5 0	4 3 7	12 10 10
80	6 0 0	4 15 7	14 6 8
90	6 15 0	5 7 6	16 2 6
100	7 10 0	5 19 6	17 18 4

TWO YEARS.

Money Advanced.	Interest Added.	Monthly Repayments.	Quarterly Repayments.
£	£ s. d.	£ s. d.	£ s. d.
20	2 0 0	0 18 4	2 15 0
30	3 0 0	1 7 6	4 2 6
40	4 0 0	1 16 8	5 10 0
50	5 0 0	2 5 10	6 17 6
60	6 0 0	2 15 0	8 5 0
70	7 0 0	3 4 2	9 12 6
80	8 0 0	3 13 4	11 0 0
90	9 0 0	4 2 6	12 7 6
100	10 0 0	4 11 8	13 15 0

A money-lender's prospectus of 1895, with his scale of interest and repayments. (Thomas Farrow)

She had received £70 in cash, repaid £35, and still owed £101 15s.

Farrow quoted a Lieutenant Colonel as saying that his neighbours knowing he had money on a Bill of Sale would mean ruin.

He gave another instance of a farmer who obtained a loan of £100 on a promissory note of £140 to be repaid at a rate of £8 a month. He had repaid £64 when the money-lender sued him and obtained judgement for £283 8s 1d which was accounted for in this way:

Promissory Note	£140
Default interest on unpaid balance at rate of 216%	£190 13s 4d
Solicitors cost of action	£12 14s 9d
	£347 8s 1d
LESS by cash paid	£64 0 0
	£283 8s 1d

THE WORST POVERTY

The farmer went bankrupt.

Magistrates said, 'If there are no borrowers, there are no lenders.' But, said Thomas Farrow, in 1895,

> The necessity for borrowing arises from a variety of justifiable causes – such as the desire to extend one's business; to take advantage of some opportunity in the market; to pay pressing accounts or to meet unexpected demands brought about by sickness, accident or death. The race of prodigal sons is of course not extinct, nor is the class of rich fools who will insist on walking into Mr ——'s office and consenting to pay £1,000 for the use of £1,000 for some useless purpose.

Farrow urged the abolition of Bills of Sale, the statutory form for which is reproduced here. He had no quarrel with the honest money-lender, only the unscrupulous extortioner. His aim in publishing his book was to ameliorate the lot of those who appeared to be victimized *because* they were honest, poor or in needy circumstances. Under the heading 'Money-Lenders' Baits' he showed his readers how the cormorants attempted to lure them into their net – advertisements from loan merchants hiding behind grand names like The Clerical and Medical Bank, in all parts of Britain, none of whom saw fit to mention the rates of interest they would charge, and some specifying Without Sureties. Plus marks to Mr Grunwell of Leeds for giving a telephone number.

Many of the minority who reluctantly chose to borrow money did so as preferable to having to spend forty days in Winson Green Gaol like Tom Broadbent, the Birmingham brass-dresser, who in 1899 was committed in default of a small debt to a coal merchant, and died there. At the inquest a fellow debtor, Harry Wood, told the coroner the routine was to rise at six and then busy themselves among the cells till breakfast at 7.15. They were locked in their cells till 8.30 when they were let out for chapel. 'The honour was accorded the poor debtors of being the first to enter the place of worship', he said. The half hour service 'was most heartily enjoyed'. After the Officer-in-Charge had inspected their cells they spent the rest of the day in the Association Room. They were never given any work to do. That year, however, at the suggestion of Admiral Tinklar, the new Governor of Winson Green, an Act of Parliament was passed providing useful work for debtors in prison – making post office bags, naval hammocks and army haversacks, grinding corn and picking oakum.

If anyone needed a small amount he could still raise it on the security of a treasured possession left with a pawnbroker. The Pawnbrokers Act of 1872 had raised the annual interest chargeable to 25 per cent – a halfpenny a month for every 2s. lent on loans under £2. For more than £2 the rate was 20 per cent or a halfpenny a month for every fraction of 2s 6d. A pawnbroker could charge a ticket fee of $\frac{1}{2}$d if less than 10s was advanced, and 1d on larger loans. By an Act of 1922 a pawnbroker could charge a 'valuation fee' of ½d for each 5s lent for pledges under £2. The cost of the ticket and valuation fee was deducted from the loan.

North of The Border the escape route provided by sanctuary in Edinburgh became redundant by the passing of the Bankruptcy (Scotland) Act of 1913, though the last entry in the court book of the Bailie of Holyrood under whose care the debtors lived, was dated 1880, when imprisonment for debt was in most cases abolished. No Act of Parliament ever repealed the privilege of sanctuary within the girth of Holyrood Abbey, but defaulting Abbey Lairds no longer occupied the area where Thomas de Quincey knew he was safe from his creditors and Walter Scott seriously thought of doing the same thing.

One way of never having to become a hostage to the tolerance of a credit-giving retailer, the patience of a money-lender, the goodwill of a pawnbroker, to surrender to the sorrow of exile or the safety of sanctuary, was to emulate Thomas Creevey of whom Charles Greville wrote in his journal in 1829:

> He possesses nothing but his clothes, no property of any sort; he leads a vagrant life visiting a number of people who are delighted to have him . . . and staying till he has spent what money he has in his pocket. He has no servant, no home, no creditors; he buys everything as he wants it at the place he is at; he has no ties upon him . . . He is certainly a living proof that a man may be perfectly happy and exceedingly poor, or rather without riches, for he suffers none of the privations of poverty and enjoys many of the advantages of wealth. I think he is the only man I know in Society who possesses nothing.

Few could be expected to assume that eccentricity. More would be likely to take to heart Samuel Smiles's advice to look their affairs in the face. It was their bounden duty, he said, to keep an account of their incomings and outgoings in money matters.

> Prudence requires that we pitch our scale of living a degree below our means rather than up to them; but this can only be done by carrying out faithfully a plan of living by which both ends may be made to meet.

Half a century later the top-hatted, side-whiskered Stingy Uncle in *Punch* was giving the same advice. 'Pay as you go, my boy! Pay as you go!' he told his nephew. No money to pay with? Then don't go.

There had always been that choice, and it was as difficult to take, and as easy to reject, in the twentieth century as it had been in any other. And still popular was the middle way of going, and shouldering the cost of it later – if anyone could be found trusting enough to allow you to. Tailors were traditionally tolerant in this

(A) Statutory Form of Conditional Bill of Sale.

This Indenture made this...............day of....................
one thousand eight hundred and.......... Between.................
of..........................of the one part, and........................
of..........................of the other part **Witnesseth** that in
consideration of the sum of £...............now paid to...........
by...........the receipt of which the said....................hereby
acknowledges, he the said.... ....**Doth hereby**
assign unto............................his executors, administrators
and assigns all and singular the several chattels and things
specifically described in the schedule hereto annexed by way of
security for the payment of the sum of £...............and interest
thereon at the rate of.. ....per cent. per annum. **And** the
said......................doth further agree and declare that he will
duly pay to the said..............................the principal sum
aforesaid, together with the interest then due by equal..............
payments of £...............on the...............day of..... ....
and the.................day of.........................**and** the said
..................................doth also agree with the said.........
.................that he will at all times during the continuance of
of this security insure and keep the said chattels and things
insured against loss or damage by fire in the sum of...............
pounds at the least **And** will pay all rent to become due and
payable by him in respect of the premises in which the said
chattels and things or any of them now are, **Provided always**
that the chattels hereby assigned shall not be liable to seizure or

to be taken possession of by the said......................for any
cause other than those specified in section seven of the Bills of
Sale Act (1878) Amendment Act, 1882. In witness whereof the
parties to these presents have hereunto set their hands and seals
the day and year first above written.

Signed and sealed by the said....................
in the presence of me

[add witness's name,
address, and description].

THE SCHEDULE.

Statutory Form of Conditional Bill of Sale, 1895. (Thomas Farrow)

(B) Form of Absolute Bill of Sale.

This Indenture, made the............day of..................
one thousand eight hundred and.....................................
between...
of the one part and..••.......
of the other part. Whereas the said.................................
has agreed with the said...
for the **absolute sale to him** of the.............................
....and effects specified in the
Schedule hereunder written for the sum of........................

Now this Indenture witnesseth that in pursuance
of the said agreement, and in consideration of the sum of
.... to the
said...paid by the said
.... (the receipt of which

the said..hereby
acknowledges) to the said............................ ....
as beneficial owner doth hereby convey and assign unto the said
....................all and singular the said..................and effects
....to hold
the said... ....and
effects unto the said..'.......
his executors, administrators and assigns absolutely.

In witness whereof the said parties to these presents
have hereunto set their hands and seals the day and year first
above written.

Signed, sealed and delivered by ⎞
the said .... |
in my presence, the effect of the |
above-written Bill of Sale having ⎬
been explained to the said........... |
....................before his execution |
thereof by me, the attesting Solicitor. ⎠

THE SCHEDULE.

Form of Absolute Bill of Sale, 1895. (Thomas Farrow)

OBVIOUS.—*Stingy Uncle (to impecunious Nephew).* " Pay as you go, my boy !—Pay as you go ! " *Nephew (suggestively).* " But suppose I haven't any money to pay with, uncle——" *Uncle.* " Eh ?—Well, then, don't go, you know—don't go ! "

[*Exit hastily.*

'Pay as you go!' *Punch* reflects the current Edwardian attitude.

respect. For a gentleman, a tailor's bill had always been very low in his priorities for settlement. Savile Row tailor R.J.W. Gieve suspects that it was an attitude born of the realization that the tailor would probably wait for his money rather than press for payment and jeopardize goodwill and the prospect of future orders.

Gieves, a business that dates back to 1785, were above all tailors to the officers of HM Navy, many of whom, the management appreciated, could not afford to buy a good quality uniform, which they had to provide themselves, and pay for it in cash. Naval officers received no help from the Treasury for their outfits, though they were given a small tax allowance. Between 1903 and 1921, when the Royal Naval College at Osborne on the Isle of Wight closed, 98 per cent of the cadets were outfitted by Gieves who then continued their service to Dartmouth cadets.

Making them pay cash too often resulted in debt, followed by embarrassment and loss of custom. So James Gieve introduced the Gieve Account and the use of credit. He organized a sales ledger which offered a credit account to naval customers, and even encouraged payment by instalment. Each officer had an account number which could be used in any of the firm's branches.

Family tradition had it, says David Gieve in his bicentenary history of *Gieves & Hawkes 1785–1985,* that it was James Gieve who first persuaded the Director of Navy Accounts to extend the allotment system from the lower deck to officers. This allowed a rating to allocate a proportion of his pay each month to be sent direct to his family. This was extended to officers who were allowed to authorize payments from source direct to naval tailors for their uniforms. In this way many kept an account going at Gieves over a period of years for a modest monthly sum of two or three pounds.

Shortly after the First World War the firm had occasion to make a loan of £27,000 – for the crew of a cruiser that sailed into Portsmouth Harbour with paying-off pennant flying, only to find that someone had forgotten to order the cash. Tempers ran high, and the dockyard authorities were unable to help. And then the Paymaster Commander had an idea. He went to the Portsmouth branch of Gieves and asked Mr Alderman, the manager, for a loan on his personal account. Lloyds Bank cashed a Gieves cheque for £27,000, the crew were paid and a crisis averted. On Monday morning an armed guard escorted the Admiralty's cash for repaying the loan to Mr Alderman's office on The Hard.

Credit was the solvent that oiled the wheels of many other retailers' businesses. The upper middle class customers of Harrods, Marshall & Snelgrove, Shoolbreds, Maples and Debenham & Freebody, and in the provinces of Kendal, Milnes and Lewis's, who spent whole mornings walking their floors, completed the inspection and sampling in each department by telling the assistant behind the counter, 'Put it down on my account.' Having 'an account' was a status symbol. Retailers were confident that they could trust such customers implicitly to pay for the goods they took away or had delivered. They were equally trusting in sending country customers goods 'on approval', selected from catalogues received in the mail which they retained and paid for by cheque, or returned. Telling shareholders of his Deferred Payment Scheme of 1901, Sir Blundell Maple said he had found no one coming to his Tottenham Court Road store with a dishonest intention to defraud. Anyone wishing to buy furniture out of income rather than capital could have it at the cash payment price plus 5 per cent commission, a quarter of which they had to deposit before the goods were delivered. They paid the balance in monthly or quarterly payments spread over one, two or three years with interest at the rate of 5 per cent a year. Anyone settling their account within twelve months had half the commission returned. Britain's first hire purchase?

Only occasionally was a management's confidence misplaced in extending credit in any of these ways. There was always the last resort of threatening to take a persistent defaulter to court, as wine merchant Henry Berry had done. Debenham & Freebody's of Wigmore Street did so in 1920, but not for tardy payment of a long outstanding account but for an order which the customer denied had ever been given. They sued the well-known actress Constance Collier for the £16 9s 3d which they said she owed them for the flowers which her maid had ordered by telephone to be delivered to the Savoy Theatre. Miss Collier told Judge Bray in Bloomsbury county court that her maid often ordered flowers on the telephone on her instructions, but that she had not done so on this occasion. Whereupon Debenham's counsel said he had no more questions to ask the actress. 'It looks', said the judge who was plainly captivated by the actress, 'as if I am the only one who would like to see Miss Collier again.'

Telling the story in his book *Fine Silks and Oak Counters, Debenhams 1778–1978* Maurice Corina says,

> The actress won the case and Debenhams, seeming to lack humour, but concerned for its prosecuting record, sought unsuccessfully to appeal. England smiled.

It was obviously desirable for such stores to have a trusting public image which invited people to indulge freely in the convenience of spending money without actually paying it out. But at the same time, away from public scrutiny, many of these same stores reduced the risk of their credit being abused through a semi-secret organization known as The Mutual Communications Society which circulated to its members the names of habitual defaulters. Though it was holding weekly meetings in the 1920s it was no new group, having started a hundred years previously in a London coffee house where members met to discuss debtors and exchange information about how best to deal with bad payers. At their 113th annual dinner in the Connaught Rooms in London in November 1920, A.E.W.

Cooper of Selfridges said the idea of the society was reciprocity. There was never a time when such a society was more important.

> A few months ago people were supposed to be worth a certain amount of money. They were *on paper*. But to-day they are not worth half as much. The society renders a lot of assistance, and should be supported.

The need for tighter control of credit was seen as vital. It was taking time for Britain to recover from the First World War. Members of the society were sending 100,000 enquiries a year to its central office about credit worthiness. Agents throughout England, Scotland and Ireland (not, for some reason, in Wales) undertook debt enquiries as part of the paid-for service of The Mutual Communications Society. A central register of information blacklisted certain people, particularly those who passed bad cheques and placed fraudulent overseas orders.

The sums which people paid Maples for furniture were very small compared with what they had to pay for a house to put it in. Very few could produce the cash to cover the cost of building a new house, and from the 1770s they started clubbing together to pool their money to buy a plot of land and pay a builder to erect houses on it. They called themselves building societies. Each member contributed so much a week to form a common fund. Each house as it was completed was allotted to a member either by ballot or auction. When every member of the society had got his house the society was wound up. The first of such groups was Ketley's Building Society known to have been operating in Birmingham in 1775.

At the beginning of the nineteenth century, building societies began to accept investments from people who did not want to buy a house, but use them as a way of investing their savings and obtaining an income in the shape of interest. As the only funds which the building society possessed were those they received as interest on the sums being borrowed by those buying houses, the payments to these non-house purchasing investors came from these 'borrowing funds'.

Building societies were legally recognized in 1812, and the first Act of Parliament to regulate them was passed in 1836, when some 150 societies were being formed every year. In 1845 the first 'permanent' society was established which accepted investments and made loans for house purchase on a continuing basis. A National Association of Building Societies was formed in 1869.

Making landed property the security for a loan – 'mortgaging' it – was what Sir Giles Overreach was hoping to do in *A New Way to Pay Old Debts*, as seen; but it was a much older ploy than that. After the First World War which ended in 1918, local authorities would also advance money for house purchase, as would a body called the Public Works Loan Board; but between 1920 and 1934 building societies lent £920 million and the others only £94 million. Between 1932 and 1939 when the bank rate was 2 per cent, a building society's advance was normally around 80 per cent of the value of the house spread over fifteen to twenty years at 4 to 6 per cent interest. The societies, which had at first been purely local became national, with branches throughout Britain.

At their 1931 annual meeting the Building Societies Association warned that prospective borrowers should have a personal stake in the property to the extent of 10 per cent – 'the limit of safe and prudent lending'. A Code of Ethics and Procedure was introduced in 1934 to curb 'uncoordinated activity and unregulated competition'. Forty societies refused to make acceptance of the Code a condition of membership and broke away to form their own rival society, but the two were merged again in 1940.

People without the ready money to buy a necessity of life like a house, who had to borrow it not from an individual with the distasteful label 'money-lender', but a non-profit mutual cooperation body called a building society, were respectable. The building society movement made borrowing respectable. It was one of the factors which transformed shameful debt into indispensable credit. 'Debt', with its overtones of fault and defaulting, embarrassment and mismanagement, gradually changed into the more significant 'overindebtedness' – though, of course, news-paper subs hung on to the monosyllabic short word which fitted more easily into headlines and made for more racy reading in the copy.

Organizing respectable credit for respectable people became the respectable part of an accountant's work, whose training enabled him to ensure that it was sound, that is, within the bounds of profitability. The Americans were one jump ahead of the British in this. They had created a race of specialist accountants whom they called creditmen. These individuals had combined into a National Association of Creditmen. In Britain, from around 1800, traders in towns had done no more than seek to control the sale of goods and services on promises to pay later by combining into Trade Protection Societies, which had grouped into a National Association of Trade Protection Societies (NATPS).

Protection against what? Buyers' abuse of their credit facilities. They created machinery to avoid extending them to those whose ascertainable record showed them to be untrustworthy and likely to default. It was important that they should *all* be seen to be doing this in a town as a matter of agreed policy, to present a common front to prospective buyers who could not therefore accuse a particular tradesman of unfairly, unjustly discrediting him as a personal vendetta.

In 1934 the British members of the NATPS took another step along this road when, after talking with officials of America's National Association of Creditmen, they planned to form an 'Institute of Creditmen', a body of individuals, which came into being in April 1939 based in London but with local societies all over Britain.

Credit management and credit assessment became a separate professional activity within accountancy, conducted by creditmen or credit managers, the term more generally adopted in the UK. A central object of the new Institute was to train these specialists in the 'sanction office', keep them up to date with legislation and accounting techniques and make credit managers as much a part of a trading company's marketing operation as sales managers who already had their association.

It took time for their role to be accepted and appreciated. In its early days in Berners Street the Institute was not recognized by Industry and Commerce, as Sir Kenneth Cork recalled in his Foreword to the Golden Jubilee issue of the *Journal of the Institute of Credit Management* (which it had become in 1989), of which he was President. As credit managers the members of the Institute were extremely badly paid. The organization of the Institute wilted and might have collapsed.

> At that time, most Credit Managers were clerks, unqualified, working in the Chief Accountant's office, and carrying no weight in the running of their firms. Dragging them from that position to being a respected senior member of management has been the real success of the Institute of Credit Management.

Credit assessment – judging the profitable amount of credit to give, in what form and who to give it to – acquired new significance with the social changes that came with and after the First World War, and the even greater upheaval with the much bigger population after the Second. Traders/sellers found themselves having to sell more sophisticated goods to more sophisticated customers, and had to fine tune credit facilities designed to increase profitable trading to ensure they did not reduce it, let alone end it. Non-traders/buyers/users – or 'consumers' as all the non-traders came increasingly to be called – needed equally to take care, in taking advantage of those facilities, not to be tempted to spend beyond home budgeting limits – economy – and by reckoning debt as part of that budget, they did not fall into or, worse, steer for overindebtedness.

The people from whom the trade protection associations of 1818 were protecting themselves, were smaller in number and simpler in their wants than their 1918 counterparts. In the Roaring Twenties there were more – and more expensive – things that people wanted, and could become overindebted for. And they were not 'luxuries' but, in the higher standard of living, had become essentials for anyone with the modest ambition of keeping up with the Jones's – wireless sets, gramophones, motor bikes, motor cars, vacuum cleaners, geysers, Oxford Bags, artificial silk stockings, tennis racquets and steel-shafted mashie niblicks. For those who asked themselves 'Can we afford it?' and knew the answer was No, there were a greater number of tempting schemes, through which they could be led to believe the answer was Yes. Which scheme they chose depended on their circumstances. As Sir Gordon Borrie, Director General of Fair Trading, explained in *Over-indebtedness* (July 1989),

> In the 19th century and into the first half of this century, different classes borrowed in different ways from different sources. People in professional and steady white-collar occupations could typically take advantage of bank loans and mortgage advances, while those in less secure industrial jobs more commonly resorted to pawn-brokers, trading checks and the hire purchase facilities which became more readily available to promote the sale of mass-produced consumer goods.

And of course there were still a few who would never have dreamt of asking themselves whether they could afford anything, with the attitude to money of an Algernon Moncrieff. According to Winston Churchill junior, until his mother married Randolph Churchill at the outbreak of the Second World War, 'she had never been even a penny in debt, but since then worries about bills and people threatening to sue had been endless.' And then on the troopship to South Africa in 1941, Randolph gambled with his rich friends and lost a fortune. Pamela Churchill had to leave their house which she had to lease out to others to get income from the rent. She sold their wedding presents and took a civil service job at £12 a week. In the telegram which Randolph sent her from Cape Town telling her what had happened, he asked her on no account to tell his father, the prime minister, but to arrange payments on the instalment plan of perhaps £10 a month to a list of the names he enclosed who had fleeced him at the cards tables. 'In the post-war years', wrote Randolph's son, 'Randolph remained for ever in debt because of his determination to live in the grand style to which he had allowed himself to become accustomed.' He had a retinue of three or four young researchers and kept a full domestic staff, entertaining lavishly.

> We would go through periodic crises when petrol could only be bought two or three gallons at a time, and purchases of whisky and cigarettes had to be restricted to a single bottle and two or three packs . . . Most mortifying of all were those occasions when the butcher, the baker, the greengrocer and the newsagent would form a desultory queue outside the back door to request payment of their accounts which were many months overdue. The only one not in the queue was the publican who sensibly insisted on being paid in cash.

But the circumstances of the Second World War lessened the gap between the privileged and the less privileged on the home front, between the rich and the poor. Those who had survived the shooting and the bombing voted Randolph Churchill's father out and Clement Attlee in, looking to a compassionate Welfare

FOR DEBT READ CREDIT

State reflecting the ideas of Sir William Beveridge and his Social Insurance Committee which, it seemed to many, could reduce their need to overspend and provide a safety net if they did. Security was the end, and Public Social Services the means – 'a set of devices' stated a Political and Economic Planning Report,

> varying widely in scope and in the means by which they are administered by providing people whose incomes are low or precarious with as many of the facilities and advantages as would be available for well-to-do families if the need arose.

Development of the social services was seen as concentrating on improving the Big Four – unemployment insurance, workmen's compensation, health insurance and old-age pensions – which provided against the 'interruption of earnings' which caused five-sixths of the want in Britain before the war. The idea, stated Donald Tyerman in the Army Education's pamphlet *The British Way and Purpose*, was to provide

> for all the individuals and families in the country a nation-wide minimum of security below which none should fall – security of work, security of remuneration and security of consumption – a guarantee that the work, the pay, the goods and the services that are needed for a decent standard of living will be forthcoming.

The key element of that standard was a decent house. A few interpreted that adjective as describing the dream home which was far beyond their present means to run, let alone acquire, but did so none the less with the aid of a mortgage from the friendly building society office in the High Street. When the breadwinner's earning curve rose, his standard of living rose to the level of his aspirations. When it fell, the property he had been encouraged to buy by government became the proverbial millstone round his neck and seen too late as a self-inflicted woe. Most prospective houseowners kept their feet on the ground and proceeded with caution, suspicious of unconvincing voices that called Don't Worry It Will All Come Right In The End.

The end of hostilities in Europe was boom time for the building societies. Their loans rose from £97 million in 1945 to £242 million in 1947, to £394 million in 1955. Harold (Never Had It So Good) Macmillan, Minister of Housing and Local Government, introduced a scheme in 1954 to help people buy houses through building societies who were allowed to advance a larger proportion of the price, now rapidly soaring, than hitherto. The risk was to be shared by central government, local authorities and building societies. That risk had become proportionately greater. Because of the role of the home in family life and because the sums involved were so much larger, getting behind with mortgage payments became a more serious potential debt trap than running up bills at retailers. It became a more serious potential debt trap than running up bills at retailers. It became comparable with lax payment of obligatory local and central government rates and income tax, and fines, which could spell real trouble – and gaol.

For Gieves the tailors, the extent to which clients indulged in running up bills regardless had become extremely serious. In the mid-1950s they had a sum of £600,000 outstanding on their sales ledger which was far in excess of any other asset. It was a left-over from the days when an admiral, who had spent the greater part of his life in debt to Gieves, none the less had the matter on his conscience and despaired of dying in that state. So, in his will, he directed that an envelope he had deposited with the firm should be opened after his death and the instructions he had given in it carried out. When opened, relates David Gieve in his bicentenary history of the famous tailors, it disclosed a small life insurance policy and a charming letter in which he said he wished the proceeds of the policy to be applied to settling his final account, and if there was a surplus he would be glad for Gieves to keep it as a modest token of his gratitude for a lifetime's service.

They sent letters appealing to customers to pay part at least of what they owed in 1955 and within a week the £600,000 had been reduced by £150,000.

A senior naval officer was heard to remark, 'We all know about the debt that this country owes to the Navy, but what about the debt which this country owes to Gieves!' Times were changing however; the need for an organised system of credit control was accepted, and the belief that Gieves never worried about money gradually passed into history.

CHAPTER SEVEN

The New Orthodoxy
– 1980 to 1990

T he most significant way in which times were changing was in the emergence of a new attitude to owing money, a new norm, a new orthodoxy. This, explained Sir Gordon Borrie in his 1986 Rathbone Memorial Lecture, was that *everyone* should be free to obtain as much credit as he could get, on the easiest terms available on the market. But that was not to say that people had a right to it, that they were *entitled* to it.

On this the National Consumer Council, the body which the Labour Government created in 1975 as an independent voice for the consumer, agreed. It had always been their view, they stated in their 1990 report, *Credit and Debt; the Consumer Interest,* that consumers did not have the right to credit.

> It must be for the lender to take the responsible decision. In this, consumers and lenders have broadly the same interest. Consumers who can manage credit should be able to get it, and those who cannot should not. Lenders will not make money out of consumers who cannot repay their loans.

Lady Wilcox, the NCC chairman, told Valerie Grove of the *Sunday Times* in September 1990 that she wanted to see responsible lending and responsible borrowing.

> The lenders of money have an obligation to lend prudently and if they do not check the creditworthiness of the borrower I think the debt should not be enforceable.

The lenders of the Consumer Credit Association, also formed in 1975, were aware of the reputation of some of them for irresponsible lending. Ian Stewart warned them not to overload, in his speech as chairman at their 1989 Conference.

> In business the objective if you sell goods is to keep selling more goods; if you lend money, to keep lending money and increase ever increasing targets. That's all very well if people/customers can repay. If they can't it is misery for both borrower and lender. My

message therefore, boring but always to be heeded, is 'watch your credit control, say NO more often, ask for increased payments more often, use the reference bureaux more often, if in doubt say no – cash in the company is better than a lazy or non repaying loan.'

This was the voice of a separate business activity, the credit industry, for which money-lending was conducted to make its own profit, not just as a means of increasing the sales of the company who employed it as part of its marketing. When Stewart said the boom in consumer credit during the previous decade had been phenomenal and some said dangerous, the danger to which he was alluding was not to the consumer/borrower who might incur overindebtedness, but to the professional finance houses. Their problem was not an increasing percentage of defaulters, but the same percentage owing more.

Their concern was that the lenders might find themselves debtors.

They had no need to worry about what the National Consumer Council called 'manageable commitment', in which the customer operated a system of precisely monitored deferred payment, only 'overcommitment' and 'unmanageable commitment'. Overcommitment was most common among younger adults before they reached peak income and in families with young or dependent children. Unmanageable commitment implied accounts three months in arrears for fuel, telephone and mortgage payments, and maybe cars and furniture were seized. When a borrower was systematically unable to meet commitments by the required date he became insolvent, the final stage when all his remaining assets were repossessed. The end result was misery – the word used to describe the final stage consistently for seven centuries, whether in or out of prison.

To enable as many as possible to run their lives on the basis of the manageable commitment which was the essence of the new orthodoxy, credit had to be available from a variety of sources from which each could make his choice to suit his circumstances. There was no lack of commercial money-lenders, who combined into bodies like the Finance Houses Association, the Consumer Credit Association, the Institute of Credit Management, to satisfy the growing urge to borrow and purchase goods and services on a credit basis.

The Macmillan era in the late 1950s and early 1960s, with its catching slogan 'You never had it so good' was an appropriate optimistic backcloth for a great surge forward in the provision of consumer credit [said Sir Gordon Borrie in that Rathbone Memorial Lecture]. The new consumer durables (TV, washing machines, refrigerators) were much in demand, and it made sound economic sense to enjoy the use and benefit of such things at once and pay for them out of rising real incomes. This was after all a period of full employment and marked growth in people's real earnings. Moreover as inflation began to rise in the 1970s it made no sense to wait before buying; the price would inevitably be higher if you did so. Two-digit inflation was a great boost to buying on credit, and buying a house on credit made the greatest sense of all because inflation ensured that the capital value of your house increased while your repayments took a gradually smaller percentage of your income.

The Conservative administration had not made it good, said Borrie; government had not created either the demand or the supply of credit. The Labour Party disagreed. It was 'irresponsible government policies' which had promoted credit, and 'Mrs Thatcher's consumer boom' had been fuelled by a credit-led economy. Government policy, stated the party's Economic Secretariat, had directly contributed to the surge of personal debt.

> Its belief in the free market mechanism has meant the scrapping of credit controls in 1982 and the abolition of the supplementary special deposit scheme (the corset) in 1980, which restricted a bank's ability to lend. This ended a long history of credit controls in Britain since the war. (*Economic Brief*, 'Household Credit – Personal Debt', 14 June 1989)

They might have added that government's encouragement of home ownership, already alluded to, had reinforced the need for credit. But if the then Prime Minister had been governing by decree based on policies formed by her own beliefs, credit might have been easy. 'My policies', *The Economist* quoted her as saying,

> are not based on some economic theory but on things I and millions like me were brought up with: an honest day's work for an honest day's pay; live within your means; put a nest egg by for a rainy day; pay your bills on time; support the police. ('Margaret Thatcher's Ten Years', 29 April 1989)

A one-time Economic Adviser to HM Treasury turned university Professor of Personal Finance, K. Alec Chrystal, gave no discernible answer to the question he posed in his Social Affairs Unit report *Consumer Debt: Whose Responsibility?* But he had no hesitation in recommending the provision of consumer credit on the widest scale – and no bars to the easiest access.

Whoever was responsible for it, Britain had grown into a credit society and looked like staying that way. Janet Ford, a Senior Lecturer in Sociology at Loughborough University, preferred to call it 'The Indebted Society', the title of the book she wrote in 1988, but her sub-title 'Credit and Default in the 1980s' showed that she meant overindebted. 'Credit' when you can afford the loan, 'Debt' when you cannot? *The Economist* called it the Consumer-Credit Snowball and pronounced it well and truly rolling. Yet in the 1960s some members of the credit industry had feared it would grind to a halt unless they could threaten promise-breakers with prison. Imprisonment for ordinary civil debt was abolished by statute in 1970 – another hundred years had had to pass since the enactment of the 1869 measure which was seen as the triumph of liberal attitudes over the centuries-long stand of the powerful trader lobby. Regret for the loss of the use of force against those who reneged on their promise to pay later may still be harboured by some in secret, but no longer publicly.

> In no circumstances can a debtor now be sent to prison for failing, no matter how deliberately, to pay a hotel bill or an account with a shop or a hire-purchase debt, yet the air has not been filled with the ululations of stricken credit traders unable to recover their money. (Lord McGregor of Durris, *Legal Fiction and Social Reality: the Case of Maintenance Defaulters*, 1979)

Contempt of Court could still bring a custodial sentence. In a well-publicized case, Judge Peck sitting in Wandsworth County Court issued an order committing the thirty-one-year-old Lord Mancroft to jail for seven days for contempt of court after repeatedly failing to meet four court orders to pay debts totalling more than £4,000 to Moss Bros the tailors, Barclaycard, a firm of vets and an international transport company. The committal order was for failing to attend court for examination of his means in proceedings to enforce judgement debts against him. In upholding Peck's committal order, Judge White said Mancroft was not protected from arrest under Parliamentary privilege or as a peer of the realm in a situation where the courts were exercising their punitive disciplinary powers. In giving his ruling Judge White said the court had more cases waiting in which judgements in default against Lord Mancroft totalling more than £16,000 had not been satisfied. He had execution of the warrant for his arrest stayed for twenty-one days to allow the young peer to appeal.

In its 1969 report, the Committee on the Enforcement of Judgement Debts chaired by Mr Justice Payne recommended the setting up of a Court Enforcement Office, the functions of which would include assisting the creditor to obtain from the debtor 'as much as he can properly afford', to liquidate the debts as soon as possible and to protect the debtor against undue hardship or harassment. It was all very much less threatening an atmosphere than Judge Furner's county court in Lewes in the 1840s.

Credit managers had had their prison threat weapon taken away from them after reports of exploitation and deceptive trading practices by certain 'loan sharks' became too numerous for the government to ignore. In 1968, to restore public confidence in the so-called finance houses, banks and other money-lending agencies, a Committee of Enquiry was appointed under the chairmanship of Lord Crowther who had been Governor of the Bank of England. The authors of the Crowther Committee Report of 1971 saw no benefit in controlling credit, though it would be socially harmful for money-lenders to risk lending money, at the high interest rates which would bring them a commercial profit, to anyone unlikely to be able to pay it back. Their main conclusion was that on balance credit is beneficial, since it makes a useful contribution to the living standards and the economic and social well-being of the majority of British people.

They were aware of the danger of individuals being tempted to enter into excessively burdensome commitments, but that was no reason to restrict access to a facility which the vast majority used with discretion. Consumer credit, they said, could help even the poorest in society with planning their household expenditure. It would be difficult to draft measures which protected the minority who borrowed unwisely without depriving the large numbers of others, who knew how to use it wisely, of its benefits. It was a basic tenet of a free society that people themselves must be the judge of what contributed to their material welfare. The Government responded to these recommendations by passing the Consumer Credit Act 1974.

There was no intention of controlling credit, only the credit givers. The object of the Act was to protect the minority of unwary consumers from possible exploitation by the minority of unscrupulous lenders who took unfair advantage for their own gain of their 'victims'' ignorance. The means was to restrict the legal provision of credit to those who applied for it and were granted a licence. The system of licensing and control was to be operated by the Director of Fair Trading.

'Fair' was the key word. Make borrowing fair and honest; bring bargaining between borrower and lender out into the open, with the borrower being given the opportunity to understand precisely what he was letting himself in for, and in that knowledge to make his choice. What he must expect, and assume, was truth in lending. So that one bargain could be fairly compared with another, the cost of borrowing – the interest charged – should in all cases and by all lenders be expressed in terms of an Annual Percentage Rate (APR), not solely in weekly or monthly interest. Sales talk and advertising must not be 'false' or 'misleading'.

Only those who were regarded as 'fit' could be trusted not to trade on the despair of people, at their wits end, reduced for the first time in their lives to seeking a loan. Fitness was the applicant's clean record, his ability to show that he had never committed fraud or any act of dishonesty or violence, or indulged in any deceitful or oppressive, unfair or improper practices. Once licensed, the lender must not make an 'extortionate' charge for the loan. If a borrower had rashly signed a credit agreement and then discovered he had committed himself to paying what he considered disproportionate interest, he could have his opinion confirmed, or shown to be unreasonable, by a court. Clause 137 (1) reads:

> If the court finds a credit bargain extortionate it may re-open the credit agreement so as to do justice between the parties.

So not only fair but just.

ELIZABETH II

Consumer Credit Act 1974

1974 CHAPTER 39

An Act to establish for the protection of consumers a new system, administered by the Director General of Fair Trading, of licensing and other control of traders concerned with the provision of credit, or the supply of goods on hire or hire-purchase, and their transactions, in place of the present enactments regulating moneylenders, pawnbrokers and hire-purchase traders and their transactions; and for related matters.

[31st July 1974]

B E IT ENACTED by the Queen's most Excellent Majesty, by and with the advice and consent of the Lords Spiritual and Temporal, and Commons, in this present Parliament assembled, and by the authority of the same, as follows:—

PART I

DIRECTOR GENERAL OF FAIR TRADING

1.—(1) It is the duty of the Director General of Fair Trading (" the Director ")— *General functions of Director*

    (a) to administer the licensing system set up by this Act,

    (b) to exercise the adjudicating functions conferred on him by this Act in relation to the issue, renewal, variation, suspension and revocation of licences, and other matters,

    (c) generally to superintend the working and enforcement of this Act, and regulations made under it, and

    (d) where necessary or expedient, himself to take steps to enforce this Act, and regulations so made.

First page of the Consumer Credit Act 1974.

A credit bargain was considered 'extortionate' if it required the debtor to make payments 'which are grossly exorbitant, or otherwise grossly contravenes ordinary principles of fair dealing.' Regard should be had, however, to the interest rates prevailing at the time, to the debtor's age, experience, business capacity and state of health and 'the degree to which, at the time of making the credit bargain, he was under financial pressure and the nature of that pressure.' Factors which applied to the lender included the degree of risk he accepted having regard to the value of the security provided, his relationship to the debtor and 'whether or not a colourable cash price was quoted for any goods or services included in the credit bargain.' A credit agreement could be re-opened, if the court thought just, on the grounds that the bargain was extortionate, on the debtor's application to the High Court, a county court or a sheriff court.

In re-opening the agreement, the court had a number of ways of 'relieving the debtor or a surety from payment of any sum in excess of that fairly due and reasonable.' They included setting aside the whole or part of any obligation imposed on a debtor, requiring the creditor to repay the whole or part of any sum paid under the credit bargain, direct the return to the surety of any property provided for security, altering the terms of the credit agreement.

Under the 1974 Act it was creditors not debtors who were liable to imprisonment. They could be jailed for two years and fined £400 for 'engaging in activities requiring a licence when not a licensee', and thirteen other offences which included inserting false or misleading advertisements, canvassing debtor-creditor agreements off trade premises, sending circulars to minors, and supplying unsolicited credit tokens. In some cases the term of imprisonment was only for one year, and the fine was £200. Presumably either a creditor or a debtor could commit the offence of 'Knowingly or recklessly giving false information to the Director', which carried a penalty of £400, two years in gaol, or both.

Except under an order of the court, a creditor could not enter any premises to take possession of goods subject to a regulated hire-purchase agreement or other such agreements. A lender who wanted to terminate an agreement, to recover possession of any goods or land, or demand earlier payment of any sum, had first to serve a notice on the debtor.

Obligatory use of Annual Percentage Rate was introduced in 1980, but the main regulations issued under the Act did not come into force until May 1985. The reaction of members of the Consumer Credit Association of the UK, whose declared aim was to promote the highest standards within the unsecured credit industry, was to produce a Code of Practice. They launched it in May 1984 (and it was updated in 1989). They also produced a range of agreement documentation written in simple English but legally correct within the terms of the 1974 Act. They held a series of seminars and workshops to indoctrinate their members in the newly defined ways of fair trading from which they should not stray. They intended, they said, to be stricter in the way they selected credit traders who applied for membership, and to distance themselves from 'rogue money-lenders'. It was, they contended, in everyone's interest to recognize 'the legitimate industry'.

Their Code of Conduct, drafted in consultation with the Office of Fair Trading, supplemented the legislation by setting out guidelines of 'good business conduct'. Any lender who displayed the Association's symbol indicating he was a member was also publicly acknowledging adherence to the Code. Continued non-appliance or a serious breach would probably lead to a warning from the Disciplinary Committee followed maybe by 'a recommendation of expulsion'. The Code enjoined members to trade fairly and responsibly, to behave at all times with integrity, comply with all relevant legislation benefiting consumers, act responsibly and prudently in their marketing and advertising, ensure that its debt collection procedures conformed to the highest ethical standards. They later added a 'Members Business Conduct Pledge' regarding selling by telephone, canvassing, harassment, and complaints and redress procedure. Honesty and courtesy were to be their guides when phoning potential customers, with no misleading statements, exaggerations or partial truths, and no unsolicited calls made to them at their place of work. It was a breach of the Code to falsely claim that criminal proceedings could be brought for non-payment, or to compel anyone to sign documents which allowed repossession of goods.

Whether or not the Association regarded the method of debt collection adopted by London Manhattan's Smelly Tramps Ltd as conforming to the highest ethical standards, it apparently had a high success rate. Ninety per cent of debtors paid up in 1979 rather than tolerate the presence of the malodorous individual in reception for another five minutes. Hiring a disgusting pretend-tramp drenched in stomach-turning chemicals to collect debts cost the creditor customer £20 a time.

The Finance Houses Association were also anxious to ensure that collection practices conformed to the highest ethical standards. In their 1985 booklet *Consumers and Debt* they listed sixteen obligations of members. They should also promote plain English in their contracts, discourage oppressive and intrusive methods of canvassing and encourage prudence in borrowing among applicants for credit. Only in the most pressing circumstances could members be expected to release customers from the binding legal contracts which they had entered into freely. Finance houses sought to promote business in a responsible manner, recognizing that only in that way would they be promoting profitable business. They also recognized that among the major contributory causes of debt problems were accident, sickness, unemployment, divorce or marital difficulty, death or other change of family circumstances.

If a customer's circumstances change adversely for reasons beyond the customer's control, the finance company will look sympathetically at the circumstances and will try, subject to any restrictions placed upon it by the Consumer Credit Act 1974, to reach an accommodation with the customer to pay off the outstanding balance in a practicable manner.

The Finance Houses Association recognized the problems caused by loan sharks often operating illegally. It was at one with consumer bodies in wishing to see their activities stopped. While the Consumer Credit Act licensing system imposed a restraint on credit traders and provided for criminal and financial sanctions against unlicensed trading, the Association was concerned in 1985 at the minority of creditors who were either unaware of, or careless of the existence of, the licensing system.

What was it that the lenders had to offer potential borrowers at this time, facilities which would help solvent individuals to meet 'special' capital expenditure – buying a boat, adding a conservatory – which they did not wish to, and maybe could not, take out of an adequate income without upsetting the household budget, and many credit traders (mostly credit brokers, agents who 'arranged' loans from money-lenders in the style of stockbrokers) highlighted as meeting the needs of those already in debt? In their advertising these firms represented their service as one that would relieve the anxiety of owing so much to others – borrowing from a single Peter to pay pressing Pauls?

PUT ALL YOUR DEBTS IN ONE BASKET

suggested one Licensed Credit Broker.

> If you're paying out every month on credit cards, on short term loans, perhaps on an overdraft too, here's a way to simplify your finances and get cash in hand. Take out one loan to cover them all. Try us. You can borrow anything from £2,000 to £50,000 secured on your home with no fuss, and no delays.

It stated 'APR 16.9% variable'. They gave the example of someone who borrowed £5,000 over ten years. He would pay back the £5,000 together with the interest in 120 monthly instalments of £82.89. By the end of the ten years he would have paid the firm £9,946.80.

Not paying on the nail could be extremely expensive. Probably some, who considered the idea of Making Ends Meet unacceptable and unbecoming, i.e. those

PUT ALL YOUR DEBTS IN ONE BASKET.

If you're paying out every month on credit cards, on short term loans, perhaps on an overdraft too, here's a way to simplify your finances and get cash in hand. Take out one loan to cover them all.

Try us. You can borrow anything from £2,000 to £50,000, secured on your home, with no fuss, no interviews and no delays.

Just look at the table below and see for yourself.

APR 16.9% Variable	EXAMPLES	MONTHLY REPAYMENTS			
	Borrow	5 years	10 years	15 years	20 years
	£2,000	£48 34	£33 15	£28 98	£27 41
	£10,000	£241 70	£165 77	£144 92	£137 03

Typical Example If you borrow £5,000 secured on your home over 10 years you will make 120 payments at £82 89 per month giving a total repayment of £9,946 80 (reduced on early settlement) Written quotations about the terms of our loans are available on request

AS YOUR LOAN WILL BE SECURED ON YOUR HOME, PLEASE REMEMBER YOUR HOME IS AT RISK IF YOU DO NOT KEEP UP REPAYMENTS ON A MORTGAGE OR OTHER LOAN SECURED ON IT.

☎ CALL US FREE ON   or post the coupon to

Licensed as a Credit Broker by the Office of Fair Trading under the Consumer Credit Act

To: The   FREEPOST, P.O. Box
(No stamp required.)

I am interested in borrowing £_____ over _____ years

Name_____Age_____

Address_____

_____

Postcode_____ Tel. No._____

BT 10/8/90

Money-lender 1990s style.

180

enjoying the thrusting Live-Now-Pay-Later lifestyle of the 1990s, would think differently if they knew that the cost of borrowing the £5,000 that would extricate them from the consequences of their cavalier attitude would cost them almost another £5,000. A sobering thought.

In the open market of credit trading there were, of course, all kinds of permutations and combinations, the main variable factor being how long the lender would wait for his loan to be repaid.

£5,000 for just £44.98 per month
WOULD YOU BELIEVE IT?
Loans secured on property

That was the cost of borrowing £5,000 over 180 months *for the first year*; after that it was £100.77 a month. And that, said the advertiser, was 'almost certainly around half of what you pay now (the total cost of £17,469.12 will be reduced on early settlement). APR 22.6% variable. Pay it back over any period between 3 and 15 years.'

In the same 1990 issue of the *Birmingham Evening Mail*, another Finance broker offered to send readers £500 to £100,000 over two to twenty-five years with interest rates fixed until 1992 and 'nothing to repay until 7 months'.

Some Mortgage Arrears and Court Judgements are acceptable. All problems considered sympathetically. Homeowners and mortgage payers may borrow without proof of earnings – including self-employed.

Their APR for borrowing £3,500 over thirty-six months was 20.9 per cent. Borrowing £30,000 over twenty years would be repaid plus interest at 16.9 per cent APR in monthly instalments of £411.99.

One of nine lenders advertising in half a page of the *Daily Mirror* in June 1990 asked

NEED CASH? NEED IT FAST?
Decision Today!
Loan Refused?

Whatever your needs or circumstances give us a ring now!
Even if you've been turned down elsewhere.

Every day the London *Evening Standard* carried two or three small classified advertisements headed LOANS from lenders who only gave their telephone numbers, viz:

Plenty of easy credit any day of the week – typical enticing advertisements in the *Daily Mail* (17 September 1990).

182

THE NEW ORTHODOXY

UNSECURED Loans £1000 – £10,000, payout 4 – 8 days, no bad debtors 081 000 0000 up to 8 pm. Written quotations on request. Licensed Credit Brokers.

Some 35,000 still used one of the 140 Credit Unions operating in Britain in the 1990s as cooperative savings and loan clubs. These were groups of people with a common bond who had joined together to make regular contributions into a pool from which they could borrow at low rates of interest. Most of them would also have borrowed in the open market, maybe from a clearing bank where they had a current account and the manager had allowed them to draw over and above what was in it – an overdraft (the cheapest way of borrowing?) – or perhaps a Personal Loan. Banks promoted such services by press and television advertising. And other firms with 'Bank' in their title also offered to lend, viz:

CREDITPLAN FLEXI START BANKLOAN

was the headline of a large advertisement of such a bank. The borrower had three ways of repaying his loan, either starting at once, in three months or nine months time. 'You'll find our current interest rate – 20.9% variable – very competitive. Let's say you take out a £5,000 loan over two years and you elect to start your payments right away. You'd pay £130.26 a month with a total amount payable being £7,815.60.' The loan would be secured by a mortgage on the borrower's property. Borrowers under sixty got free life insurance. 'Quick, confidential, no arrangements fee'.

In another advertisement the same firm proclaimed

IF YOUR MONTHLY PAYMENTS ON CREDIT CARDS, STORE CARDS AND PERSONAL LOANS ADD UP TO SAY £200

they could halve them to £100 or even £50 a month.

Some manufacturers had themselves licensed as credit brokers, and in their advertisements offered INTEREST FREE CREDIT to any who purchased their goods – 'over a period of 12 months APR 0%'.

Retailers relied more on bank credit cards or their own 'store cards' to maintain and increase their sales with the smallest risk of default. A customer who produced a credit card could take away goods without payment on the implied promise to pay within a month, and if they did (which the vast majority did) they would not be charged interest for being lent the amount they would otherwise have had to pay across the counter. The check-out girl gave the customer an invoice listing the purchases and their cost, which was stamped with the credit card, and added to the monthly account. Anyone failing to pay the total amount shown on that account when they received it (the end of the 'free credit' period) would have to pay what he owed plus interest, which in 1990 was on average 2.2 per cent monthly or 29.8 Annual Percentage Rate (risen from 23.1 per cent in 1988).

Numerous people ran into debt from being unable or unwilling to settle their credit card accounts at all or in full each month, and allowing their purchases to grow in price as every month passed, but the sums people in Britain owed in this way was a very small proportion of the total outstanding personal credit granted, which in 1987 Janet Ford reckoned in her book *The Indebted Society* was £30,000 million. It was the lowest cause of overindebtedness, less than two per cent of people's commitments.

The credit card schemes were run by the banks who charged *their* customers – retailers, restaurants, theatres, hotels, travel agents – for the service. The card belonged to the bank who issued it under a Credit Agreement, regulated by the Consumer Credit Act 1974, to those who gave what they considered satisfactory answers to the questions put in their application forms. The applicant had to sign agreement to a statement that confirmed he or she was not less than eighteen years of age, and they understood that the bank reserved the right to decline the application without being required to state any reason, and that no correspondence would be entered into in those circumstances. 'We may ask for references.' So not everyone could become a cardholder and admit himself to another potential source of overindebtedness.

The ways cards made spending – and overspending – so easy and painless made it difficult for people not to treat the plastic rectangles as money. And their novelty. In the mid-1960s they were unknown. The first was introduced by Barclays Bank in January 1966 – the 'Barclaycard'. By 1990 there were twenty-eight million cardholders, mostly 'Barclaycards' and 'Access' cards, owned by the Midland, Lloyds, National Westminster and the Royal Bank of Scotland (recently renamed 'Signet' and up for sale), but since a Monopolies and Mergers Commission investigation in 1989, there are a whole lot more. Britain was the most credit card conscious country in Europe, but less than ten per cent of all payments were made with them. The banks added to the conventional credit card schemes and others with names like 'Connect', a Visa debit card, and 'Switch', an electronic-only debit network. But profits from their credit card schemes slumped; they took advantage of a new government ruling that they could charge for the cards, but felt their schemes were newly threatened by the Government's agreement to allow shops to charge lower prices when customers paid in cash. The next best thing was being given a month's free credit, and by most people taking this they knocked the wind out of the banker's sails. When, in an attempt to arrest the drop in profits from their schemes, Lloyds unilaterally changed the terms of its Access credit card by introducing a £12 annual fee, they received a severe reprimand from the Office of

Fair Trading. From 1 March 1991 they increased the interest rate from 1.9 per cent a month to 2 per cent, raising the APR from 26.8 to 28.3 per cent.

Apart from making it easier for customers to shop at their stores, retailers started their own store card or charge card schemes as a way of adding to their ancillary profits – and reducing outgoings by not having to pay the banks so much for their credit card schemes.

Customers who declined to pay cash across the counter with 'real' money, a cheque or by direct debit, or produced a bank credit card, found the price of their purchases greatly increased if they were a store card holder. Virginia Matthews, Consumer Correspondent of the *Daily Telegraph* reckoned there were almost eleven million store cards in circulation in Britain in December 1989 with an average APR of 34.5 per cent which compared unfavourably with the 29.8 per cent charged by Barclaycard.

Marks & Spencer, the House of Fraser and the Burton Group had some six and a half million store cards between them. Burtons were the biggest with a card portfolio of £580 million and profits in 1989 of £40 million. They were planning to sell Burton Group Financial Services to General Electric of America for £183 million. They were not the only retailers to be bankers as well. Marks & Spencer Financial Services offered Personal Loans 'to help you spread the cost of almost any major purchase . . . and because it's an unsecured loan, you won't be asked to offer your home as security.'

> We will, of course, make sure you're not overstretching yourself. The checks that we make are quick but thorough as we take our responsibilities seriously – no one wants to add to an existing debt problem.

Fool's Paradise – *Sunday Times*, 22 July 1990.

THE WORST POVERTY

In spite of the high cost of store credit, said Virginia Matthews, many families were multiple store card users and had accounts at as many as five separate shops. The number of store cards rose by 1.4 per cent in the six months to September 1989. However, with other banks following Lloyds' lead to charge for their credit cards, many began to show a preference for 'debit cards', cheque equivalents. The Retail Consortium, which represented 90 per cent of Britain's retailers, said they were cheaper for traders to operate than credit cards.

Few were tempted by credit cards, debit cards, store cards or account cards to overstretch themselves, but 'in several moments of madness' Allison Battye was able to do so at Harrods, the House of Fraser store in Knightsbridge, to the tune of £2,300 on a card which Harrods had given her on the strength of her claiming on the application form that she was in employment, which was not true. Charged at Horseferry Road Magistrates Court in January 1989 with dishonestly inducing Harrods to forego payment, she heard the magistrate Eric Crowther say it was not entirely her fault. She had been treated with the utmost stupidity.

> They just let you go on buying on the never-never. This is just the kind of system that encourages crime. If Harrods hadn't in this ridiculous way offered you a credit card, no crime would have been committed. Harrods is the author of its own misfortune. It blatantly encourages young people to live on credit which is extremely undesirable, and brought about by their greed in getting people to buy their goods in every possible manner.

Allison Battye's behaviour was as unrepresentative as that of the sales engineer earning £10,000 a year who ran up debts of £141,590 and was said in St Albans Crown Court in March 1990 to have eighty-nine credit accounts; or as that of the thirty-seven-year-old doctor from Gwent, made bankrupt in 1988 with total debts of more than £1½ million and still owing £780,000, who used his credit card to buy £6,000 worth of furniture for his girlfriend.

Living in a fool's paradise? Nothing new. The doctor and the engineer were but the latest to follow the folly and beggary route, the minority which every generation throws up thinking they can beat the system. And of course some do.

From the research which they commissioned into consumer attitudes Mintel concluded there were millions of people in Britain living in a fool's paradise in the 1990s, continuing to borrow money to the very limit on credit cards, store cards, bank loans and mortgages, yet refusing to accept they were 'in debt' – mainly because of their ignorance of how money was borrowed and paid back. Marie Jennings of the Money Management Council thought it unfair to expose people with little knowledge of sales techniques to 'offers' such as holiday homes and trying out cars. 'Someone becomes overcommitted and, before the position is recognized, starts slipping into debt in other areas without their prior knowledge of what could be involved.' Young and ignorant? A Halifax Building Society survey found most elderly people with financial difficulties did not resort to credit as a panacea – 'their generation does not approve of credit.' British and ignorant? 'Give the Germans five Deutschmarks and they will save it', said John Major as Chancellor of the Exchequer, 'but give the British five pounds and they will borrow £25 and spend it.' If he had a good fairy on hand he would ask her to wave her wand and change British spending habits.

Protecting retailers, banks, building societies and other lenders from exploitation by a heady few set on having a spree was the function of Credit Reference Agencies. Any organization, in the business of issuing credit cards or lending, employed them to assess the likelihood of applicants for cards being able and willing to keep their implied promise to pay later, and the level of risk that they would not – their credit-worthiness in other words. It was a precaution any lender had always had to take. In the 1990s the report of these professional organizations who constituted a separate industry, was based on what they could discover about the applicant's known record to date as regards prompt and full payment, on the applicant's own assertions and, controversially (because of possible contravention of the Data Protection Act) information volunteered upon questioning by third parties. Most agencies took into consideration the credit rating of other members of the applicant's family, cross-checking which, believed Michael Cronin, chairman of the Independent Forum on Data Protection, was highly relevant. The National Consumer Council had the impression that consumers wanting to borrow money felt agencies automatically regarded them as 'guilty' and that they had to prove their innocence. They should be able to read the agency's report, the Council thought, and point out what they considered mistakes in it before it was disseminated as fact. Apart from anything else, agencies had to make absolutely sure they had the applicant's correct name and address, mistakes in which, claimed Simon Moulton, Assistant Data Protection Registrar, accounted for more than 100,000 people being refused credit every year. Mistakes of that sort apart, it would seem that, as had always been the case, some sort of checking system was needed to give lenders the required degree of confidence to carry on, and that the more thorough and 'scientific' it was the better for both borrower and lender, the more effectively it reduced the incidence of overindebtedness, and saved borrowers from overstretching themselves and indulging in mad bouts of impulsive buying.

Few bought a house on impulse. Much larger sums were involved, almost inevitably in five, or maybe six, figures. Some paid in cash, most borrowed the whole or 90 per cent of the price from a building society or other mortgage lender. For the latter the risk was high and he took even more stringent steps to protect himself against default. As a result many would-be house purchasers never qualified for a loan. 'Probably the relatively low level of heavy commitment in the case of mortgages', stated the Office of Fair Trading report *Overindebtedness* (July 1989), 'can be attributed to the detailed investigation into incomes and other circumstances which usually precedes the granting of a mortgage.' Most of those whom the investigations showed to be credit-worthy justified the faith put in them and stayed the course.

The Policy Studies Institute preliminary report *Credit and Debt in Britain* (February 1990) emphasized that mortgages did not result in problem debts for the vast majority of borrowers. The most common debts were rent arrears. The National Consumer Council report *Credit and Debt; the Consumer Interest* (May 1990) noted that the number of mortgage repossessions still only represented a tiny proportion of all people with mortgages.

However, in spite of stringent credit referencing precautions, loans in arrears between six and twelve months rose from 24,000 in 1982 to 83,000 in 1988 according to the Building Societies Association statistics, but came down to 58,000 in 1989. Those in arrears by more than a year rose from 5,000 to 21,000 between 1982 and 1988. The number of repossessed properties rose from 6,000 in 1982 to 23,000 in 1987, though in 1988 the figure dropped to around 13,800. 'Underlying factors which affected the growth in arrears and repossessions', stated the Office of Fair Trading, 'were increasing unemployment, relaxation of building society lending criteria, competition in the mortgage market and easier availability of credit.' More than 136,000 mortgage payers were taken to court in 1990, a 63 per cent rise on 1989, according to the Lord Chancellor's Department; but only 55,000 possession orders were made (49,000 in 1989). The Council of Mortgage Lenders reckoned that at least 40,000 homes were actually repossessed in 1990. Most were within the first three years of taking out a mortgage and among people who bought property early in 1988 on over-generous terms that stretched monthly payments to the limits. Most lenders waited until payments were three to six months in arrears before seeking repossession orders, and by the time a court order was granted most families had moved out. As *The Economist* pointed out, 'only a few go through the final humiliation of meeting the bailiff at the door and watching him change the locks'.

For the Government the scale, not of the commitment but of the arrears, was unacceptably large, and in 1990 Michael Spicer, Housing Minister, asked the Council of Mortgage Lenders 'to develop a code of practice for dealing with people borrowing money and getting into trouble.' The first general principle of their *Handling of Mortgage Arrears* code of practice issued in May 1990 was:

Mortgage loans should be made only to people who have the capacity to repay them.

THE NEW ORTHODOXY

The problem of a borrower who fell into arrears through no fault of his own should be handled sympathetically and positively. But the borrower must co-operate with the lender, particularly by answering correspondence and making contact at the earliest possible moment. The most important factor in keeping arrears down to the lowest possible level was exercising proper care in granting mortgage loans, checking the applicant's income, his previous borrowing record, verifying that the property was relevant to the borrower's needs and his ability to maintain it in good order. It might be in order to lend three times the income of an applicant whose wife was also working, there were no children, a significant salary increase was likely and he had no outstanding hire purchase commitments, but not in less favourable circumstances.

Borrowers do, of course, have a responsibility to ensure that they are not over-committing themselves, and the vast majority do so.

Lenders sought to take possession only as a last resort, but sometimes there was no alternative. If the borrower could no longer afford to keep up the payments, the longer he stayed in the home the more the interest bill mounted. But by handing over the keys he did not necessarily escape his debts. A borrower had a personal covenant with the lender who could still sue for outstanding debts.

The Building Societies Association were well aware that if interest rates rose sharply, some borrowers might find it difficult to increase their payments in step. In such cases borrowers with repayment rather than endowment mortgages might be allowed to extend the length of their mortgage instead of increasing the payments. In extreme circumstances borrowers might be allowed to pay interest only for a while. Building societies' basic rules of operation were designed for home buyers to repay loans over periods of twenty to twenty-five years without over-committing themselves. They lent up to 100 per cent of valuation although normally they would ask for a deposit of at least 5 per cent in 1990. The Association reckoned that in 1986 one third of first-time buyers received an advance for 100 per cent of the purchase price of their houses.

Banks now competed with building societies in mortgage lending. One of them, the Midland Bank, advertised

FINALLY. A MORTGAGE THAT RECOGNISES MY POTENTIAL

They offered the person, whose salary did not reflect how handsomely he would be paid in the future, a Professional Mortgage. 'If you're a first-time buyer we'll lend you every penny you need to buy the place.' Over-readiness to lend to households contributed to the drop in profits of the Midland Bank whose chairman Sir Kit McMahon resigned in March 1991. At the beginning of the year they began an advertising campaign encouraging people to save rather than spend. Chancellor John Major introduced a Savers Budget in 1990. By abolishing the composite rate tax in his 1991 Budget his successor Norman Lamont enabled 15 million savers on low earnings to gain at least a quarter more interest on bank and building society deposits. Thrift was back in fashion.

Britain's largest building society, the Halifax, offered a Fixed Rate Mortgage at APR 14.9 per cent fixed for a full two years, after which monthly repayments reverted to their normal variable rate of APR 16.8 per cent.

Many were tempted to relieve the immediate pressure by obtaining a Re-Mortgage. 'For homeowners like you,' advertised a licensed credit broker,

> high interest rates can turn a wise investment into an uphill struggle. Repayments and other financial commitments (loans, credit cards etc) can suddenly turn your comfortable lifestyle into a tunnel of relentless worry. But it doesn't have to be. A simple re-mortgage can release the value tied up in your bricks and mortar . . . more often than not we can REDUCE your monthly repayments.

It was all made very attractive. But to keep overindebtedness as low as possible – and in October 1990 Sir Gordon Borrie said the level of default had risen, and was significant and disturbing – the government ruled that every advertisement of a mortgage lender carried the warning:

YOUR HOME IS AT RISK IF YOU DO NOT KEEP UP REPAYMENTS ON A MORTGAGE OR OTHER LOAN SECURED ON IT

A borrower risked more than his home if he chose the wrong lender. In the autumn of 1990, the Office of Fair Trading warned some thirty High Street estate agents, mortgage and insurance brokers for 'targeting' known debtors and bankrupts with offers of credit and for failing to explain the fees involved. In March 1991 the OFT invited people in trouble over credit to send for *Credit Wise*, a sixteen-page guide telling them where to go for help, what to look for and what to avoid. The Consumer Credit Association expelled six companies for contravening their rules. Credit brokers, said its Director, Michael Liley, were using a loophole in the statutory regulations to charge extortionate rates of interest by manipulating credit protection insurance. All imposed or compulsory charges, he insisted, should *always* be included in the APR.

Anyone who looked for a way out of stopping short of the tunnel of relentless worry could telephone Simon Johnson, manager of the Housing Debtline. Created with a grant from the Government's Department of the Environment (DoE) in 1987 to

The Office of Fair Trading tries to redress the balance in 1991.

give financial advice to people with housing problems, it ran a free and confidential service under the aegis of the Money Advice Association and the Birmingham Settlement. Financial support also came from the credit industry.

> Women make up almost 60 per cent of all first callers to Housing Debtline [said Simon Johnson in 1988], and are usually willing to discuss their problems frankly and be guided by their adviser. Male callers however are far more likely to be looking for easy solutions to a debt problem, usually a further loan or re-mortgage which in the long term will often make the problem worse.

Since then, as the National Debtline, the service has broadened its scope to give advice on how to stabilize any apparently unmanageable debt, not just on how to save the home. The Retail Credit Group agreed to fund the service when in 1990 the DoE withdrew its grant of £32,500 a year. In his report *Living in Debt*, produced by Birmingham Settlement Money Advice Services, John Brady showed how families lived under tremendous stress, which increased as the situation worsened.

THE WORST POVERTY

Using credit in today's society is a symbol of sensible financial management. However, allowing credit to turn into debt is still viewed as a result of inadequacy or recklessness on the part of the individual. Debtors feel shame and guilt by their continuing inability to pay their creditors, which is made worse by the never ending demanding letters that fall through the letter box and the inability to get proper legal advice due to lack of money.

In Manchester a similar service was offered by Support in Debt founded, also in 1987, by Stuart Giles who three years later was appealing for £500,000 to keep it going.

The National Consumer Council saw the need for a greater effort, particularly in regard to funding, to give advice to the 560,000 households in Britain who at any time had three or more 'problem debts', and the 170,000 who had five or more. The Money Advice Funding Working Party under the chairmanship of Lord Ezra agreed that existing services were not capable of coping with the demand for advice. They reckoned that some £9.9 million would be needed to finance a plan for educating consumers in the basics of credit and provide funding for rescue services. When in November 1990 Sir George Blunden, who had been Deputy Governor of the Bank of England, was appointed chairman of The Money Advice Trust (created in January of that year), the aim was to raise £6 million for the purpose.

The contribution of the National Consumer Council was to commission a report by Tim Young of the Community Information Project, on *Debt Advice Provision in the United Kingdom* (May 1990), listing what services were operating and how, and under whose auspices, they were funded.

One of many such services was the Money Management Council formed in 1985 'to advance the education of the public in the efficient management of their own personal financial affairs . . . to promote financial literacy among the general public.' They were putting into action the words of Sir Gordon Borrie:

> There has been precious little attention to giving basic education to the general public on the art of wise borrowing. It is all in our interests to see that credit is used wisely and prudently. Otherwise our credit society could easily go sour on us, with repercussions for the country's industry and commerce which would not be to our benefit. (*1987 Office of Fair Trading Annual Report*, published July 1988)

The Money Management Council dispensed its advice through, *inter alia*, a series of Factsheets. That on Personal Budgeting advised, 'Never borrow more money to pay off existing debts; there is always a better solution.' Debts could be negotiated; decide what of your debts are priority debts. 'We have to help ourselves by never stretching ourselves to the limit when taking out a mortgage or borrowing money.'

THE NEW ORTHODOXY

'The main thing is to keep the roof over your head, the electricity on, and you out of prison for the rates', the Citizens Advice Bureau money adviser tells Sue and Tony in Polly Bide's Thames Television play *Not Waving But Drowning* of August 1990.

Consumer borrowing advice was offered to the public by the Citizens Advice Bureaux to be found in towns all over Britain. In London their 135 bureaux were informed by the London Money Advice Support Unit which in March 1990 reported that consumers then owed £26.7 billion on credit commitments, *excluding mortgages*, but that in spite of high interest rates, borrowing continued to grow. The Office of Fair Trading's Consumer Use of Credit Survey showed that the Citizens Advice Bureaux were seen as far the most obvious place to turn to for advice on problems of meeting credit payments with 69 per cent of the 2,155 respondents to the survey.

Typically, debt problems are not presented as the major problem when people in debt seek advice; the nature and scale of indebtedness gradually emerges. Debt, as experienced by clients is often seen as an aspect of another problem. Mixed feelings of fear, embarrassment, anxiety, distress, inadequacy and guilt must be overcome before the debt problem can be properly tackled.

193

THE WORST POVERTY

In the study which Teresa Hinton and Richard Berthoud made of *Money Advice Services*, they showed how much the development had been a response to the increasing demands for help at a local level. 'There is no general policy and this had led to a pattern of provision which is diverse, fragmentary and localised.' But, as Roger Lawson of Southampton University has pointed out, more efforts have been made to counter this localism by the Money Advice Association (founded in 1984) and the National Association of Citizens Advice Bureaux.

> With the growing concern with debt problems, and the difficulties of dealing with new forms of over-borrowing and multiple debt, the credit industry appears to be accepting more responsibility for encouraging and funding money advice services. There is some scepticism and much caution, based on past experiences. In one way or another however the credit industry now sees the need to adjust its attitudes and behaviour to incorporate more advice work, and to build on its shared interests with advice agencies.
> (*Problems With Debt: A Survey of Creditors' Perceptions and Practices*, May 1989)

Those in financial trouble who knew of the money advice services but chose to ignore them, or who were unaware of their existence, and as a result let their indebtedness, once just manageable, become unmanageable, were heading for real trouble. Their debts were on the verge of managing *them*. They were risking falling foul of the law whose edge they would not find as rough as their ancestors had, but would soon discover was hurtful enough. If, having chosen not to take advice, they took the same tack with the process of law once started, and thought that by ignoring it or defying it they could halt it, they were laying themselves open to an even ruder shock.

They were no longer committed to a debtors' prison at the instance of the man to whom they still owed money, to suffer indignities at the hands of a Thomas Bambridge. But they could still be summoned to appear in court to answer the allegations of their creditor, to admit or give good reasons for disclaiming them – if the sum involved was less than £5,000 in a county court, if more in the High Court.

Not to answer the summons made matters worse, as it had always done, and particularly if it concerned a mortgage. In 1986 153,870 possession actions were started in county courts in England and Wales. Of these, 46 per cent were brought by mortgage lenders such as banks and building societies; 38 per cent by landlords such as local authorities and housing associations. Three quarters involved unpaid rent or mortgage arrears. According to the National Consumer Council's report *Ordinary Justice* (1989), from which these figures are taken, few attended the court hearing to defend themselves against the claims. Researchers for the Lord Chancellor's Civil Justice Review found that three quarters of local authority tenants, half the private tenants and two-fifths of mortgage borrowers failed to go

PERSONAL FINANCE

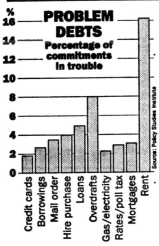

Sunday Times, 6 May 1990.

to court. And only eight per cent of those that did had engaged a lawyer to speak for them 'even though, where defendants are represented, they are more likely to receive a favourable outcome.'

For the unhappy family the process began with Mr Dunn the debtor receiving a summons form (or writ, as it once was), and a reply form on which he was invited to write down whether he admitted owing Mr Rich the creditor the sum he claimed was still outstanding. Yes or No? If Yes, was he willing and able to offer to pay some of what Rich said he owed? If No, what reason did he put forward for non-payment? Or did he think Rich owed *him* money?

If Dunn admitted he owed Rich the money he claimed, and he had it – he was always going to pay but just forgot – he paid it over and that was the end of the matter. If he disputed Rich's claim, then he had to set down his reasons.

Dunn should then have returned his reply to the court that issued the summons. In two-thirds of the cases however, the person receiving such a summons never returned it. In that event his creditor was entitled to ask the court to register the borrower's indebtedness to him for the sum claimed as a fact without further to-do, and without the borrower's case being heard. To this request the Registrar of the court acceded by 'entering judgement' for the lender who received it in writing. In 1987, 2.16 million summonses were issued under this Administrative Default Procedure, two thirds of which were for less than £500 – there were only 1.98 million in 1983.

That ended the Registrar's connection with Rich's plaint. Armed with that written judgement Rich was legally entitled to extract what he said Dunn owed him, in whichever of two ways appealed to him most. For either he had to obtain another document for which he had to apply to the court and would be given by its clerk. Most applied for a 'warrant of execution'. This empowered him to send bailiffs (county court employees) to the house of the man who owed him money and had made no reply to his allegations. He would instruct them in the first instance to threaten to seize the man's belongings to the value of the money owed. If Mr Dunn the debtor refused to be cowed by this threat, Mr Rich the creditor would tell the bailiffs to take the belongings out of the house – and for that service he paid the bailiffs a fixed fee.

In 1987 county courts issued 160,000 warrants of execution but only in 2,882 cases were goods actually seized and sold. A similar procedure took place when the claim was for more than £5,000 and the case was adjudicated in the High Court, where in 1987 another 67,054 warrants were issued called 'writs of fieri facias' shortened to 'fi fa'.

It was in Mr Dunn's interests to return the summons with his answers, because if he did not he would never know of judgement made against him in court declaring he owed Mr Rich the sum he claimed. He would never be officially informed that Rich had applied for a warrant and to expect a bailiff at his door next week. If he should come to hear of all this, however, he still had the right to apply to the court for a 'stay of execution'.

If Mr Rich found that way of recovering what he had lent Mr Dunn in good faith unpalatable, he could apply to the county court for an 'Attachment of Earnings Order' instructing Dunn's employer to make weekly or monthly deductions from his earnings. In 1987, 103,078 applications were made for one of these, and 53,297 issued.

A number of other ways were open to him for recovering what was owed him. He could obtain a 'Charging Order' giving him a charge over Dunn's house so that when it was sold his debt was paid out of the proceeds. He *could* force the sale of the house, but very few ever did. Another option was obtaining a 'Garnishee Order' requiring money to be paid out of Dunn's bank or building society account.

If Dunn did elect to return his summons and to appear in court, he found himself caught up in a drama in which he had been cast as The Defendant, facing the man he had known as Rich whom everyone called The Plaintiff, and being called to order by someone he had never heard of before called The Registrar and his right hand man The Clerk of the Court – and all in the unfamiliar setting (set) of a courtroom. His affairs had become a 'case' which were being given 'a hearing'. Or was he on trial? It was highly disconcerting and unnerving, if not alarming. The language was comprehensible only by the greatest concentration; the issues mind-boggling; the logic of past actions difficult to recollect and harder still to articulate.

In *Ordinary Justice* the National Consumer Council were scathingly critical of such court proceedings which in practice, they said, became a rubber stamp. The documents the court sent out were difficult to understand and no guidance was given on completing it. The 'defendant' was not asked about his personal circumstances. The Civil Justice Review found that a third of banks and building societies, and a fifth of local authorities, did not enquire about the debtor's circumstances before the hearing. Three quarters of local authorities did not follow up the Department of Environment's advice and carry out checks to see if the tenant was receiving the right benefits. Sixty-seven per cent of creditors had no knowledge of the debtor's financial state at the time of the original transaction, and 77 per cent did not obtain any further information before or during the proceedings.

For the inexperienced debtor the arrival of a bailiff at the front door could be a harrowing experience, said the National Consumer Council. In a study of 150 debtors by Queen Mary College, a third said their health had suffered; just under a third said their family's health had suffered; and two debtors had taken drug doses following the bailiff's visit.

The Worst Poverty

Debt enforcement is a case of every creditor for himself. Some creditors have far greater sanctions than others. Landlords and mortgage lenders can threaten to repossess the debtor's home; the gas and electricity boards can threaten to disconnect the supply; non-payment of the rates can lead to imprisonment; hire purchase companies can repossess the goods. The non-secured county court creditor is at the bottom of the hierarchy.

In her foreword to *Ordinary Justice*, Mrs Sally Oppenheim-Barnes, chairman of the National Consumer Council, said the Council wanted all consumer debts (even up to £25,000) dealt with in county courts, and the threat to seize goods used as a last resort rather than a first step in the enforcement process. Debtors who showed the courts that they had made their best efforts to pay, and also showed they were not fraudulent or reckless in incurring debt could be given relief from liabilities after three years.

The multiple debtor can face a bewildering array of different creditors using different courts, different procedures and different threats. The county court, the magistrates court, and the high court may all be involved. Generally, debtors must negotiate with each creditor separately, and must face the ordeal without advice. Debtors have difficult choices about whom to pay first; often they will pay the person at the door at the time. This can make it very difficult to keep to the repayment plans, and the loss of home and fuel becomes more likely. It also contributes to debtors' sense of hopelessness, because as soon as one crisis is sorted out, another hits them.

It was happening only to a minority. But that made it no less a dire experience for those who found their world gradually being pressurized, slowly becoming conditioned by a series of events beginning with the familiar friendly knock on the door – as dramatized in Thames Television's play *Not Waving But Drowning*, produced and directed by Polly Bide, based on a real-life case history.

JACQUI.	Hello, Mrs Walker?
SUE.	Yes.
JACQUI.	Oh, hello. I'm Jacqui Hurd from Oxford City Council. I'm here about some outstanding rates of 26 Elizabeth Close which you lived at last year. There's a small amount still outstanding, the amount of £178.84 pence. We sent you a couple of letters throughout April.
SUE.	I think that – I think there might have been some mistake here, because actually I know that we did get a letter about it, but my husband said he was going to ring and sort it out.
JACQUI.	Do you know if he has rung, because I haven't spoken to him.
SUE.	Well, as far as I know he has . . . but . . .
JACQUI.	Would it be possible for me to discuss it with you, because it's got to a position now that we've actually had a distress warrant issued against you and your husband by the Magistrate's Court.

198

SUE.	Distress warrant?
JACQUI.	Yeah. It's actually where we've actually taken the case to initial here at the court, ask for a distress warrant . . .
SUE.	I think you'd better come in, actually.

And then, via Composition Orders and Administration Orders, the encirclement gathers momentum, the pressure rises. Sue's husband, Tony, can no longer keep back the full extent of his overindebtedness from her.

TONY.	Susan. We've got to talk. Sit down. I don't know where to begin. I don't know where to begin. [*He cries*] You know there's been something wrong. You know there's been something wrong.
SUE.	Yeah. Are you seeing someone else?
TONY.	No. No. No. No. I had this letter this morning from the bank, and it's been going wrong. We owe thousands. There's been people coming round here. You've seen them. You've seen one bailiff, haven't you? I mean we got all this stuff on credit.
SUE.	So we don't just owe money to the bank?
TONY.	No. God no. No. We owe over a grand to Barclaycard. There's the gas and electricity, the rent . . .
SUE.	The rent?
TONY.	Yeah.
SUE.	We owe rent? How much do we owe? How much rent do we owe Tony?
TONY.	It's just about a month or so . . .
SUE.	A month! We owe a month's rent?
TONY.	Yes.
SUE.	So have they been round? Have they been round asking for money?
TONY.	I'm sorry.
SUE.	Right. Have the council been round asking for rent? Have they? Just tell me have they? Have they, Tony?
TONY.	Yes. Yes. Yes.
SUE.	Right! So we're about to be out on the streets. Is that what you're trying to tell me? Tony! And we haven't got the money in the bank to pay the rent? Right!*

[*both passages reproduced from the Post Production Script by kind permission of Thames Television PLC.]

On the night the piece was shown in August 1990, and the following day, Thames Television ran a Help Line staffed by experienced money advisers for viewers who had found themselves in the same situation as Sue and Tony. They also made available a booklet *Coping With Credit, Dealing With Debt* prepared by the Money Advice Association.

Reducing the emphasis on 'selling him up' and making it more possible for creditors' claims to be met out of a debtor's future income was one of the main objectives of the Insolvency Law Review Committee chaired by Sir Kenneth Cork which was appointed by the Government in 1977 and reported in 1982. Another was to relax the severity of the law towards the individual debtor who might be incompetent but not dishonest.

The end of the road. Sue and Tony move out of their house to stop incurring more debts – in Thames Television's *Not Waving But Drowning*.

The Committee recommended replacing Deeds of Arrangements, by which an insolvent individual could execute a deed assigning his assets to a trustee for the benefit of creditors, by Voluntary Arrangements. By these, creditors would meet to consider proposals for a voluntary arrangement which would be binding on a dissenting minority, and approve a trustee.

In the proposals which the Government made in 1984 in a White Paper, *A Revised Framework for Insolvency Law* (Cmnd 9175), largely based on the Cork Report, they indicated that they did not intend introducing a debt counselling service, but referring any debtor with liabilities less than £15,000 to an 'insolvency practitioner'. That, stated Coopers & Lybrand/Cork Gully in their guide to the Cork Report, would go a long way towards remedying the shortcomings of the present system.

> It should however be noted that by virtue of the automatic discharge from a first bankruptcy after three years irrespective of the debtor's conduct (short of criminal offence), an individual debtor will be treated far more leniently than a company director guilty of wrongful trading, who can be disqualified for up to 15 years.

For many 'a simple way of raising money quickly with no questions asked', as Steven Squire of the London Pledge Company put it, was still the pawnbroker whose business in 1991, according to the *Sunday Times*, was 'riding high'. 'We have people working in banks coming in because their managers refuse to give them a loan. And being able to get money on the spot to deal with an emergency can be the difference between coping and despair for some people.' Some pawned their cars, others their video recorders and televisions along with time honoured pawns like silver candlesticks and family portraits. There were 3,000 pawnbrokers in Greater London in the 1960s, but in ten years the number dropped to 150. The National Pawnbrokers Association kept a register of operators they approved.

Insolvency, bankruptcy – in passing from one generation to another, the terms never lost their dread significance. In the 1990s it was the end of the road that started with living on credit like everyone else on the scale of everyone else, became slightly more extended than most and then wholly unmanageable. It cast a shadow from which nothing could escape. Labelled 'bankrupt' the whole family which had been at one with their neighbours found themselves set apart. John McQueen had no reason to belittle its effects. He was so shocked by the case of his businessman brother who was forced into bankruptcy by the Inland Revenue in 1983, that he founded the Association of Bankrupts to help others in the same position.

Until he was granted a discharge, any income which a bankrupt earned in excess of what he needed to cover basic living expenses had to be paid to the trustee in bankruptcy. He could not own property which was not necessary for every day living. But John McQueen learnt it had more serious effects.

THE WORST POVERTY

Besides all these difficulties, the bankrupt also faces problems with the social stigma still attached to going bankrupt. In the public eye the bankrupt is seen as a sort of quasi-criminal. This image is eagerly developed by the popular press, which almost daily produces the most ridiculous and exaggerated accounts of the tiny minority of bankrupts who have run up extremely large debts. As a result bankrupts often have to face the ostracism of their friends, and sometimes even of their own families. (*Taxation*, 31 July 1987)

John McQueen himself had a hard struggle to remain solvent as a twenty-six-year-old university student with a wife and three children. How he disciplined himself to make ends meet in that difficult time he explained in his book *What To Do When Someone Has Debt Problems, A Practical Survival Guide* (1985), in the Introduction to which he wrote:

During my own life I have experienced many occasions when debt burdens have dominated my thoughts. Debt burdens nearly always bring with them a sense of imprisonment. They also often bring a great sense of humiliation and frustration.

It might be that 'the climate of opinion' had changed. The mortgage debt had grown so fast, explained Robin Leigh-Pemberton, Governor of the Bank of England in June 1990, and was both a symptom and a cause of a wider cultural change in Britain's society.

Thrift has gone out of fashion. Indeed the all too prevalent outlook on life has become I want it and I want it now. (Speech at the tenth anniversary dinner of the Association of International Savings Banks in London, 14 June 1990)

The increase in credit had considerable and undesirable effects, he said. Some people were undoubtedly in difficult situations. Very often arrears mounted just when borrowers were least able to cope with the situation; they felt vulnerable and confused. The distress suffered by individuals and their families was obviously a matter of concern for everybody, whether or not they were directly affected.

Being the prevailing wind did not make a storm less stormy; having bubonic plague during a Black Death which affected half the world did not make it less painful; being overindebted at a time when cultural change had made it fashionable neither excused it nor mitigated it. Reflecting that a lot of other people were in the same boat, that he was in good company – the Overindebted Minority – might bring temporary comfort and make relations with friends less strained. But it was unlikely to remove what John McQueen called the sense of imprisonment, which might however generate, as it did for Walter Scott and Benjamin Haydon, a determination to escape.

THE NEW ORTHODOXY

Not self-pity but exertion was what they told themselves was the first requirement, applying their skills to return to normal, to restore the status quo. In the 1990s there were many more at hand to help them escape, people who might have been more profitably employed than in these negative exercises if there had been fewer who needed their services.

Pundits decried the successful methods taken by the majority, who not only wanted to live within their means but did so, as old-fashioned and 'Victorian', out of step with 1990s climate of opinion. However, the surest way of never having to experience the misery – the most frequently occurring word associated with debt – the misery of debtors down the ages in Britain from Tom Verney to Sue and Tony, was to follow the time-honoured, still practical advice of Lord Chesterfield, Samuel Smiles *et al* that made boring but good sense in any age. Pay Your Way.

Up to 1950, said the authors of *Social Trends 20*, the respectable were never in debt. But Paying Your Way was not respectable, any more than Keeping To The Left. For most it was the air they breathed. For them there was nothing tame about not living in the fast lane; nothing sanctimonious about unconsciously keeping clear of the edge of the cliff. None thought of themselves as prudent – the word beloved of the philosophic writers – let alone prudes. They had no machinery for making ends meet. The sustained discipline required to keep accounts was boringly time-consuming and beyond the capabilities of most. In February 1990, a Gallop Survey, found that most people did not know how to manage their money, and just muddled through.

> In spite of most people perceiving themselves as planners, the survey reveals that in some of the most important and fundamental areas of life they have not made even the most minimal plans.

They steered their way by instinct. If they had given the matter any thought, however, and some incident had alerted them to the dangers of being too relaxed, there was no doubt they would have strained every muscle to elude the worst poverty.

Appendix

The Measure of Rising Overindebtedness in Britain, 1980–1990

(i) Key Findings of the Policy Studies Institute preliminary report *Credit and Debt in Britain* by Richard Berthoud and Elaine Kempson (1990)

> The volume of personal credit advanced by banks, building societies and finance houses more than doubled during the 1980s. There have been several signs that this has been accompanied by an increase in the number of people experiencing difficulty in repaying their commitments. Recent rises in interest rates have focused attention on the problems of debt.
>
> The independent Policy Studies Institute has undertaken a substantial survey of the uses of personal credit and the problems of debt in Britain. The research has been supported by a consortium of private sector financial institutions and public agencies, led by the Joseph Rowntree Memorial Trust.

- More than two million households had a problem repaying a debt in 1989.

- The average problem debt was more than £600 in arrears; together they mounted up to £2.9 billion in Britain.

- 560,000 households had serious debts, with arrears to at least three creditors.

- Although rising interest rates have focused interest on mortgage payments, the most common debts are rent arrears; in Scotland many report difficulties with their poll tax; but the survey also identified more than one million consumer credit agreements in difficulty.

204

APPENDIX

- The younger people are, the more likely they are to be in debt.

- The poorer people are, the more debts they face.

- Overuse of credit does not seem to cause a problem for well-off households; but arrears are strongly associated with the number of credit commitments taken out by low income households.

(ii) A table from the National Consumer Council's report *Credit and Debt; the Consumer Interest* (HMSO 1990)

CONSUMER CREDIT AND OTHER PERSONAL SECTOR BORROWING OUTSTANDING, 1980–88

Year	Personal borrowing — Lending for house purchase	Consumer credit — Monetary sector	(credit cards)	Retailers	Others	Total	Total
	£bn	£bn	£bn	£bn	£bn	£bn	£bn
1980	52.3	6.7	(1.2)	1.6	3.3	11.6	64.0
1981	62.0	10.3	(1.5)	1.7	1.4	13.2	75.2
1982	76.2	12.6	(2.0)	1.8	1.6	16.0	92.2
1983	91.2	14.8	(2.6)	1.9	2.1	18.9	110.1
1984	108.5	17.4	(3.3)	2.0	2.9	22.3	130.8
1985	127.6	20.4	(4.1)	2.2	3.6	26.1	153.7
1986	154.0	24.0	(5.2)	2.2	4.4	30.5	184.6
1987	183.5	28.8	(6.0)	2.6	5.1	36.6	220.1
1988	225.0	34.4	(6.7)	...	...	....	.....

Source: *Financial Statistics*, nos. 283, November 1985 and 322, February 1989, HMSO.

(iii) In December 1990 the Central Statistical Office said that total individual debt, excluding mortgages, had nearly doubled in five years from £26.1 billion to £49.8 billion – more than £860 for every man, woman, and child in the country.

Bibliography

up to the end of

the sixteenth

century

Braudel, Fernand, *Capitalism and Material Life 1400–1800*, translated by Miriam Kochan, Weidenfeld & Nicolson, 1973. Chapter 7: 'Money'

Chute, Marchette, *Shakespeare of London*, Secker & Warburg, 1951, Four Square, 1962

Cohen, Jay, 'The History of Imprisonment for Debt and its Relations to the Development of Discharge in Bankruptcy', *The Journal of Legal History*, vol. 3, Frank Cass, May 1982

Hardaker, Alfred, *A Brief History of Pawnbroking*, 1892

Hume, David, *History of England*, vols. 1 & 2, 1848

Johnson, Paul, *A History of the Jews*, Weidenfeld & Nicolson, 1987

Miller, Madeleine S. and Miller, J. Lane, *Black's Bible Dictionary*, A & C Black, 1973

Oxford English Dictionary re 'Interest'

Routledge, R.A., LLB, 'The Legal Status of the Jews in England 1190–1790', *The Journal of Legal History*, vol. 3, Frank Cass, May 1982

Runciman, Steven, *A History of the Crusades*, vol. 1, The First Crusade, Cambridge University Press, 1951

Scott, Walter, *The Fortunes of Nigel*, 1831 (The Waverley Novels, vol. 3; Edinburgh, Adam and Charles Black, 1868)

Shakespeare, William, *The Merry Wives of Windsor*, G.R. Hibbard (ed), Penguin Books, 1973; *The Merchant of Venice*, W. Moelwyn Merchant (ed), Penguin Books, 1967

Tawney, R.H., *Religion and the Rise of Capitalism*, 1926 (Pelican 1972)

The Oxford Dictionary of the Christian Church

Traill, H.D. (ed), *Social England*, A Record of the Progress of the People, vol. 1, 'Commerce' 1066–1216, Cassell, 1894

Wheatley, Henry B., *London Past & Present*, vols. 1 & 2, John Murray 1891 – re Alsatia

Wilson, Sir Thomas, *A Discourse Upon Usury*, 1572 (with Introduction by R.H. Tawney, 1925, George Bell; reprinted Frank Cass 1962)

seventeenth century

Blackstone, Sir William, *The Commentaries on the Laws of England*, vol. 2 'Of The Rights of Things', 1876

Book of Christian Discipline of the Religious Society of Friends in Great Britain, consisting of Extracts on Doctrine, Practice and Church Government from the Epistles and other

BIBLIOGRAPHY

documents issued under the sanction of the yearly meetings held in London from its first
institution in 1672 to the year 1883, Chapter IX (Lambeth Palace Library)

Burton, Robert ('Democritus'), *The Anatomy of Melancholy*, vol. 1, 1621, Introduction by
Holbrook Jackson, no. 886 Everyman's Library, Dent, 1932

Holdsworth, Sir William, *History of English Law*, vol. 1, 7th edition edited by A.L.
Goodhart and H.G. Hanbury, Methuen, 1903 (original 1750s)

Macaulay, Thomas Babington, *The History of England from the Accession of James II*,
1848 (J.M. Dent, Everyman's Library, Ernest Rhys (ed), 1906)

Massinger, Philip, *A New Way to Pay Old Debts*, 1633

Petition: *Imprisonment of Men's Bodyes for Debt as the practise of England now stands*,
1641 (Lincoln's Inn Library)

Pitt, Moses, *The Cry of the Oppressed*, 1692

Powel, Tho., gent., *The Mistery and Misery of Lending and Borrowing*, 1636 (from The
Somers Collection of Tracts, A Collection of Scarce and Valuable Tracts on the most
interesting and entertaining subjects, 2nd edition revised, augmented and arranged by
Walter Scott Esq., vol. 7, 1812) 'Tracts During the Commonwealth: Miscellaneous
Tracts' (Lincoln's Inn Library)

Steel, Richard, *The Tradesman's Calling*, 1685

Verney, Sir Harry, Bt. (ed), *The Verneys of Claydon, A Seventeenth-century English
Family*, Pergamon Press, 1968

eighteenth century

*An Account of the Rise, Progress and Present State of the Society for the Discharge and Relief
of Persons Imprisoned for Small Debts*, containing the original sermon by Dr Dodd, 1774
(Lambeth Palace Library)

Anon, *A Letter to Trevor Lloyd Esq concerning a bankruptcy bill*, from Collections of Cases,
Memorials, Addresses and Proceedings in Parliament relating to Insolvent Debtors, etc.,
1757 (Hill's Law Tracts vol. 2, Lincoln's Inn Library)

Ashton, John, *The Fleet, Its River, Prison and Marriages*, Fisher Unwin, 1879 & 1888
(Guildhall Library)

Ashton, T.S. (ed), *An Economic History of England, the 18th Century*, Methuen, 1955

Beckett, J.V., BA, PhD, *The Lowthers at Holker, Marriage, Inheritance and Debt in the
Fortunes of an Eighteenth-Century Landowning Family* (Lancashire Record Office)

Bindman, David, *Hogarth*, Thames & Hudson, 1981

Bruce, Henry, *Life of General Oglethorpe*, New York, 1890

Burges, James Bland Esq., of Lincoln's Inn, *Considerations on the Law of Insolvency, with
a Proposal for a Reform*, 1783 (Lincoln's Inn Library)

Forster, John, *Life and Adventures of Oliver Goldsmith*, Hutchinson, 1848

Gisborne, Thomas, MA. *An Enquiry into the Duties of Men in the Higher and Middle
Classes of Society in Great Britain*, 1795. Chapter XIII 'On the duties of Persons
Engaged in Trade and Business'.

Hanoverian, A., *A Letter to the House of Peers on the Present Bill depending in Parliament
relative to the Prince of Wales's Debts*, 2nd edition, 1795

Hoare's Bank, A Record 1672–1955, Collins, 1955

Howe, Captain G.R., *Drums and Drummers*, Medici Society 1932, re Crying Down the
Credits ceremony in the army

Kettlewell, Reverend Mr John, *The Great Evil and Danger of Profuseness and Prodigality*, in a letter to a friend, 1705

'Moderation and Temperance' 1757, *Extracts from the Minutes and Advices of the Yearly Meeting of Friends, 1782* (Society of Friends Library)

Nelson, Robert, *The Whole Duty of a Christian by way of Question and Answer*, 6th edition, 1719

New Candid and Practical Thoughts on the Law of Imprisonment for Debt & c. 1788, (Law Pamplets 26, Lincoln's Inn Library)

'Orestes', *An Enquiry into the case of the Prince of Wales*; or Reflections on the Pretended Insolvency of the Heir Apparent for the Consideration of the Nation and for the Satisfaction of the Prince's Creditors. To a discerning and liberal public. With a dedication to Alexander Lord Loughborough, Lord Chief Justice, Temple, 22 July 1780 (Lincoln's Inn Library)

Paulson, Ronald, *Hogarth's Graphic Works*, The Print Room, 1989

Reitzel, William, (ed), *The Autobiography of William Cobbett*, the Progress of a Plough-Boy to a Seat in Parliament, Faber 1967 (Chapter 9, p. 120 re his imprisonment in 1810, culled from *Political Register* XVIII & LXIX, and *Advice to Young Men*.)

Selected Letters of Lord Chesterfield (1694–1773), with an Introduction by Phyllis M. Jones, Oxford University Press, The World's Classics, 347, 1929

Sheridan, R.B., *The School for Scandal*, (*Two Plays of Sheridan*, Guy Boas, (ed), Edward Arnold, 1961)

Small Debts Act 1748 & 1759, re Southwark Court of Requests (Southwark Public Library, Local History and Archives)

Smiles, Samuel, *Self-Help*, 1859, re Admiral Jervis and the Duke of Wellington

Smith, Adam, *The Wealth of Nations*, vol. 2 'Of Public Debts' Book V, 1776

The Gentleman's Magazine, 1737, 1745, 1748, 1753, 1759, 1760, 1765, 1780, 1804

The Spectator, no. 82, 4 June 1711 and no. 174, 19 September 1711

The Statutes at Large from Magna Carta to the Union of the Kingdoms of Great Britain and Ireland, vol. IX from 1 George II AD 1727 to 15 George AD 1742, 1811 – 'An Act for the Relief of Debtors with respect to the imprisonment of their persons', 1729, Geo II cap 21, 22 (House of Lords Record Office)

Turberville, A.S., *English Men and Manners in the Eighteenth Century*, Oxford, 1929

Vox Dei & Naturae, Shewing the Unreasonableness and Folly of imprisoning the Body for Debt from the Laws of God and Reason, Custom of Nations, Human Policy and Interest, 1711 (Cooper Collection 5, Lincoln's Inn Library)

Walters, John, *Splendour and Scandal*, The Reign of Beau Nash, Jarrolds, 1968

Woodforde, Revd James, *The Diary of a Country Parson* 1758–1802, (John Beresford (ed), Oxford University Press, The World's Classics, 514, 1949)

nineteenth century

Anon, *Thoughts on the present state of the law of Arrest and Imprisonment for Debt*, 1828 (Cooper Collection 45, Lincoln's Inn Library)

Ashton, John, *The Dawn of the XIXth Century in England*, a Social Sketch of the Times, with 114 illustrations drawn by the author from contemporary engravings, Chapter LIII, pages 453–6 'Debtors Prisons'; T. Fisher Unwin, 1886

Bagehot, Walter, *Lombard Street, A Description of the Money Market*, John Murray, 1873

BIBLIOGRAPHY

Barty-King, Hugh, *The Baltic Exchange, the history of a unique market*, Hutchinson
    Benham, 1977

Birrell, J.F., *An Edinburgh Alphabet*, 1980, re Holyrood sanctuary

Brougham, Lord, *Imprisonment for Debt*, speech in the House of Lords, 5 December, 1837
    (Cooper Collection 10, Lincoln's Inn Library)

Buchan, John, *Sir Walter Scott*, Cassell, 1932

Buxton, Thomas Foxwell, *An Inquiry whether Crime and Misery are produced or
    prevented by our Present System of Prison Discipline*, 1818 – review in the *Edinburgh
    Review*, 1818, Art. IX

Corley, T.A.B., *Huntley & Palmers of Reading 1822–1972*, Quaker Enterprise in Biscuits,
    Hutchinson Benham, 1972

Cornish, W.R., LLB, BCL, FBA, and Clark, G. de N. *Law and Society in England
    1750–1950*, Part 2 'Debt, Bankruptcy, Insolvency', Sweet & Maxwell, 1984

Dickens, Charles, *Pickwick Papers*, Chapter 43 re Insolvent Court; *The Uncommercial
    Traveller*, 'Night Walks'; *Little Dorrit*

Edinburgh Review, 1814, Art. VII, review of book by James Neild

Eliot, George, *Middlemarch*, 1872, Book III, Chapter 23

Elwin, Malcolm (ed), *The Autobiography and Journals of Benjamin Robert Haydon, 1853*
    Macdonald Illustrated Classics, 1950

Farrow, Thomas, *The Money-Lender Unmasked*, 1895 (Guildhall Library)

Gray, W. Forbes, 'Palace of Holyroodhouse', *The Scotsman*, 19 September, 1935

Fraser, Flora, *Beloved Emma*, The Life of Emma Lady Hamilton, Weidenfeld, 1986

Gaskell, Mrs, *Cranford*, 1851

Grant, James, *Pictures of Popular People*, 1842

Loan Societies Bill 1835 (Journal LXVII); 1840 (Journal LXXII) – Journals of the House
    of Lords (House of Lords Record Office)

McClaren, Moray, *Sir Walter Scott, The Man and Patriot,* Heinemann, 1970

*Memoirs of the Life of the Rev Charles Simeon MA with a selection from his writings and
    correspondence*, 1847 (Lambeth Palace Library)

Memorial of the Governors of the Society for the Relief of Persons imprisoned for Small
    Debts to the Lord Mayor of London and the Court of Aldermen, 22 July 1828, –
    complaining about the conduct of James Spencer, Keeper of the New Debtors Prison.
    (Corporation of London Record Office, Repertory 232); and Report of the Committee
    thereon, with the Resignation of the Keeper and a Letter from Mr Balnianno, Secretary of
    the Society

Meymott, Frederick William, *An Analysis of the Acts of Parliament relating to the
    Southwark Court of Requests*, 1830 (Southwark Public Library)

Mill, John Stuart, *Principles of Political Economy*, 1848 (Pelican 1970)

Minutes of Judgements, Orders and Other Proceedings at a Court held at Lewes . . . before
    William Furner Esq., Judge of the said court, 1847 and 1869 (East Sussex Record Office)

News-Cuttings, Winson Green Prison 1880s–1920s (Birmingham Reference Library, Local
    Studies, ref. L. 43.93)

Number Three St James's Street, house magazine of Berry Bros & Rudd, wine merchants

Oman, Carola, *The Wizard of the North*, the Life of Sir Walter Scott, Hodder, 1973

Reitzel, William (ed), *The Autobiography of William Cobbett*, Faber, 1933

Rose, June, *Elizabeth Fry*, A Biography, Macmillan, 1980

Rose, Kenneth, *King George V*, Weidenfeld, 1983 – re the Tecks

---

Sussex Express, 1 May 1847. Report of proceedings in Insolvent Debtors Court in County Hall, Lewes, 27 April 1847 (East Sussex Record Office)

Tebbutt, Melanie, *Making Ends Meet*, Pawnbroking and Working-Class Credit, Leicester University Press, 1983

The Quarterly Review, vol. LXXVII, December 1845 – March 1846. Art. VIII: 'An Act for the better securing the payment of small debts', 9 August 1845

The Royal Criterion or A Narrative of the Transactions relative to the Loans Made in London by the Prince of Wales, Duke of York, Duke of Clarence and their Advisers, and negotiated upon the Continent, 1814 (Tract in British Library)

Tours, Hugh, *The Life and Letters of Emma Hamilton*, Gollancz, 1963

Trollope, Anthony, *The Way We Live Now*, 1875

Udall, Henry, *The New County Courts Act 1846* (Lincoln's Inn Library)

Welbourne, E., 'Bankruptcy Before the Era of Victorian Reform', *Cambridge Historical Journal*, vol. 4, 1932 (British Library)

Wetherfield, G. Manley, *A Manual of Bankruptcy and Imprisonment for Debt under the Bankruptcy and Debtors Act 1869*, Longmans, 1869 (Lincoln's Inn Library)

Wilde, Oscar, *The Importance of Being Earnest* (four-act version), 1895

twentieth century

Anderson, Susan, 'Credit and Debt – A Consumer Overview of Mortgage Overlending', *Housing Finance,* quarterly journal of the Council of Mortgage Lenders, August 1990

A Revised Framework for Insolvency Law, HMSO Cmnd 9175, 1984

Aris, Stephen, *Going Bust*, Andre Deutsch, 1985

Army Education Bureau, *The British Way and Purpose*, 1945

Berthoud, Richard, and Kempson, Elaine, *Credit and Debt in Britain*, First Findings from the PSI Survey, Policy Studies Institute, 1990

Borrie, Sir Gordon, QC, *The Credit Society of the 1990s*, lecture to Dundee University, 25 February 1989; 'The Credit Society; Its Benefits and Burdens', Rathbone Memorial Lecture printed in *The Journal of Business Law*, May 1986; *Overindebtedness*, A Report by the Director General of Fair Trading, July 1989

Brady, John, *Living in Debt*, Birmingham Settlement Money Advice Services, 1987

Chrystal, K. Alec, *Consumer Debt: Whose Responsibility?*, Social Affairs Unit 1990

Churchill, Winston S., *Memories and Adventures*, Weidenfeld, 1989

Consumers and Debt, Finance Houses Association, 1985

Council of Mortgage Lenders, *Handling of Mortgage Arrears*, May 1990

Credit Management, The Institute of Credit Management Golden Jubilee 1939–89

Cutler, Peter, *Get out of Debt and Prosper*, Thorsons, 1991

Debt and Money Advice – the CAB Experience, R & D Briefing, National Association of Citizens Advice Bureaux, 1990

Debt, a Survival Guide, Office of Fair Trading, September 1989

Economic Secretariat, The Labour Party, *Economic Brief*, 14 June 1989

Ford, Janet, *The Indebted Society*, Credit and Default in the 1980s, Routledge, 1988

Gieve, David W., *Gieves & Hawkes 1785 – 1985*, The Story of a Tradition, 1985

Hinton, Teresa and Berthoud, Richard, *Money Advice Services*, Policy Studies Institute, 1988

Journal of the Institute of Credit Management Jubilee Number, 1989

BIBLIOGRAPHY

Lawson, Roger, *Problems With Debt: A Survey of Creditors' Perceptions and Practices*. Occasional Paper 18, Citizens Advice Bureaux, 1989. Findings of survey conducted by researchers of Department of Sociology and Social Policy at the University of Southampton

McGregor of Durris, Lord, *Legal Fiction and Social Reality: the Case of Maintenance Defaulters*, 1979

McQueen, John, *What To Do When Someone Has Debt Problems, A Practical Survival Guide*, Eliot Right Way Books, 1985

Money Advice Association, *Coping with Credit, Dealing with Debt*, 1990

Money Management Council Factsheets

National Consumer Council, *Credit and Debt; The Consumer Interest*, 1990

Office of Fair Trading Annual Report, July 1988

Ordinary Justice, Legal Services and the courts of England and Wales: a consumer view, National Consumer Council, HMSO, 1989

Report of the Money Advice Funding Working Party, January 1990

Small Claims in the County Courts of England and Wales, National Consumer Council, February 1987

The Cork Report, a guide for bankers, finance directors and others concerned with the provision of credit to businesses. Coopers & Lybrand/Cork Gully, 1982

The Economist, 29 April 1989

The Enforcement of Debt, the National Consumer Council's Response to the Civil Justice Review, April 1987

Understanding Building Societies, The Building Societies Association, September 1987

Young, Tim, *Debt Advice Provision in the United Kingdom*, Community Information Project, National Consumer Council, May 1990

Index

INDEX

INDEX